New Directions for Writers

VOLUME 1
College Writing and Beyond

Carol Ann Ellis
Pennsylvania State University

Cheryl Reed
Research Analyst, MTS Technologies
Senior Research Fellow, Teachers Without Borders

Longman

New York San Francisco Boston
London Toronto Sydney Tokyo Singapore Madrid
Mexico City Munich Paris Cape Town Hong Kong Montreal

To Bill and Elizabeth, who always help me see things more clearly, and find worth in what I'm doing.

—*C. A. E.*

To my dad, W. L. Lehmberg, who hooked me on finding out how things work, and why people do the things they do.

—*C. R.*

Vice President/Editor-in-Chief: Joe Terry
Senior Acquisitions Editor: Steve Rigolosi
Development Editor: Laurie Brown
Senior Marketing Manager: Melanie Craig
Senior Supplements Editor: Donna Campion
Production Manager: Charles Annis
Project Coordination, Text Design, and Electronic Page Makeup: Pre-Press Company, Inc.
Cover Design Manager: John Callahan
Cover Designer: Joan O'Connor
Cover Photos: upper and lower, Andrew Yan; background, Erin Babcock
Manufacturing Manager: Roy Pickering
Printer and Binder: R.R. Donnelley and Sons Company
Cover Printer: Lehigh Press, Inc.

For permission to use copyrighted material, grateful acknowledgment is made to the copyright holders on pp. 341–342, which are hereby made part of this copyright page.

Library of Congress Cataloging-in-Publication Data

Ellis, Carol Ann.
  New directions for writers / Carol Ann Ellis, Cheryl Reed.
    p. cm.
  Includes index.
  Contents: v. 1. College writing and beyond--v. 2. College writing and the world of work.
  ISBN 0-321-06747-9 (v. 1)--ISBN 0-321-06751-7 (v. 2)
    1. English language--Rhetoric. 2. Business writing. 3. Report writing. I. Reed, Cheryl,
  1952- II. Title.

PE1479.B87 E45 2003
808'.042--dc21

2002030158

Please visit our website at http://www.ablongman.com

0-321-06747-9

1 2 3 4 5 6 7 8 9 10—DOH—05 04 03 02

BRIEF CONTENTS

DETAILED CONTENTS

Preface • xv

PREFACE

New Directions for Writers, Volume 1: College Writing and Beyond is the first of two writing books designed to be student-oriented and geared to the requirements of the real world as well as the college classroom. With such innovative features as **interviews** with people whose professions require that they write every day, *New Directions, Volume 1* explores the lifelong benefits of being able to express oneself clearly in varied situations. As its title implies, this text takes a fresh approach to the question of how best to pique students' desires to express themselves in writing while giving them the skills to do so.

By guiding the student through the **writing process** and emphasizing the value of writing well, *New Directions for Writers, Volume 1* makes it possible for would-be writers to gain the necessary tools to express themselves effectively as well as an appreciation for the process.

The text shows that acquisition of writing skills is both possible and enjoyable. For example, grammar skills are taught without the unnecessary baggage of confusing terminology. In the Hub section, **grammar is explained from the students' point of view.** Students will find it easy to understand these examples and explanations that emanate from their world and exemplify their experiences. In addition, **student writings** are used throughout to illustrate the writing principles being taught.

Conceived and written by two college teachers who like to write and who have spent a total of over 40 years in the classroom, this book reveals an innovative, knowledgeable approach to teaching writing for varied audiences and purposes.

ORGANIZATION

New Directions for Writers, Volume 1: College Writing and Beyond is divided into six parts. Each part contains chapters dealing with the specific aspect of learning to write that is the focus of that part. Each chapter includes internal as well as concluding **exercises** under the heading *Applying What You've Learned.*

Five chapters feature interviews with people whose professions require writing on a daily basis. One interview is with a student who emphasizes the role that writing has played in her life in college and in several paid positions.

Part I, Understanding the Importance of Writing Basics, discusses and explodes myths concerning writing and explains the necessity of considering subject, purpose, and audience when writing.

Part II, Discovering the Writing Process, explains the overall process of writing and covers getting started: understanding assignments, generating ideas, freewriting, focusing, and journal writing. Part II also explains how to write lucid sentences, how to use those sentences to develop coherent paragraphs, especially introductions and conclusions, and identifies paragraph shapes. It clarifies the difference between a topic and a thesis, and provides tips for writing a rough draft.

In addition, Part II also defines and illustrates patterns of organization within essays including comparison/contrast, narration, description, example, process (how-to), and persuasion. Assignments for papers that use these patterns and sample student papers written in response to these assignments are provided.

Part III, Refining Your Writing, explains the process of peer review and makes suggestions for getting the maximum benefit from these sessions. The revision process is explained in detail and applied to rough drafts as well as later versions of papers. The value of revision is emphasized, and the point is made that virtually all good writing involves revision. A chapter on the importance of punctuation illustrates how punctuation can change meaning and how correct punctuation is crucial to clear writing.

Part IV, Writing for a Specific Purpose, discusses the art of writing a successful essay test and gives suggestions on how to do well on this type of exam. Samples of students' answers to questions on a literature exam are critiqued.

The Hub explains grammar, punctuation, and other essentials of writing from the student's point of view. Examples of student writing illustrate the points discussed.

Readings includes readings about jobs that involve writing and illustrate some of the modes of organization discussed in the text. For example, John Updike's article "Early Inklings" tells how a summer job on a newspaper helped him discover his "element, ink on paper." Other readings show American life from multicultural points of view and can be used, for example, to analyze how writers bring their readers into their world.

Appendixes A and B provide a formal outline and a list of proofreaders' marks.

THE TEACHING AND LEARNING PACKAGE

Each component of the teaching and learning package has been crafted to ensure that the course is a rewarding experience for both instructors and students.

The **Instructor's Manual** contains answers to in-text exercises and suggestions for teaching. Ask your Longman sales representative for ISBN 0-321-06750-9.

For additional exercises, resources, and Internet activities, be sure to visit the book-specific Web site at **http://www.ablongman.com/ellis.**

In addition to the instructor's manual discussed above, many other skills-based supplements are available for both instructors and students. All of these supplements are available either free or at greatly reduced prices.

For Additional Reading and Reference

The Dictionary Deal. Two dictionaries can be shrinkwrapped with this title either free or at a nominal fee. *The New American Webster Handy College Dictionary* is a paperback reference text with more than 100,000 entries. *Merriam Webster's Collegiate Dictionary*, tenth edition, is a hardback reference with a citation file of more than 14.5 million examples of English words drawn from actual use. For more information on how to shrinkwrap a dictionary with your text, please contact your Longman sales representative.

Penguin Quality Paperback Titles. A series of Penguin paperbacks is available at a significant discount when shrinkwrapped with any Longman English title. Some titles available are Toni Morrison's *Beloved*, Julia Alvarez's *How the Garcia Girls Lost Their Accents*, Mark Twain's *Huckleberry Finn*, *Narrative of the Life of Frederick Douglass*, Harriet Beecher Stowe's *Uncle Tom's Cabin*, Dr. Martin Luther King, Jr.'s *Why We Can't Wait*, and plays by Shakespeare, Miller, and Albee. For a complete list of titles or more information, please contact your Longman sales consultant.

The Pocket Reader and The Brief Pocket Reader, First Edition. These inexpensive volumes contain 80 brief readings and 50 readings, respectively. Each reading is brief (1–3 pages each). The readers are theme-based: writers on writing, nature, women and men, customs and habits, politics, rights and obligations, and coming of age. Also included is an alternate rhetorical table of contents. Ask your Longman sales representative for more information about these and other inexpensive readers from Longman.

100 Things to Write About. This 100-page book contains 100 individual assignments for writing on a variety of topics and in a wide range of formats, from expressive to analytical. Ask your Longman sales representative for a sample copy. 0-673-98239-4

Newsweek Alliance. Instructors may choose to shrinkwrap a 12-week subscription to *Newsweek* with any Longman text. The price of the subscription is 59 cents per issue (a total of $7.08 for the subscription). Available with the subscription is a free "Interactive Guide to *Newsweek*"—a workbook for students who are using the text. In addition, *Newsweek* provides a wide variety of instructor supplements free to teachers, including maps, Skills Builders, and weekly quizzes. For more information on the *Newsweek* program, please contact your Longman sales representative.

Electronic and Online Offerings

[NEW] The Longman Writer's Warehouse. This innovative and exciting online supplement is the perfect accompaniment to any developmental writing course. Developed by developmental English instructors specially for developing writers, The Writer's Warehouse covers every part of the writing process. Also included are journaling capabilities, multimedia activities, diagnostic tests, an interactive handbook, and a complete instructor's manual. The Writer's Warehouse requires no space on your school's server; rather, students complete and store their work on the Longman server, and are able to access it, revise it, and continue working at any time. For more details about how to shrinkwrap a free subscription to The Writer's Warehouse with this text, please consult your Longman sales representative. For a free guided tour of the site, visit **http:// longmanwriterswarehouse.com**.

The Writer's ToolKit Plus. This CD-ROM offers a wealth of tutorial, exercise, and reference material for writers. It is compatible with either a PC or Macintosh platform, and is flexible enough to be used either occasionally for practice or regularly in class lab sessions. For information on how to bundle this CD-ROM FREE with your text, please contact your Longman sales representative.

GrammarCoach Software. This interactive tutorial helps students practice the basics of grammar and punctuation through 600 self-grading exercises in such problem areas as fragments, run-ons, and agreement. IBM diskettes only. 0-205-26509-X

The Longman Electronic Newsletter. Twice a month during the spring and fall, instructors who have subscribed receive a free copy of the Longman Developmental English Newsletter in their e-mailbox. Written by experienced classroom instructors, the newsletter offers teaching tips, classroom activities, book reviews, and more. To subscribe, visit the Longman Basic Skills Web site at **http://www.ablongman.com/basicskills**, or send an e-mail to **Basic Skills@ablongman.com**.

For Instructors

Electronic Test Bank for Writing. This electronic test bank features more than 5,000 questions in all areas of writing, from grammar to paragraphing, through essay writing, research, and documentation. With this easy-to-use CD-ROM, instructors simply choose questions from the electronic test bank, then print out the completed test for distribution. CD-ROM: 0–321–08117–X. Print version: 0–321–08486–1.

Competency Profile Test Bank, Second Edition. This series of 60 objective tests covers ten general areas of English competency, including fragments; comma splices and run-ons; pronouns; commas; and capitalization. Each test is available in remedial, standard, and advanced versions. Available as reproducible sheets or in computerized versions. Free to instructors. Paper version: 0–321–02224–6. Computerized IBM: 0–321–02633–0. Computerized Mac: 0–321–02632–2.

Diagnostic and Editing Tests and Exercises, Fifth Edition. This collection of diagnostic tests helps instructors assess students' competence in Standard Written English for the purpose of placement or to gauge progress. Available as reproducible sheets or in computerized versions, and free to instructors. Paper: 0–321–11730–1. CD-ROM: 0–321–11731–X.

ESL Worksheets, Third Edition. These reproducible worksheets provide ESL students with extra practice in areas they find the most troublesome. A diagnostic test and post-test are provided, along with answer keys and suggested topics for writing. Free to adopters. 0–321–07765–2

Longman Editing Exercises. 54 pages of paragraph editing exercises give students extra practice using grammar skills in the context of longer passages. Free when packaged with any Longman title. 0–205–31792–8. Answer key: 0–205–31797–9.

80 Practices. A collection of reproducible, ten-item exercises that provide additional practice for specific grammatical usage problems, such as comma splices, capitalization, and pronouns. Includes an answer key, and free to adopters. 0–673–53422–7

CLAST Test Package, Fourth Edition. These two 40-item objective tests evaluate students' readiness for the CLAST exams. Strategies for teaching CLAST preparedness are included. Free with any Longman English title. Reproducible sheets: 0–321–01950–4. Computerized IBM version: 0–321–01982–2. Computerized Mac version: 0–321–01983–0.

TASP Test Package, Third Edition. These 12 practice pre-tests and post-tests assess the same reading and writing skills covered in the TASP examination. Free with any Longman English title. Reproducible sheets: 0–321–01959–8. Computerized IBM version: 0–321–01985–7. Computerized Mac version: 0–321–01984–9.

Teaching Online: Internet Research, Conversation, and Composition, Second Edition. Ideal for instructors who have never surfed the Net, this easy-to-follow guide offers basic definitions, numerous examples, and step-by-step information about finding and using Internet sources. Free to adopters. 0–321–01957–1

Teaching Writing to the Non-Native Speaker. This booklet examines the issues that arise when non-native speakers enter the developmental classroom. Free to instructors, it includes profiles of international and permanent ESL students, factors influencing second-language acquisition, and tips on managing a multicultural classroom. 0–673–97452–9

Using Portfolios. This supplement offers teachers a brief introduction to teaching with portfolios in composition courses. This essential guide addresses the pedagogical and evaluative use of portfolios, and offers practical suggestions for implementing a portfolio evaluation system in a writing class. 0–321–08412–8

[NEW] The Longman Guide to Classroom Management. Written by Joannis Flatley of St. Philip's College, the first in Longman's new series of monographs for developmental English instructors focuses on issues of classroom etiquette, providing guidance on dealing with unruly, unengaged, disruptive, or uncooperative students. Ask your Longman sales representative for a free copy. 0–321–09246–5

[NEW] The Longman Instructor Planner. This all-in-one resource for instructors includes monthly and weekly planning sheets, to-do lists, student contact forms, attendance rosters, a gradebook, an address/phone book, and a mini almanac. Ask your Longman sales representative for a free copy. 0–321–09247–3.

For Students

Researching Online, Fifth Edition. A perfect companion for a new age, this indispensable new supplement helps students navigate the Internet. Adapted from *Teaching Online,* the instructor's Internet guide, *Researching Online* speaks directly to students, giving them detailed, step-by-step instructions for performing electronic searches. Available free when shrinkwrapped with this text. 0–321–09277–5

Learning Together: An Introduction to Collaborative Theory. This brief guide to the fundamentals of collaborative learning teaches students how to work effectively in groups, how to revise with peer response, and how to co-author a paper or report. Shrinkwrapped free with any Longman Basic Skills test. 0-673-46848-8

A Guide for Peer Response, Second Edition. This guide offers students forms for peer critiques, including general guidelines and specific forms for different stages in the writing process. Also appropriate for freshman-level courses. Free to adopters. 0-321-01948-2

Ten Practices of Highly Successful Students. This popular supplement helps students learn crucial study skills, offering concise tips for a successful career in college. Topics include time management, test-taking, reading critically, stress, and motivation. 0-205-30769-8

Thinking Through the Test, by D. J. Henry. This special workbook, prepared specially for students in Florida, offers ample skill and practice exercises to help students prepare for the Florida State Exit Exam. To shrinkwrap this workbook free with your textbook, please contact your Longman sales representative. Available in two versions: with answers and without answers. Also available: two laminated grids (one for reading, one for writing) that can serve as handy references for students preparing for the Florida State Exit Exam.

[NEW] The Longman Writer's Journal. This journal for writers, free with any Longman English text, offers students a place to think, write, and react. For an examination copy, contact your Longman sales consultant. 0-321-08639-2

[NEW] The Longman Researcher's Journal. This journal for writers and researchers, free with this text, helps students plan, schedule, write, and revise their research project. An all-in-one resource for first-time researchers, the journal guides students gently through the research process. 0-321-09530-8

[NEW] The Longman Writer's Portfolio. This unique supplement provides students with a space to plan, think about, and present their work. The portfolio includes an assessing/organizing area (including a grammar diagnostic test, a spelling quiz, and project planning worksheets), a before and during writing area (including peer review sheets, editing checklists, writing self-evaluations, and a personal editing profile), and an after-writing area (including a progress chart, a final table of contents, and a final assessment). Ask your Longman sales representative for ISBN 0-321-10765-9.

ACKNOWLEDGMENTS

First, I want to thank my husband and daughter for putting up with me during the more than three years that this manuscript was coming into being, as well as for providing technical assistance and constructive advice. It was a long gestation period.

My coauthor, Cheryl Reed, deserves credit for coming up with the idea for this project and convincing me that not only could we do it but that it was worth doing.

This book could not have been written without the generous students who donated their writings to be used as illustrations and the people who gave of their time and thought to grant the interviews which prove that to be successful in the world of work, one must be able to write well.

Ultimately, I thank the staff at Longman Publishers for their support and guidance. Laurie Brown, my developmental editor, and Steven Rigolosi, Senior English Editor, were especially supportive and helpful, and I am grateful for their dedication to this task.

I'd also like to thank those colleagues who reviewed both texts in the *New Directions for Writers* series:

Bob D. Akin, Houston Community College
Cathryn Amdahl, Harrisburg Area Community College
Vivian Brown, Laredo Community College
Jo Ann Buck, Guilford Technical Community College
Judy C. Davidson, The University of Texas - Pan American
Kevin Davis, East Central University
Eileen Eliot, Broward Community College
Dawn M. Formo, California State University, San Marcos
Patrick M. Haas, Glendale Community College
Lois Hassan, Henry Ford College
Mary C. Hutchinson, Penn State University
Joan Mauldin, San Jacinto College South
Pianta, San Diego Mesa College
Deneen M. Shepherd, St. Louis Community College
Sherry Shurin, Cambria County Area Community College
Richard C. Taylor, East Carolina University
Alice Trupe, Bridgewater College

Carol Ann Ellis

ABOUT THE AUTHORS

Carol Ann Ellis

Carol Ann Ellis recently retired from the Pennsylvania State University, where she directed the Writing Laboratory and taught writing and speech communication. She has taught at The Ohio State University, The University of Puerto Rico, and Bloomsburg University. She has also worked in publishing, including being the production editor for the literary journal, *The Kenyon Review*. Currently, she is a columnist for *Panorama* magazine and a faculty member with the Center for Distance Learning, Empire State College, New York.

Dr. Cheryl Reed

Dr. Cheryl Reed, who formerly taught writing at Penn State University, researches the use of telecommunications technologies to deliver medical care for MTS Technologies, Inc. She is a Senior Research Fellow at Teachers Without Borders, currently collaborating to develop the Certificate of Teaching Mastery. Dr. Reed has also developed curriculum and training for an educational software company, and worked in smoking cessation and drug prevention programs.

PART I

Understanding the Importance of Writing Basics

CHAPTER 1

Why Should I Learn to Write Well?

You may ask, "Why should I learn to write well?" In a society where you are bombarded with sound and sight 24 hours a day, it may be hard to see the value in learning to be a better writer. You probably don't see many people just sitting down and writing in your day-to-day life. So you may see writing solely as a classroom exercise, another one of those requirements that you have to fulfill.

Writing, however, is not just a classroom exercise. Being able to write well has far-reaching real-world as well as academic applications. For example, many jobs require that you be able to express yourself effectively. A recent advertisement for a manufacturing management trainee states, "Qualified candidates will have a bachelor's degree in engineering or related fields, excellent time management and problem-solving skills, superior written and verbal communication skills . . ."

You may not be aware that professionals in fields that are not directly related to writing (such as newspaper reporting or publishing) do a great deal of writing on their jobs every day.

However, the classroom *is* the place to learn and practice those writing skills that you will need not only in your college years, but also thereafter. Many instructors, including those outside of English or communications, will expect you to be able to express yourself well in writing. You are probably aware that some professors test your knowledge of course material by giving essay tests and assigning term papers, reaction papers, reports of group projects, lab reports, and other forms of writing. Your instructors may not know you as a person, so they must judge you as a student by

1

your writing. It is not enough to know the material; you must be able to demonstrate that you have learned and can apply the subject matter of the course, often by expressing yourself in writing.

Even getting a job requires that you be able to present yourself well and convincingly in writing. A clearly written, complete resume that outlines your education and experience in terms that the prospective employer can understand and a convincing letter of application aimed at the job you want are required for virtually every professional position. Like the college instructor who only knows you through the work you produce for his or her class, the employer only knows you from what you have said about yourself and how you have presented yourself on paper.

Like it or not, people judge you by how you communicate. Poor spelling, incomplete sentences, incorrect verb tenses, a messy format, lack of organization, or unclear purpose make a poor impression on prospective employers. Messy resumes end up in the wastebasket. The person who submits a well-written, neat resume and application letter is much more likely to get an interview than the one who sends in a messy, hastily thrown together application.

This book will teach you the foundations of all good writing and show you how to apply these principles to various types of written communication. Being able to write effectively is a skill that will serve you well in many situations in life.

As you read this text, especially the interviews with writers in real life, think about how what they say relates to what will be required of you as a writer outside the classroom. Read the following advertisement for a process engineer at a snack food manufacturer. Notice the emphasis on communication skills, including writing. Even entry-level jobs require excellent communication skills.

PROCESS ENGINEER

Throughout the region, the name **Wise Foods** stands for the highest quality snack food products. Currently, our Berwick, PA facility is seeking a team-oriented professional to administer the process development of new products and line extensions as well as cost and quality improvement projects.

You will develop and implement product and process specifications, coordinate plant trials, and document project work through *concise written and oral reports including criteria design, experimental plans and technical summaries.* You will work closely with Marketing, Operations, and R&D [research and development] personnel to *complete projects within an expected timeframe* and direct the work of technicians, consultants, and contractors as needed.

To qualify, you must have a Bachelor's degree in food, chemical, or mechanical engineering . . . . *Excellent verbal/written communication skills* and computer efficiency are essential. (Italics ours)

Process Engineer, Advertisement, *Times Leader* [Wilkes-Barre, PA], 24 Sept. 2000: 6F.

EXERCISE 1.1   ANALYZING THE PROCESS ENGINEER ADVERTISEMENT

(A) Why do you think that this position requires excellent communication skills? What kind of communicating do you think you would be doing as a process engineer?

_____

_____

(B) Can you think of other jobs where you would need similar skills?

_____

_____

(C) Once you have completed your degree, what field do you see yourself entering, and how important do you think having excellent writing skills will be to your career success?

_____

_____

Writing on the Job

Jane Robinson Meggers, a social worker in Roanoke, Virginia, who specializes in finding employment for her clients, does a great deal of writing on her job.

Jane was born in Welch, West Virginia, grew up in Bristol, Virginia, and graduated from Radford University, Radford, Virginia. She has worked in the area of social services and mental health in the city of Roanoke for the past 27 years. She says she spends "90 percent" of her day writing.

In a typical day, she may do one or more of the following types of writing:

Jane Robinson Meggers

Social Worker

- social histories of her clients
- work histories of her clients
- service plans for clients
- scheduling letters
- informational letters to community agencies

- letters of recommendation
- resumes
- brochures and flyers
- "running dictation"—a sort of diary or contact sheet with her clients. Jane emphasizes that these records are very important and have to be accurate because they can be reviewed even for court cases. She also makes the point that any information that is second- or third-hand has to be labeled as such. In other words, she has to report her sources even as writers of research papers do.
- evaluations of employees under her immediate supervision
- strategic plans—These consist of setting annual goals and the means for reaching them. Jane compares them to a lesson plan or a syllabus. These strategic plans help justify staffing needs and current positions as well as fit into the Mission Statement for the City of Roanoke. Many businesses require that you formulate objectives and the ways that you intend to attain them.
- memos—interdepartmental communications to workers in other areas, often done by e-mail (but still written)
- grant writing—documenting the needs of certain populations of clients
- operating manuals—standard operating procedures for her office, generally written by a group and revised annually
- presentations to the community and to clients concerning services that are provided

As you can see, Jane is responsible for many types of writing which, as she says, have to be "precise, concise, and factual." She emphasizes, "The written word is your record; it represents the work that you do. In a way, it is *you*."

Jane makes the comment that when she started this job, over 27 years ago, the written records were not nearly as crucial as they are now. For example, the City Manager now requires that each unit of the government account for itself in writing. Each department has to develop a mission statement (what it hopes to accomplish each year and how it intends to do it). She added that the Manager demands accuracy in writing and will not tolerate typos or careless mistakes. Today, the accurate written word is the standard.

When asked what advice she has for college students, Jane says, "Someone will be looking over your shoulder. What you write has to make sense to someone else." In other words, you have to be able to *communicate* well. She also explains that if you are absent from the office for a day or even for an hour, someone else should be able to understand and work from your records. "No one is irreplaceable." She emphasizes the importance of having "the ability to communicate in a meaningful way." Jane adds that you will need to justify your own performance in order to move up in your organization.

Jane says that when she was in college she never realized how important writing would be to her in her career. She says, "Now everyone from the garbage collector to the city manager is taught keyboard skills and is expected to be able to write reports."

So, if you think that your English teacher is just being fussy or that you will never need the skills that you are learning in basic English, think again. Having these skills may mean the difference between keeping and losing a responsible job. ✑

EXERCISE 1.2   **RESPONDING TO WRITING ON THE JOB**

Jane Meggers says, "The written word is your record; it represents you. In a way it is *you*." Write a paragraph on a separate piece of paper that explains in approximately 150 words what you think she means by this. How is it possible that you are what you write?

MYTHS ABOUT WRITING

Over the years, many myths about writing have developed. These distorted views concerning the importance of learning to write well and the nature of writing itself have been voiced so many times that people have come to believe them. Therefore, no one thinks to check their validity. When you take a hard look at these popular beliefs, you will find little or no truth in them.

Myth #1: *I won't have to write on my job. I'm going into engineering, banking, etc.*

As you have seen from Jane Robinson Meggers' comments, some kinds of writing will no doubt be required for any job that you get.

Myth #2: *There will be someone such as a secretary who will correct my mistakes. All I will have to do is dictate what I want to say to this person, and he or she will make the necessary corrections.*

While this idea may have been true in the past, today it is unlikely that you will have someone to catch your mistakes. It is much more likely that your company will give you a nice computer, which will faithfully record what you type into it, mistakes and all. Even spelling and grammar checkers won't make up for having the skills to say what you mean, clearly and effectively. Beginning writers often use strange, unidiomatic expressions (words used in an unusual way) and explain them by saying that this was what their grammar checker told them to say. To the experienced writer, these usages are clearly wrong. In other words, you, the writer, have to be able to judge what is right or wrong, regardless of what the software tells you.

Myth #3: *State-of-the-art technology makes it unnecessary to have good writing skills.*

Wrong! Today's technology makes it even more imperative that you be able to write well. With the greater reliance of businesses on communicating via e-mail and instant messaging, you may find yourself doing more writing on the job than ever before. And while verbal mistakes made during a telephone conversation may be overlooked, or not even detected, mistakes made in writing on e-mail and particularly on such services as Instant Messenger are readily detected and may be preserved long after they were written. Also, it is easy to misinterpret a written message that has been stated unclearly or incompletely. Thus, use of current technology makes it more important rather than less important to write clearly.

Myth #4: *It really doesn't matter whether I use English correctly. Today any usage is acceptable; only grammarians and English teachers get upset about things such as double negatives (I don't have no money).*

The truth is that the language is dynamic; it is constantly changing. For example, people needed a whole new vocabulary in order to deal with computers (a *byte* used to be a *bite*). And grammar rules have been relaxed somewhat. Your teacher no longer tells you that you can't put a preposition such as *with* at the end of a sentence.

The English statesman Winston Churchill allegedly said that if he could not put a preposition at the end of a sentence, he would say, "This is the sort of English up with which I cannot put." Some rules, when applied rigidly, result in this sort of ridiculous construction. On the other hand, most educated readers still tend to judge writers who say, "I don't have no" or "I have went" as being uneducated or of a lower class. So there are standards of usage that you have to abide by if you want to be considered an intelligent, educated writer. Similarly, errors that obscure understanding have to be overcome. The bottom line is that you write to communicate, and whether you like it or not, rules enable you to do so.

EXERCISE 1.3 **EXPLORING MYTHS ABOUT WRITING**

(A) Make a list of any other myths about writing you can think of.

_____

_____

(B) On a separate piece of paper, in a paragraph of approximately 150 words, explain which of the myths discussed in this chapter, in your opinion, is the most important to avoid. What tips can you can think of to help writers avoid falling victim to this myth?

APPLYING WHAT YOU'VE LEARNED

1. Read the job ads in the classified section of the Sunday _New York Times_ or your local paper. Note how many ads specify that applicants need good written and verbal communication skills. Highlight at least five of these and make a note of the types of jobs that require writing.

2. Interview someone who is working in the field you're interested in. Ask questions about the type of communication skills, including writing, that are required for the job.

3. Talk to someone who you think would _not_ have to write on the job. Ask what kind of writing or communicating this person does at work. You may be surprised at the amount of writing and other types of communication that the job involves.

4. Read through the course descriptions in your college catalog. Note how many classes _outside of English or journalism_ require writing—term papers, reports, essay exams, and the like. Often, these are labelled _W_ to indicate writing-intensive courses.

5. Check the syllabi for the courses you are presently taking. Note how many assignments involve writing, such as term papers, journals, lab reports, reaction papers, e-mail reactions to readings and lectures, and other correspondence.

6. Log onto an online source of job listings such as Monster.com and look for a job that interests you. Then read carefully to see what communication skills are required for this position.

Write a paragraph of approximately 150 words discussing how the skills you have would qualify you for this job and/or how you could acquire the skills necessary to obtain this position.

7. Visit a local employment agency (government or private) and ask to see a list of jobs that may be appropriate for you. Note how many of these jobs require excellent communication skills.

Make a list of the communication skills needed. Then try to determine objectively which of these you already have and which you would have to acquire. Write a short paragraph (100 to 150 words) summarizing what you would have to do to qualify for one of these jobs.

CHAPTER 2

Why Should I Consider My Subject, Purpose, and Audience?

Writing, by and large, is not a "closet" experience. Most writing is meant to be read by other people. There are exceptions, such as diaries. But even some of these, such as Anne Frank's account of life in Nazi-occupied Amsterdam during World War II and Mary Chesnut's observations about her life as the wife of General James Chesnut, Jr. during the Civil War were eventually published and widely read. While you probably don't have to worry about publishing your writing (unless you want to), you still have to consider your reader.

All good writing is done with subject, purpose, and audience in mind. You can remember this by using the first letters of these words, SPA.

Even the simplest note on the refrigerator at home has *subject, purpose,* and *audience.* "Feed the dog" has the family pet as its subject, getting the dog its supper as its purpose, and the first person who comes home as its audience.

Knowing *what* you want to say, *why* you want to say it, and to *whom* you want to say it are crucial first steps to successful writing. You should ask these three questions the next time you are writing:

1. What do I want to write about?   (subject)
2. Why am I writing?   (purpose)
3. To whom am I writing?   (audience)

SUBJECT

Sometimes the subject matter is determined for you. Your instructor tells you what to write about. Or you are writing a letter of application that asks you to talk about yourself. Often, though, you have the chance to choose a topic, within certain limits. Suppose, for example, that your instructor asks you to comment on a decision you made that turned out to be wrong. You should "tailor the assignment to yourself" and write about something that is meaningful to you. After all, you are going to be spending several hours on this paper. You should choose a subject that interests you and that you truly wish to express on paper.

Something else to consider when choosing a subject is whether it will interest your readers. No one wants to read about something that is dull, boring, preachy, or overly familiar. For example, a paper on how to make a peanut butter and jelly sandwich would hold no interest for students who learned to do that in kindergarten.

You should also choose a subject that you know something about already and that, if necessary, you are willing to learn more about (that is, do research). It is extremely difficult and usually unnecessary to try to write on something you are totally unfamiliar with.

EXERCISE 2.1

Be ready to discuss the following questions.

What is the subject of the following paragraph? Do you think the writer chose an interesting subject? If so, what do you find appealing about it? If not, what do you think would be a better subject?

> Let us turn, for a moment, to the problem of plastic bags stuck in trees. It and I go back a long way. I began to notice it about 10 years ago when the larger vexations of adulthood—don't get me started—were becoming real to me for the first time. Pushing my daughter in her stroller and thinking perhaps about the fact that my health insurance payments had just doubled, I heard a rustling sound overhead. When I looked up, I saw it: a milky-white plastic bag stuck to the bare branch of a tree. As I watched, the flapping bag took on a last-straw quality. It irritated me no end.

Ian Frazier; "Free the Trees," *Modern Maturity* Mar.–Apr. 2002: 12.

PURPOSE

Why are you writing this paper or letter? Hopefully, you won't answer, "because my instructor or employer requires it." It may well be that you are required to produce this piece of writing, but it should have purpose beyond getting the assignment (or the job) done.

Common purposes include the following:

- To express an idea or share feelings
- To teach someone how to do something
- To persuade someone to agree with your point of view or to do something
- To explain or clarify a position or topic

Whatever the purpose, you must have it clearly in your mind before you start to write. If you don't, it will be apparent to your reader that you really did not have a good idea of what you were trying to do.

EXERCISE 2.2

Be ready to discuss the following questions.

Imagine you are applying for a job posted by a major manufacturer in your hometown. Of the preceding stated purposes, which do you think would be the most effective one to use in an application letter to get an interview? Why have you chosen this purpose?

AUDIENCE

Your *audience* will differ from one piece of writing to another. Accordingly, what you write must be suited to the audience for which it was intended. No one would confuse the audience for a love letter with the audience for a job application letter (at least, we hope not). But writing that letter with the audience in mind takes some thought.

Ask yourself the following questions:

- What is the age of these people?
- What is their gender?
- What is their level of education?
- What are they interested in?

- What do they know about my subject?
- Are they likely to agree or disagree with me?

The answers to these questions help determine what you will say and how you will say it. It is absolutely necessary to think about these questions and their answers before you start writing. While you can never completely determine the reaction of your audience or sometimes even who your audience will ultimately be, considering these questions will help you focus your writing and tailor it to your intended audience.

Once you have a pretty good idea who your audience is, you should also consider what kind of writing would be most appealing to them. Here are a few more questions to consider:

- What words should I use to persuade my significant other that I truly love him or her?
- What words should I use to convince a potential employer that I am the right candidate for the job?
- How long should my sentences or paragraphs be?
- How long should the whole letter be?
- Do I want to be candid or should the reader be able to read between the lines?
- What tone of vocabulary should I use with this person (formal, slangy, ironic)?

All of these things and more are determined by your audience. You cannot predict completely how your audience will interpret your writing, but you can try to anticipate the reader's response and work toward getting the reaction that you desire.

EXAMINING SUBJECT, PURPOSE, AND AUDIENCE IN WRITING

Which of the following letters is more likely to prompt a favorable response from Ellen? Keep in mind that the writer's purpose is to convince Ellen, the object of his affections, that he loves her.

(1)

Ellen,
    You are the sun of my days and the moon that lights my nights.
Without you, there is no day or night.
        Love, Steve

(2)

> To: Ellen
> From: Steve
> Subject: Love
> This note is to inform you that I believe I'm in love with you.

You get the idea—Ellen may find the first letter a bit flowery, but she doesn't want to be treated as the subject of an interoffice memo!

EXERCISE 2.3   Imagine you are Ellen. Respond to the second letter from Steve. Before you begin to write, what should you consider about Steve (your audience) that will determine how you say what needs to be said?

_____

_____

_____

_____

DETERMINING VARIOUS AUDIENCES

Consider the audience for the following excerpt. Where might you find this, and to whom would it be directed?

> Since you are more financially responsible these days, you need more security. Now you can bring your financial security up to date, easily and economically. You can get $100,000 in life insurance for yourself. This is affordable protection designed by women like yourself.

What can you tell about the audience (subject and purpose) for this short paragraph?

First you know that it is persuasive writing, advertising to be exact. You can also tell that it is aimed at women. But women of what age and status? Probably working women (age 25 to 45) who are supporting themselves and often a family. You can make a shrewd guess that these women are making a fairly good salary, and that they have an income and lifestyle to protect. In addition, you can detect a note of respect for women: ". . . protection designed by women like yourself." On the whole, it is flattering and a bit threatening, with its underlying question: What would happen if you and/or your family did not have the benefit of your income?

You were able to find out a great deal about the subject, purpose, and audience for this paragraph because the authors wrote it with these things in mind. They chose their words carefully. *Easy, economical,* and *security* all are used to appeal to the needs and desires of the women they hoped would respond to their advertising. The sentences are short and to the point. The writers do not waste their readers' time. In short, it is a well-written advertisement which should attract the audience it is designed for.

You may be thinking at this point, "But I don't plan to go into advertising." Perhaps not, but the same principles apply to other kinds of writing. Consider the following situation:

- You had been partying earlier in the evening.
- You left one party to drive to another across town.
- A blue Chevy pickup slowed down 500 feet in front of you to make a right-hand turn.
- You were busy putting a CD in your player so you didn't notice that the truck had slowed down.
- You hit it!

First, imagine that you are writing an account for a friend, a friendly letter or e-mail. What would you say? Second, imagine that you are writing an account of this accident for the trooper who is investigating at the scene. What would you say? How would you phrase this explanation for an audience that represents the law (a completely different audience from the first one)?

While your subject may be the same, you may find you need to add details according to your audience and purpose. You also may find that you want to omit a detail or two, depending on your audience. Choose the appropriate level of language usage and tone (formal/informal). Feel free to be creative while being true to the situation; try to think of what you would honestly say if this were a real-life situation.

You may be interested in what two of our students wrote when given this situation.

E-mail to a Friend

Hi Pete,

Man, you are never going to believe what happened to me. I was going from Jake's to Sammy's. I was reaching under my seat to find my favorite CD (you know the one) when this nut passed me and caused me to spill my soda. I was taking my shirt off to wipe up the spill when this jerk stopped in the middle of the road. I hit him, and he wasn't happy.

His name was Bubba, and he had on tan suspenders. He was about 6'7", 300 pounds, and he was mad about me scratching his favorite Lynyrd Skynyrd bumper sticker. After he beat me to a bloody pulp, I spoke to the cops.

Statement to the Police

I was cautiously driving down the road. The blue Chevy pickup in front of me suddenly slapped on his brakes in order to make a hard right turn. Even though I was following at a safe distance behind him, the lack of his use of a turn signal and the wet roads from the storm that had been going on all day caused me to hydroplane into the back of the truck. This is why I feel that I was not at fault for this accident.

As you can see, there is a vast difference between these two accounts. As might be expected, in the first one, the driver admits to his friend that he had not been paying attention to his driving. He also uses some colorful language to describe the other driver. In effect, he presents himself as a normal young man and the other driver as a big bully. In the second account, he places the blame on the other driver (not using his turn signal) and the weather. In neither account does he take responsibility for his own lack of attention to driving. But this is not a lesson in responsible driving; it's a wonderful example of how the same information can be changed radically for different audiences and purposes and, therefore, have very distinct effects.

Here is another situation where considering your audience may make the difference between getting what you want and being turned down: You have learned that some universities are offering noncredit courses free to people 60 years old and older. You decide to find out why the local campus of the state university is not offering this option to senior citizens. Which of the following letters is more likely to get a favorable response from the administrator to whom it is addressed? Why? Be prepared to defend your choice.

Letter One:

Dr. Janice Ellington
Director of Continuing Education
State University
Anytown, Any State
February 25, 2003

Dear Dr. Ellington:

What's this I read in the newspaper about our campus of State University deciding not to offer the Elderschool program? What the devil is wrong with you people?

We seniors have worked hard all our lives and paid local, state, and federal taxes. This money is what keeps your school open. If you didn't have our money, you'd have to close your doors.

Other colleges around here are offering similar programs. If they can do it, why can't you? I read that State is offering this option at all its campuses. So why the heck doesn't our campus have it? Aren't we as good as the upstate campus only 25 miles from here? Don't we support our campus just as much as anybody else does? Why are we denied our rights?

I'd like to take a course myself. Since I'm a retired policewoman, I'd like to take a course in criminal justice. Maybe I could teach these young cops a thing or two. Get those teachers of yours busy and make them earn their salaries.

Nobody in this area gives a darn about us senior citizens. Now your campus seems to have jumped on the bandwagon. You need to give your decision not to offer these courses a second look. You guys are really missing the boat, as usual.

Signed:

Amy Purpledress

* * *

Letter Two:

Dr. Janice Ellington
Director of Continuing Education
State University
Anytown, Any State
February 25, 2003

Dear Dr. Ellington:

I was reading the newspaper yesterday and came across an article regarding the decision of our local campus not to offer the Elderschool program to senior citizens. As I understand it, this is an opportunity for people 60 and up to take courses free. Personally, I think this is a wonderful chance for people to engage in lifelong learning. Many seniors are living on limited budgets but have time on their hands, so this program would look very attractive to them.

I think the campus should reconsider its decision not to offer this program for the following reasons:

1. Families in our area are very tightly knit. For example, you often see grandparents and even great-grandparents at school functions, such as plays and sporting events.

2. These elders have a great deal of influence on their children and grandchildren. If they took a course on campus and liked it, they might be more likely to recommend that their grandchild go to the local college. Their thinking might go along the lines of, "Oh, that nice place gave me a free course last year. You really should look into it."

3. No doubt other colleges in the area that are competing for students are already offering these free courses to seniors or are planning to.

4. If the problem is that this program would make more work for teachers, some restriction could be made that people could sit in on classes but that they would not have to take all the tests or do all the papers. This could be done on a case-by-case basis, at the discretion of each instructor. The faculty could be polled, and the instructors who don't mind having an extra person or two could volunteer to open their classes to the program.

5. The presence of adult learners in classes tends to have a positive effect on younger learners. These people are good role models since they generally come to class on a regular basis, pay attention, and respect the instructor.

6. Looking at this from a broader, more altruistic point of view, a better educated citizenry is likely to be more supportive of education in general. This could be a chance for seniors who have never been inside a college classroom to learn what goes on there on a daily basis.

7. Personally, I would love to take a criminal justice course since I am a retired policewoman. It would be an advantage to me to learn about the latest developments in the field.

Thank you for your consideration of this request. I do hope you will think about offering Elderschool in the future.

Sincerely,

Amy Purpledress

Here are two more examples to analyze:

Passage One:

"Catching on to What's Catching"

Some infectious diseases were (and are) slow to be recognized. If we can scan modern medical history a few decades at a time, we can see a pattern that is still evident today: The more obscure (or "cryptic") the chain of infection, the more slowly the medical community comes to recognize a disease as infectious.

In some cases, transmission from person to person is easily observed. Take chickenpox: Johnny was playing with Susie the day that Johnny came down with chickenpox; two weeks after that, Susie got it; and two weeks after that, Susie's little brother got it. It is no surprise that diseases with overt signs and symptoms—like chickenpox, with its red lesions and fever—were recognized as infectious decades and even centuries before the causative agents were identified.

Paul W. Ewald and Gregory Cochran, "Catching on to What's Catching," *Natural History* 108 (Feb. 1999): 34, 36.

Let's try to analyze this passage: What is the subject? Well, it's talking about germs and contagious diseases and how they are detected.

What is the purpose? It seems informative and descriptive.

Who is the audience? This question is a little harder to answer, harder to pin down. But you can make some educated guesses. While some of the language is formal (*transmission, cryptic*), much of it is informal. Consider the example: a common childhood disease affecting children with two ordinary names, Johnny and Susie. So you can rule out a strictly professional audience because they would know these things already. Yet the author seems to be assuming a certain level of education and intelligence; it is clearly not aimed at children, for example. Therefore, you come to the conclusion that it is a piece from a popular (as opposed to purely scientific) magazine designed to appeal to educated adults with an interest in science in general and germ theory in particular. And in fact, it is from the popular science magazine *Natural History*. Most readers of this magazine would find it easy to follow this style of writing because, once again, the authors have carefully considered their audience.

Passage Two:

Radials

The other approach to tire construction is the radial. Cord plies run almost parallel from side to side without the friction-causing criss-cross. The radial also uses belts which surround the tire just under the tread, allowing the tread to work independently from the sidewalls. This "tank-track" construction greatly reduces friction, giving more miles, cooler running tires, and increased gas mileage. The strong footprint and flexible sidewalls give that glued-to-the-road feeling, puncture resistance, and handling response other types lack.

The subject of this paragraph—radial tires—is clear. The purpose and audience may be a little harder to figure out, so we have to ask some questions.

What seems to be the purpose of this passage? In some ways it is informative; it tells the reader how radial tires are constructed and how they perform on the road. In other ways it is persuasive: "This 'tank-track' construction greatly reduces friction, giving more miles, cooler running tires, and increased gas mileage."

Who is the audience for this passage? At first you might think that it was written for engineers since it talks about the construction and performance of tires. On closer look, however, you may notice that it really doesn't give any specifications for the tires such as thickness of ply, sizes, or materials. So you have to consider another possible audience.

The consumer or person buying the tires comes to mind. How can you tell that this is a good guess? For one thing, the language is nontechnical. Terms such as *tank-track*, *strong footprint*, and *glued-to-the-road feeling* are used deliberately to make the driver feel safe. Also, references are made to the way the car handles with these tires. An appeal to economy is used in the reference to increased gas mileage.

The sentences are fairly short and easy to understand.

Also, the paragraph is short and to the point, increasing the possibility that the buyer (or potential buyer) will actually take the time to read it.

This is an excerpt from an informative booklet published by Michelin, written especially for the owners of these tires.

APPLYING WHAT YOU'VE LEARNED

1. Read an article in your favorite magazine. Decide what the author's subject, purpose, and audience are. Then write a one-page explanation of why you feel the style of writing is appropriate for its intended audience or not.

   Don't be afraid to be critical. Just because it is in print doesn't mean that an article is necessarily well written or appropriate for its audience and purpose.

2. You want to start a new club on campus. In order to do this, you have to write a proposal outlining why this organization is necessary and why it would benefit the campus community. You have to convince the administration that it should approve your proposal.

   To make this more practical, you could choose an organization or activity that you would really like to see introduced on your campus.

   Before you begin, outline what you would include in the proposal. Consider including a background of the present situation, why this new activity is needed, and who would benefit from it.

   Write a one-page proposal, keeping in mind your subject, purpose, and audience.

3. Find two articles on the same subject in two separate publications aimed at different audiences; for example, an article on employment in a magazine such as *Parents,* whose audience is young adults with children, and an article on the same subject in a magazine such as *Seventeen,* whose readers may just be entering the work force (or *Modern Maturity,* which is aimed at older adults who may be considering retirement or part-time work).

    Write a one-page paper explaining the difference in purpose and audience between the two articles. Decide if the authors have successfully adapted their writing to their apparent audience and purpose.

4. Your college has banned smoking inside all campus buildings. You and your friends who smoke object to having to go outside to smoke, regardless of the weather, and feel a smoking area should be established in the dormitories where most students live.

    Write a one-page letter to the director of student housing, explaining the situation and outlining why you feel an inside smoking area should be provided for students who choose to smoke. The director is your audience; be sure to consider your subject and purpose.

5. You have recently been transferred to a foreign country by your company. Unfortunately, you don't know yet that times are only approximate in this culture. In fact, you will soon learn that when you really have to be on time, "hora Americana" [American time] will be specified.

    One day you are invited to a noontime luncheon at your boss's home as well as dinner at 6 p.m. at the home of an American friend who also lives in this country. Although your friend's house is two hours away from the boss's residence, you figure that you can easily make both events. What you don't know is that "lunch" will actually be served some time after 4 p.m. Because you are contributing a casserole for the dinner (which will be served promptly at 6 p.m.), you have to make apologies and leave before lunch is served. Your boss and his wife are embarrassed and insist that you at least eat a snack before you go. As a result, you arrive late at your dinner.

    Write a note or e-mail to your boss, apologizing for having to leave early and missing what promised to be a delicious lunch.

    Write a note or e-mail to your American host, apologizing for being late and forcing people to eat part of their meal separately from the rest.

    Note: Remember that your lack of knowledge of cultural differences influenced both situations.

6. You have a term paper due on Monday that will be worth one-third of your final grade in the course. Your significant other invites you to go on a week-

end ski trip. You just can't turn down the offer; therefore, you don't have your term paper done on Monday morning.

Write an e-mail to your professor asking for an extension on the due date and giving an explanation of what happened over the weekend that prevented you from finishing the paper.

Write an e-mail to your best friend back home, describing the weekend and telling him or her why you didn't finish your term paper.

Compare the two written accounts. How do they differ in purpose and audience?

PART II

Discovering the Writing Process

CHAPTER 3

How Do I Get Started?

Many beginning writers think that they do not have anything to say. They cannot see themselves as authors; therefore, they often parrot trite, tired ideas that have been used over and over rather than trusting their own instincts and their unique abilities as writers.

First you must see yourself as a writer, as someone who has something worthwhile to say. Your writing should reflect your thinking and personality, not someone else's. You need to develop your own style and find your voice as a writer. If you use clichés and write in vague abstractions, you will end up with what Professor Parke Muth of the University of Virginia calls "Big Mac" essays, predictable and the same around the world. You may not realize it, but you have experiences and ideas which no one else has, and which are worth writing about.

ANALYZING YOUR ASSIGNMENT

Your instructor gives you an assignment, or your manager asks you to write a report, and you are wondering how to go about doing it. First, make sure that you understand what is being asked of you. If necessary, ask for clarification in class or at work. When you are asked, "Do you understand what you are supposed to do?" or "Does anyone have any questions?" speak up. Even though you may feel hesitant about asking what you consider a stupid question, your instructor or manager will be glad that you took the initiative to clarify the assignment. It is much better to ask questions at the beginning than to go ahead with the task and perhaps do it incorrectly.

The next thing is to decide how you can tailor the assignment to you. This does not mean changing the assignment to fit what you would like it to say or to make it easier for you. In the case of a writing assignment for a class, it does mean choosing a topic that you are truly interested in, one that you would prefer to spend time exploring rather than one that bores you.

For example, if you are assigned a process or how-to paper, and you are an avid skier, why not write a paper on how to keep those expensive skis in good shape by waxing them or doing other preventive maintenance? If this is more interesting to you than, say, writing about how to take a test, by all means pick the topic that you find appealing. You should choose one that is familiar or one that piques your interest enough that you are willing to find out more about it. Most instructors will give you some leeway on your choice of topic as long as you fulfill the objective of the assignment—that is, do what the assignment asks so that you learn the skill that it was designed to teach you.

EXERCISE 3.1   **TAILORING YOUR ASSIGNMENT TO YOU**

You are asked to write about an experience that changed the way you live your life. On a separate piece of paper, make a list of incidents that have influenced you greatly. Then pick one that you would actually like to write about, one that would be worth developing. Analyze why you chose this particular incident.

Understanding Your Assignment

If you do not understand your assignment, you have a number of options.

First, you could ask the instructor or supervisor to clarify the assignment and answer any questions you have. He or she will be glad you asked, rather than trying to do the assignment without a clear idea of what you are supposed to do. This is the best approach.

Second, if your college has a writing assistance center, you could go there for help. Remember to take your assignment with you, because the tutor needs to know what your instructor asked you to do. Usually these services are very helpful and free! Also, keep in mind that some of the best students use these services; they should not be thought of as remedial.

Third, if your instructor or a tutor is not available, you could check with a class member. Perhaps that person understood the assignment better than you did; be sure to pick a person who does well in the class, however, and whose opinion you respect.

Fourth, you could reread the section in your text that deals with this type of assignment. In many cases, the writing tasks will be closely related to the skills you are studying in your text.

Whichever method you choose, do not just go ahead and hope that it will turn out okay. Getting the assignment straight at the beginning will save you time later.

STEPS TO SUCCESSFUL WRITING

After you have picked a topic that you can live with, you need to think of writing as a series of steps, not just a one-shot, get-it-on-paper deal. Many writers do not see the value of spending a fair amount of time up front, before they put actual sentences on paper, and they find it even harder to proofread and revise, but experience has shown us that spending more time in the beginning saves time in the end.

Successful writing can be achieved by following a logical process, a series of steps that will enable you to come up with the end product (the finished paper) that you want. In most cases, if you take the time to carefully and thoughtfully complete each step in the writing process, you will be able to create a piece of writing that satisfies you and successfully fulfills the assignment:

- **Step 1:** Brainstorm ("Think in the Shower"): make a list of possible topics to write about.

- **Step 2:** Choose one topic that you can live with and form a main idea or thesis.

- **Step 3:** Organize your material, according to the main ideas and supporting details. Making a formal or informal outline is one way of doing this. See Appendix A for an example of a formal outline.

- **Step 4:** Write a rough draft, keeping in mind that you will make changes in it. Let it jell for several hours or a day before you revise this draft.

- **Step 5:** Revise and proofread your rough draft, using peer and professional review if available. Many instructors will provide time for peer editing.

- **Step 6:** Write a final draft, keeping in mind that this, too, can be revised.

- **Step 7:** Proofread for "typos" and mechanical errors (spelling, tenses, agreement, etc.).

- **Step 8:** Type a clean copy to hand in.

GENERATING IDEAS BY BRAINSTORMING

We have given you these steps so that you can see what the complete process looks like. We will discuss the various steps in the following chapters, but for the moment we are going to concentrate on the first step, **brainstorming**, which means searching your mind for any and all possible ideas that you could use in your writing.

Again, remember you have to think of yourself as a writer, someone who has something worthwhile to say. Most writers get their ideas from their own experience. Think of the writers you may have read. In *I Know Why the Caged Bird Sings,* Maya Angelou writes about growing up in the small town of Stamps, Arkansas, at a time when the South was still segregated. Ernest Hemingway writes about his experiences in Africa in *The Snows of Kilimanjaro,* and F. Scott Fitzgerald writes of his young, wild days in Paris in novels such as *This Side of Paradise* and about the life of the rich on Long Island in *The Great Gatsby.*

Now, you are saying to yourself, "But I can't write about Africa or Paris or even Long Island; I haven't been to these places." Maybe you don't know about the South if you grew up in the North and vice versa. However, you *do* know a great deal about where you grew up, trips you have taken, your friends, your family, your school (classes, sports, clubs), your interests, and jobs you may have held. All of these areas are rich sources for ideas. The question is, "How do I access these resources?" And the answer is by thinking about them, by searching your brain for material. It's there; you just have to access it. The following are some suggestions for how to do just that—search your brain.

Thinking in the Shower

Understand the assignment. Think through what you need to do before you start writing. We call this step "thinking in the shower" because the shower is an ideal place to sort out your ideas. Generally, you do not have other distractions there and are able to think through what the assignment or request is actually asking you to do. Any quiet place will do, however. The important thing is that you take this step, that you thoroughly understand what you are supposed to do.

Searching Your Five Senses: Freewriting

While you are aware that you have five senses, sometimes it is easy to take them for granted. When you are getting ready to start a writing assignment or work project, it is a good idea to consciously tap your senses and what they tell you about the world surrounding you.

One way to do this is by jotting down all that is going on around you. Write down what you see, feel, hear, smell, and even taste. Don't worry about spelling or putting your observations in sentences. Just jot them down in a list as they come to you. When you have a page or so of observations, stop and look at what you have. You will no doubt be surprised at the quantity and variety of what you have written. Depending on where you are (for example, on a busy street), one or two senses such as sight and sound may predominate; that's okay. The purpose of this exercise is to make you more aware of what is going on around you, to access your sensory observations. Here's a list one student made:

Observation List

orange juice carton on table	TV blasting
cars passing	sleepy
birds chirping	hot
sun shining	odor of burned coffee
bones ache	tired
spilling coffee	dishes in sink
kids screaming	cereal box torn open

Reading this list, you can see that some of the observations are related to hearing—*birds chirping, kids screaming, TV blasting*. Others are related to seeing—*cars passing* (may also involve hearing), *sun shining, spilling coffee, dishes in sink, cereal box torn open*. Others are related to feeling—*hot, sleepy, tired, bones ache*. And one is related to smelling—*odor of burned coffee*.

Here is the student's focused paragraph, based on selected observations from the list. Note that the student chose only two related observations to discuss. The main idea for this paragraph, which pulls the observations together, is highlighted.

Focused Freewriting

Every morning Americans wake up and prepare to face the day ahead of them. After convincing themselves that they have to get up, most people head for the kitchen. They are looking forward to that first cup of coffee, which will jump-start their bodies for the day. That jolt of coffee through their system wakes them up and keeps them going until they can get to work, where they get a second or third cup to get them through to lunch. **Morning coffee has become an American tradition**. Millions of Americans drink several cups daily, in spite of warnings from health professionals about the dangerous physical effects of caffeine on the body. Coffee seems to have a positive psychological effect on people. It helps them face the day. However, spilling one's coffee seems to signal a lousy day ahead. If you spill that first cup, maybe the best thing to do is stay home. Whatever happens, it is unlikely that Americans are going to give up their morning coffee any time soon.

—*Lois Herron*

In this paragraph, the writer has used two of her observations to make comments about the coffee drinking habits of Americans and some positive and negative effects of these habits. This is a well-focused, honest, even humorous look at a tradition which most adult Americans can relate to.

EXERCISE 3.2   **USING YOUR FIVE SENSES TO GENERATE IDEAS FOR WRITING**

Choose a place (either indoors or outside) where some action is going on. Find a place to sit, and for about ten minutes write down on a piece of paper everything that you see, hear, smell, taste, and feel. Don't worry about spelling or expressing your ideas in sentences. Just jot them down. You will be surprised at how much is going on around you that you were not aware of. Keep your list; you will need it later.

EXERCISE 3.3   **USING YOUR OBSERVATIONS TO GENERATE IDEAS FOR WRITING**

To get the most out of your list, leave it for a short time and then go back to it. Read through the list carefully and pick *one* observation that you would like to write about. Choose something that would be interesting to you and think about what you can say to make it meaningful to your audience. Write a sentence, based on that observation, which expresses the main idea of your paragraph. Use this sentence to write the paragraph described in the Applying What You've Learned section at the end of this chapter.

_____

_____

Searching Your Memory

Another way to generate ideas is to freewrite about your memories. You may recollect things that happened long ago, fairly recently, or both. All of these can be useful as subjects for writing.

This time, pick a quiet spot where you can be alone and think. Now you are going to access what is inside of you rather than outside. You may find yourself thinking about your first day of school, your first date, your first day on a new job, celebrating a certain birthday, losing a friend, breaking up with your significant other, or making a big mistake. Your memories may be happy, sad, or both. The idea is to get them out in the open where you can use them. Here again, don't worry about form; just write these down in a list. Also, don't try to edit them as you go. Later you can take out the very personal things that you don't want to talk about. Again, keep your list so that you can use it for a focused writing. Here's a list one student jotted down:

Memory List

grandmother's swimming pool	playing soccer and basketball
velcro he-man sneakers	for school
first friendship in preschool	starting high school
finger painting in kindergarten	sophomore summer
birth of my sister	working--tough balance among school,
getting used to grade school	friends, job, relationships, social life
playing little league	paying own bills, managing money
Nintendo--"new wave technology"	starting college--starting over

As you read through his list, you see that the memories are chronological, starting with preschool and continuing through college. While this is fine for this writer, not all students' lists will be organized the same way. Some students will concentrate more on recent memories, others on older memories. The point is that the basic process works for everyone—sitting down in a quiet place and just letting the memories come to you. The next step is to choose a memory that is interesting to you and to your intended audience and write about it. A word of warning: don't try to write about all the memories; the result will be just a boring list.

Here is the focused paragraph the student wrote based on one of his memories. Note the main idea, which is highlighted.

Focused Freewriting

Finger painting in kindergarten was an experience I will never forget. That was the first time I ever painted, let alone with my fingers. I remember that I used my Dad's old, white, button-down shirt as a smock. It was a crazy day at school because everyone was so wound up, and the teacher even threatened to cancel the big event [painting]. When the moment finally came, toward the end of the day, I think everyone was more excited about getting messy than creating the actual artwork. The assignment was to paint your favorite place during your favorite season. I painted the Little League field during the summertime. I was never so proud of my work, but now, looking back on it, it was really nothing more than a giant green blob. So whenever I look back on my old artwork, it takes me back to a time I miss, when I enjoyed life with the innocence of childhood.

—Bill Conklin

EXERCISE 3.4   **USING YOUR MEMORIES TO GENERATE IDEAS FOR WRITING**

For about ten minutes, write down on a separate piece of paper all the memories that you can think of. What did you do on your tenth birthday? What was the first day of school like? of college? of a new job? In the past, what made you very happy? very sad? What was your wedding day like? Here again, don't worry about form; just write these down in a list. Keep the list; you'll need it later.

EXERCISE 3.5   **FOCUSING AND WRITING**

Using the list you created in Exercise 3.4, pick one memory and develop it into a sentence that expresses a main idea about that memory. Choose a memory that is meaningful to you and that will interest your audience. Use this topic sentence to write the paragraph described in the Applying What You've Learned section at the end of this chapter.

_____

_____

Searching for the Unexpected

Yet another way to generate ideas is to freewrite about unexpected happenings or situations that you encounter.

Every day unexpected, odd things go on around us; most of the time we don't pay any attention, probably because we are used to people acting strangely or we are preoccupied with our own concerns. However, if we keep our eyes open for these things, we discover that they surround us. Everyone, including us, has foibles and idiosyncrasies, and strange things can be observed every day. Some of these are visual, such as a sign with incorrect spelling ("House for Sail"), while some are behavioral. For example, a person may get dressed up just to go to the gym or wash the dishes in hot water and soap before putting them in the dishwasher! Here are some examples that students have observed:

- An overweight person comes into a fast-food restaurant, orders a double cheeseburger with extra-large fries, and then says, "I'll have a diet Coke with that."
- A sign says "No Parking During Snow Emergencies" but is covered with snow and can't be read.
- Two people are IMing [instant-messaging] each other in the same room, on side-by-side computers.
- A "pound" cake weighs only 11 ounces.

EXERCISE 3.6   **USING THE UNEXPECTED TO GENERATE IDEAS FOR WRITING**

Keep your eyes open for the unexpected, unusual things that go on around you every day. These observations may be visual (signs, labels, written policies, people's actions), auditory (odd things that you hear), or a record of something you have observed about people's behavior in the past. This way of generating ideas for writing incorporates the other methods we have discussed. You have to use your senses, and you can use your memory as well. You have to be alert, but you can also recall the peculiar actions of the people you know, such as friends, family, and co-workers. Write these things down when you see, hear, or think of them. Keep a small notebook handy for the purpose.

This exercise should be fun; it makes you more aware of what is happening and generally provides a laugh at the same time. For example, it's hard not to giggle when your roommate or spouse gets up, showers, styles her hair, puts on makeup, and heads off to the gym to work out. An hour or so later she is back, repeating the same procedure. And guys can look fairly silly, spending a half hour getting their hair "just right" before going to a fitness center. In response to this assignment, one student came up with the following:

List

My dog turns around in circles before she lies down.
A lady bought a big bag of dog food and had a little dog.
A sign that said Ped Xing
People go to Wendy's and order a side salad with lo-cal dressing, a
small diet drink and a double cheeseburger.

| EXERCISE 3.7 | FOCUSING AND WRITING |

Using the list of unexpected happenings you created in Exercise 3.6, pick *one* observation and develop it into a main idea by saying something about that unexpected situation or action. Choose something that has meaning for you and that will appeal to your audience. Use this sentence to write the paragraph described in the Applying What You Have Learned section at the end of this chapter.

_____

_____

Focused Freewriting

When I was in Giant [supermarket] one day, I noticed a lady buying a very big bag of dog food. I thought to myself that she must have a big dog. The lady left; then I left. As I walked out to the parking lot, the lady was going to her car. When she got there, I saw that there was a small dog inside, and the lady said, "Look what Mommy bought for you!"

—*Wendy Witkowski*

This paragraph is funny and effective, because it is focused and leaves the conclusion (big bag of food/little dog) to the reader.

Another student responded to the assignment this way:

List

Why are there 10 hot dogs in a package but only 8 buns?
Why does Carol, a deaf teenager, go to dances to "hear" the music?
Why does a poor man give away his only jacket to someone he felt was less fortunate, in the middle of winter?

Focused Freewriting

Hot dogs are one of America's biggest conspiracies! They are widely enjoyed at sporting events, picnics, and parties, and generally with any meal, but hot dogs are involved in one of the greatest secret conspiracies. Hot dogs, you see, come in packs of 10 while hot dog buns come in packs of 8. Therefore, you would need to buy 80 or 160 hot dogs and buns to make your purchase thoroughly cost effective; if you do not buy that many hot dogs and buns, you will always have some left over. Families all over America are being affected by this conspiracy. So next time you have a family picnic, think twice about serving hot dogs, and instead grill up some hamburgers.

—Seth Hueter

This student has kept his eyes open, thought about what he sees, and used one of his observations to come up with a humorous, clever piece of writing that not only his teacher but also his peers can relate to.

Keep in mind that the purpose of this and the other brainstorming exercises is to make you aware of all the useful ideas that you have stored in your mind. These exercises are designed to get you started. Later on, of course, you will have to do more research to develop and support your ideas, but by then you should feel more confident about your writing because you already know how to do it.

Keeping a Journal

Another way of generating ideas is by keeping a journal. Many instructors recommend that you write several days a week in a separate notebook that you keep for this purpose.

Even if you are not required to do this, it is a good idea to write in your journal on a regular basis anyway. Writing regularly is like playing tennis every day or doing aerobic exercises to stay in shape or to become a better athlete. You hone your skills by practicing them. Similarly, you become a better writer by writing. A journal gives you a convenient, portable way to practice your writing any time you wish. You should spend 15 to 20 minutes (more if you wish) four or five days a week, or daily, making journal entries. (Your instructor may specify how much time you should spend on your journal.)

The more you write, the more comfortable you will become with the process of getting your ideas on paper. It's as simple as that. Writing gives you a channel to explore your impressions of what you are reading or hearing, or allows you to clarify your dreams and ambitions and get your frustrations out in the open where you can deal with them. There are two kinds of journals: *reaction* and *personal*.

In a *reaction journal*, you write your responses to assigned readings and/or class presentations and lectures. When writing this type of journal, you must give evidence that you have read and understood the assignments as well as paid attention in class. The instructor wants to see that you have understood the material clearly enough to make perceptive comments on it.

In a *personal journal*, on the other hand, you write about your ideas, feelings, and events in your life. These may or may not be related to classes you are taking. In a way, a personal journal is like a sophisticated diary.

As you write either type of journal, you are consciously (or subconsciously) generating and refining topics and ideas that you can use in your writing. In a nutshell, you can clarify your ideas, express your wildest dreams, release some of your frustrations, come up with topics to write about, and improve your writing skills, all for an investment of 15 minutes a day and a notebook. Why not try it?

<table>
<tr><td>EXERCISE 3.8</td><td>STARTING YOUR JOURNAL</td></tr>
</table>

If you don't already keep a journal, start one today. Find a time each day when you feel you will be able to write without interruption for about 10 minutes. For the next week, try to write at that same time every day. You can explore your dreams, plan your future, examine a character flaw, or try to organize your schedule. Since it's your journal, all topics you choose to write about are acceptable.

WRITING ON THE JOB

Joyce Steinman

Magazine Editor

Joyce Steinman spends most of her professional (and private) life writing. She is the editor of *Panorama,* a monthly magazine that covers life and events in Hazleton and surrounding areas of North-eastern Pennsylvania.

Joyce was born and brought up in Hazleton, a small city near Wilkes-Barre, Pennsylvania. Joyce's enthusiasm for writing started early. She says, "I've always wanted to write, ever since the first time I knew there were things called words. Writing is something I have to do."

Her parents encouraged her to write by giving her a new diary each Christmas from the time she was eight years old. Her first brush with "professional" writing came in third grade when her teacher started a class newspaper. She remembers that it was "great fun" putting together that paper. From this experience she knew that she was hooked. She had a "tremendous desire to write."

She continued to write, and in high school she received the Kline Essay Award, a coveted prize, for comparing student life in Russia and America. She says that when she graduated from high school, about 40 years ago, girls were not generally encouraged to attend college. Regardless of a lack of formal training, she knew that she wanted to write. She comments that when she told people about her plans, though, they laughed and doubted she would be able to get a job writing.

Fortunately, after graduation, she became a copy writer for a local radio station. After holding this job for several years, she went on to five other radio stations, including two on Long Island, New York. During her radio career she wrote commercials, public affairs notices, public service announcements, material for special promotions, and editorials. During this time, she earned various awards, including the prestigious Pennsylvania Association of Broadcaster's Excellence Award.

Currently, as editor of *Panorama*, Joyce

- writes articles for advertisers
- pens a nostalgia column about the area entitled "Long Ago and Not So Far Away"
- edits all articles for the magazine
- supervises the rest of the editorial staff
- corresponds with advertisers and contributors

She says that in the 18 years that *Panorama* has been published it has grown from 16 pages to 128 pages and now has a circulation of 30,000. Joyce suggested the name for the magazine and has been with it since the beginning.

Joyce's writing is not confined to her professional life, however. She points out that she keeps a journal, writes poetry and letters as well as reports for her church council, and recently completed a booklet commemorating the two-hundredth anniversary of her church.

Her advice to college students is to "write, write, write." In other words, you learn by doing. She encourages people to "put down on paper what you feel." Even if an idea comes to you in the middle of the night, get up and jot it down. She also feels that if you have the opportunity to get a formal education, you should definitely do so. She says, "Go to school and acquire a knowledge of the English language." She also suggests that people read whatever interests them. Generally, good writers do a great deal of reading and learn from other writers.

So, as it turns out, Joyce was able to do something with her writing. For many years, she has followed her own advice to "write, write, write," and she doesn't show any signs of stopping. As she says, "I love words, and I love the way they make me feel."

EXERCISE 3.9   **RESPONDING TO WRITING ON THE JOB**

Answer the following questions.

1. What events in your younger life affected the career and hobby choices you have made?

_____

_____

2. How did your parents and/or other adults influence the way you live your life today?

_____

_____

3. What have you read lately that would give you some ideas for writing?

_____

_____

4. What childhood hobbies or interests do you still pursue today?

_____

_____

5. Use some of the answers to the previous questions to generate ideas for writing.

_____

_____

APPLYING WHAT YOU'VE LEARNED

1. Using the main idea that you wrote for Exercise 3.3, write a 150-word paragraph. Do *not* try to use everything on your list; if you do, the result will still be a list rather than a focused paragraph. Put the sentence containing your main idea at the beginning of the paragraph. Make it the first or second sentence. See Lois Herron's writing on pages 27–28 for an example of a well-focused, funny, sensory-based paragraph.

2. Using the main idea that you wrote for Exercise 3.5, write a 150-word paragraph. Do not try to use everything on the list. Use only the ideas that are relevant to your main idea. See Bill Conklin's writing about his kindergarten experiences for an excellent example of this type of paragraph.

3. Using the main idea that you wrote for Exercise 3.7, write a 150-word paragraph. Focus on the one oddity that you have chosen and comment on that. Briefly summarize the unexpected action. You may want to give a reason for it, but don't overanalyze why people behave this way. Keep it light and funny. See Wendy Witkowski's paragraph about the dog on page 36 and Seth Hueter's writing about hot dogs on pages 32–33 for good examples of discussions of the unexpected.

4. Read the following two observation paragraphs on the subject of people's attitudes toward losing. Which paragraph is more focused? Be ready to discuss which paragraph indicates that the writer has clearly focused on the main idea and developed it in a logical way. Which paragraph is easier to understand (indicating that the writer has considered what her audience needs to know)?

A. Everybody hates to lose, whether it is at a sport or a video game. I think they were playing for money, which makes losing even harder. I watched two people play each other at a video game. When the game was over, you could tell who won and who lost just by looking at them. I think he would have rather lost to the computer than to his friend. At least, the computer can't tell anyone. Sitting here I notice that the men take losing much harder than women do. Perhaps it is because of their egos or from playing sports as boys, but I think men definitely take losing worse than women do.

B. I spent part of last Saturday night at the video arcade. While there, I noticed that men react differently than women to losing. Everybody hates to lose, whether it's a sport or a video game, but men seem to get more upset about not winning than women do. I saw two guys playing a video game. After the game you could tell who won and who lost by the looks on their faces. The loser acted very sulky. My friend Sarah just laughed when I beat her at several games. I guess men just have bigger egos or feel that they have to defend their male images.

—Leah Portman

5. Keep a journal. Use a blank or lined notebook for this purpose. Write in it for about 15 minutes daily (or longer if you have more to say). If you're writing for yourself, put down whatever seems important to you. If you are doing this for an assignment, follow the instructor's directions. The idea is to keep writing on a regular basis.

CHAPTER 4

How Do I Write a Clear Sentence?

Aclear sentence starts with a clear idea of what you want to say. Knowing correct grammar and syntax will not help you until you know exactly the thought you want to convey. Once you have the idea distinctly in mind, however, certain conventions of English sentence construction will help you.

DEFINING A SENTENCE

A sentence, strictly speaking, can be as short as one word: *Stop!* The subject of this command (you) is understood. Since it would be limiting for the writer and boring for the reader to create a paragraph containing nothing but commands, most sentences consist of a subject, a verb, and a completer (SVC):

(S)   **(V)**   **(C)**
The snowplow **cleared** the <u>street</u>.

Simply put, the *subject* is the doer of the sentence or the person or thing to which something is done. The *verb* indicates active or passive action, and the *completer* does just what its name implies—completes the sentence.

- The completer may be the object of the action done by the subject:

Juan filled out the application.

- The completer may say something about the subject:

Juan was qualified.

- The completer may be a word which means the same as the subject:

Juan was a qualified applicant.

However, many variations on this basic pattern exist and are correct as long as they follow the generally accepted rules of sentence structure. For a more detailed explanation of SVC, see page 171 in the Hub.

BUILDING A SENTENCE

Let's build a sentence. Start with these three words: *The store opened*. Now say something about what kind of a store it is: *department? grocery? discount?* Let's try *discount*.

The discount **store opened.**

Notice that we put this modifier or descriptor right in front of the subject. Where is this store?

The discount store on Green Street **opened.**

Notice that we put this information right after the subject, as close to it as possible. When did it open?

The discount store on Green Street opened yesterday.

Notice that we put the time indicator at the end of the sentence. You could also put it at the beginning, depending on how much you want to emphasize it. It usually would not go in the middle, though.

What else do we know about this store?

The discount store on Green Street, which had been closed for two months**, opened yesterday.**

We have added a *which* clause (a clause is a group of words that contains at least a subject and a verb) right after the subject because it tells us something about the subject. We have also put commas around it because it does not change the meaning of the sentence significantly. (For more information on clauses, see pages 186–190 in the Hub.)

What information or thought about this store do we want to add?

The discount store on Green Street, which had been closed for two months, opened yesterday, and its old customers were overjoyed.

Here we have added a whole new sentence and connected it to the original one with *and*. Be sure to put a comma before *and* when you are adding a new, independent set of ideas.

We now have a 21-word sentence, containing a great deal more information than the three-word sentence we started with. Yet this sentence is grammatically correct, because we added to it in acceptable ways.

| EXERCISE 4.1 | **FORMING SENTENCES** |

Choose one group from each column to make a logical sentence. Start with the subject groups on the left. The other groups do not necessarily have to be used in the order they appear. Use each group just once. Write the new sentences on a separate piece of paper. When you are finished, your sentences should form a unified paragraph.

SUBJECT GROUPS	VERB GROUPS	COMPLETER GROUPS
1. Bikers	keeps	the roadways for the woods.
2. Many riders	have left	peace and tranquility.
3. Bikers	have traded	riders on their toes.
4. The ever-changing terrain	has resulted	their thin tires for fat ones.
5. The growing popularity of mountain biking	find	in clubs for riders.

RECOGNIZING FRAGMENTS

Many students have trouble with fragments, or parts of sentences masquerading as real sentences. Usually a fragment results when a writer doesn't complete a thought or tries to make two sentences out of a group of words that should be only one sentence.

A colleague of ours, Kathie Kemmerer, came up with a sentence recognition trick. When you are faced with a group of words and are unsure whether it is a sentence or a fragment, try this easy test:

Imagine that you are in a room when a person you care about (and who always makes sense) walks in, says that group of words, and walks out. Does what that person said make sense, or are you concerned about his or her mental health?

For example, if your sensible person walked into the room and said, "Cars on the highway," and walked out, because you care about this person, you might wonder, "What's wrong with him or her?" In contrast, if your person said, "Joe was in an accident," you might ask, "Was he injured?" In this case you would not be worried about the speaker; your concern would be for the content of the message, which made sense but lacked an important detail. The first group of words sounds crazy and is not a sentence; the second one is a sentence. Thus, if a group of words does not make sense on a very basic level, you can be confident that it is not a sentence.

Think about the following paragraph. Are the highlighted word groups sentences or fragments?

> Being able to write well and having a background in political theory opens many doors for careers. Such as being a lawyer or a legislator. I will definitely be writing in my chosen career. Either as a lawyer preparing cases or in the legislature, writing speeches and drafting laws. I feel that the importance of my writing will be to convey my ideas. To a judge or to the public.

The highlighted words illustrate the most common types of fragments—groups of words that belong to the thought that comes before them (or sometimes to the thought that comes after them). Reading sentences aloud can help you to avoid these mistakes. Don't conclude the sentence until you have completed the thought that you wanted to express. Here is the corrected paragraph:

> Being able to write well and having a background in political theory opens many doors for careers, such as being a lawyer or a legislator. I will definitely be writing in my chosen career, either as a lawyer preparing cases or in the legislature, writing speeches and drafting laws. I feel that the importance of my writing will be to convey my ideas to a judge or to the public.

For more information on fragments, see pages 175–181 in the Hub.

EXERCISE 4.2   RECOGNIZING SENTENCES AND FRAGMENTS

Decide whether the following groups of words express a complete thought and form a sentence. Remember that a sentence also needs a clear subject and a verb. Write *S* in the blank if the group of words forms a sentence; write *F* (fragment) if it does not. Then revise the fragments to make complete sentences.

_____   1.   People fear things that are unfamiliar to them.

_____   2.   Stop!

_____   3.   The one person I really relate to.

_____   4.   A shooting lane to the left with a well-lit target at the end.

_____   5.   Because he remained quiet and shy.

_____   6.   I have been to many record stores, but none were quite like Camelot.

_____   7.   A woman of great distinction to her country because she aided countless poverty victims who had almost lost the will to live.

_____   8.   Not having to worry whether they have enough money to do their laundry.

_____   9.   The pilot checking his landing gear before takeoff.

_____ 10.   After the concert, which lasted until midnight.

AVOIDING RUN-ON SENTENCES AND COMMA SPLICES

While the term *fragments* describes sentences that are too short or incomplete, the term *run-ons* indicates the opposite problem—sentences that are too long. These sentences result when a writer does not stop at the end of a complete thought and start over. Rather, the person writes in a stream-of-consciousness manner, putting down whatever comes to mind with no thought to punctuating these ideas so that they will make sense to the intended reader. Writing down whatever comes to mind works for brainstorming but not for a formal draft.

The following sentence about a music store is a run-on:

You can ask for anything you want they know where everything is from the least popular band to the most popular.

If you read this sentence aloud, you will probably stop at the word *want*. You may decide to add a comma to clarify what is being said. In that case, the sentence would look like this:

You can ask for anything you want , they know where everything is.

Unfortunately, you now have a *comma splice,* a comma that splices—or holds together—two main ideas. This won't work either, so how do you correct the run-on sentence and avoid the comma splice? Here are some solutions:

1.   Break the sentence into two shorter ones:

You can ask for anything you want. They know where everything is.

You can use a period or a semicolon to separate the two sentences. They both signal a break in thought, although the semicolon shows a somewhat closer relationship, and the next word is not capitalized. Our example with a semicolon looks like this:

You can ask for anything you want; they know where everything is.

2.   Use a connector called a *coordinating conjunction,* such as *and, or, for, nor, but, yet,* and *so.*

You can ask for anything you want, for they know where everything is.

Note: You need a comma before the connector.

3.   Use a connector called a *subordinating conjunction,* such as *because, since, before, after, while, as, if, even if, as if, though, although, as though, even though, so that, in order that, unless, until,* and *unless.*

You can ask for anything you want, because they know where everything is.

Note: You need a comma before the connector here too.

For more information on run-ons, see pages 175–180 in the Hub.

EXERCISE 4.3   RECOGNIZING AND REVISING RUN-ONS

Read the following paragraph and determine which sentences are run-ons and/or have comma splices. Then, using the four methods described in this section, revise the sentences on a separate piece of paper to make them grammatically correct. (There are several ways to do this, and your solutions may differ from those of your peers.)

The feeling you get when you order the food makes your mouth water, it's unreal that you can get this sensation even before the food arrives. When your meal comes, the fillet of fish covered with bread crumbs and fried in olive oil with a touch of lemon looks delicious all you want to hear is the crunch of your teeth biting through the crispy crunchy breaded outside of the fillet and the fish just melts in your mouth. The taste of this fish just blows the competition out of the water, there is no comparison with fish served anywhere else.

WRITING ON THE JOB

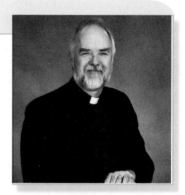

The Rev. Thomas J. Beam

Pastor and Writer

The Reverend Thomas J. Beam is pastor of Emmanuel Lutheran Church in Nuremberg, Pennsylvania, and Mt. Zion Lutheran in Zion Grove, Pennsylvania. He is also a writer and editor. In both of his professions, Tom writes almost daily.

Tom was born in Plymouth, Pennsylvania, and has spent most of his life in eastern Pennsylvania. He lived in Hulmeville, Pennsylvania, and attended Neshaminy High School.

After high school, Tom joined the Air Force, where he studied electronics. After leaving the service, he worked in various areas of the automotive industry; he was a tool and die maker, an auto mechanic, and a service manager for a car dealership.

At age 30, Tom decided to go to college, where he studied automotive engineering. He says his favorite courses were history and literature, though.

After college, he taught automotive technology courses at Spring Garden College in Philadelphia and Pennco Technical College in Bristol, Pennsylvania.

While he was doing all of this, Tom was writing for automotive magazines and became a technical editor for *Motor Age Magazine*. But Tom had wanted to become a pastor for a long time, and interestingly, the publishers of his magazine offered to pay some of his seminary expenses if he would continue to write for them. So in 1980, he graduated from the Lutheran Seminary in Philadelphia and combined his two careers—ministering and writing.

Today he serves his two churches, and his book, *Consumer's Digest Automotive Advisor,* was published in 2000.

So what kind of writing does Tom do on a regular basis? As a pastor, Tom writes

- sermons
- the congregational newsletter
- annual reports
- letters of recommendation
- general church correspondence

As a technical writer, he pens monthly articles for automotive magazines as well as books.

Tom's advice to new writers (who may be thinking about becoming published) is to "Write, whether it sells or not; the more you do it, the better the quality becomes." He also urges you to develop your own style, your own voice, because people will actually recognize your writing by its style.

Regarding technology, Tom says use your spell and grammar checkers, but don't let them dictate your style. Within the bounds of clear comunication, develop your own style. Don't be identified by the word processing program you are using.

Tom continues to write for fun and profit. He is currently writing what he calls some "fact-based fiction." He often weaves real-life stories into his sermons to help illustrate his points.

As you can see, writing is a very real, everyday experience for Tom. He says, "Writing is an endeavor of immersion; you can swim in it, you can get lost in it." And when he's lost in it, he's where he wants to be. ✍

EXERCISE 4.4   **RESPONDING TO WRITING ON THE JOB**

Tom's writing covers a wide area, from inspirational and theological to technical and even fictitious. What skills do you think are required to write in these various styles? How do you think one learns to write across so many different areas? How do you think Tom would answer this question based on what he has said? In terms of your own life, what kind of writing do you do or can you see yourself doing in the future? How would you learn to do these various types of writing?

_____

_____

_____

_____

_____

_____

_____

_____

_____

_____

APPLYING WHAT YOU'VE LEARNED

1. Revise the following fragments so that they become complete sentences. You may move the words around or put these word groups (or phrases) at the end of your sentences.

   (a) All the players being well trained . . .

   (b) Unlike yesteryear when women were stereotyped as being homemakers and bearers of children . . .

   (c) For example, the housewife whose job is to clean, take care of the children, and have dinner on the table . . .

   (d) Independent individuals who feel they can do whatever a man can . . .

   (e) Also, the saying, "Blondes have more fun!" . . .

   (f) Because of a simple lie . . .

   (g) Being a crafty person at the time . . .

   (h) When the teacher turned around fast . . .

   (i) Because everyone knows that sooner or later the truth will come out . . .

   (j) Which is why the attitude of the television newscasters has changed . . .

2. Read aloud a piece of your own writing or that of a friend and be alert for fragments masquerading as sentences. Mark the fragments and decide how they could be revised to express a complete thought that makes sense.

3. Develop each of the following sentence starters into complete, sensible sentences by adding the five parts (a–e) to each sentence. Move the original words around as necessary. See the sentence about the discount store on pages 39–40 as an example.

(a) a word that tells something about (describes) the subject

(b) a word or phrase that tells where the subject is or where the action happened

(c) a word or phrase that tells when the action happened

(d) a group of words that tells something else about the subject (use *which* or *that*)

(e) a group of words that add a complete, additional thought about the subject (use *and* or *but*)

The store closed . . .

The university opened . . .

The semester started . . .

Exams began . . .

The party ended . . .

4. Read the following paragraphs and underline the fragments. Then revise these groups to make clear sentences; combine ideas and add words if necessary.

Is knowing about the private lives of public officials a good or bad thing? Can life in public service ever be private? There is one fundamental fact about this debate. Which is that the attitude of the news media has changed drastically in the last few years. There has been a shift in the way news is presented. This shift is called "tabloidization." Which has been defined as changing from factual reporting to gossiping and making suggestive remarks. Basically from using valid sources to using hearsay.

The public craves gossip and information about the lives of its public servants. Especially the president. One prominent senator commented, "The reality now is that a president's life is public." This is a prerequisite for being a politician. Accepting that one's private life is no longer private. Although a tough realization, an unavoidable one.

Perhaps there is some good in this situation. This lack of privacy in politics may make officials think twice before doing something questionable. Because everyone knows that eventually whatever was done will become public knowledge.

5. Rewrite the following sentences to remove the comma splice. (1) Use a coordinating conjunction or connector (*and, or, for, nor, so, but, yet*) to create two independent clauses. (2) Use a semicolon between the two sentences. (3) Make two sentences. (4) Use a subordinating

conjunction or connector to create an independent and a dependent clause (*because, since, before, after, while, as, if, even if, as if, though, although, as though, even though*). Do this for each one as indicated.

(a) He is a good player, he will win the championship.

Coordinating conjunction: _____

Semicolon: _____

Two sentences: _____

Subordinate conjunction: _____

(b) Technical subjects are easy for me, I will major in information systems technology.

Coordinating conjunction: _____

Semicolon: _____

Two sentences: _____

Subordinate conjunction: _____

(c) About half of all marriages end in divorce, that doesn't stop people from getting married again.

Coordinating conjunction: _____

Semicolon: _____

Two sentences: _____

Subordinate conjunction: _____

(d) Herbal remedies are not regulated by the government, they are still widely used.

Coordinating conjunction: _____

Semicolon: _____

Two sentences: _____

Subordinate conjunction: _____

(e) Some people like to live in the past, there is no turning back.

Coordinating conjunction: _____

Semicolon: _____

Two sentences: _____

Subordinate conjunction: _____

CHAPTER 5

How Do I Use Sentences to Create Well-Developed Paragraphs?

Paragraphs are useful to the writer because they make it possible to cluster like ideas together in a logical, organized sequence before going on to a related idea. Paragraphs are useful to the reader because they break writing into chunks that can be easily understood. Breaking essays into paragraphs is like cutting your food into pieces that can be chewed and digested. You don't have to eat the whole "steak" at once. The white space between paragraphs gives the reader's eyes a rest and makes the page more inviting to look at. Long sections of print can seem very intimidating to any reader.

A paragraph is a group of sentences, all on the same topic, which discusses or describes a certain aspect of that subject. A paragraph usually consists of a topic sentence, several body sentences, and a concluding sentence (which may also lead to the next paragraph).

TOPIC SENTENCES

A topic sentence expresses the main idea of your paragraph. Since a paragraph should have only one main idea, the topic sentence keeps you, the writer, on track and helps the reader to focus on what you are saying. Paragraphs have different shapes; therefore, the topic sentence will not appear in the same place in each one. And, yes, you can have a paragraph without a topic sentence, but it will be a lot harder to organize, so we suggest that you think about writing a clear topic sentence for now.

PARAGRAPH SHAPES

Paragraphs have three basic shapes: the triangle, the inverted (or upside-down) triangle, and the hourglass. They look like this:

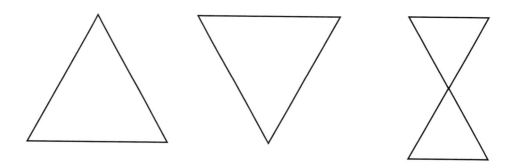

Where do you think the topic sentence would be in the triangle-shaped paragraph? If you said, "at the top," you are right. Then the details of the paragraph flow out from this topic sentence.

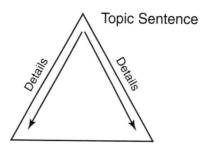

One example of this type of paragraph would be a persuasive passage. Your topic sentence would state what you would like your readers to believe, and you would follow with the reasons that support this idea. A student reviewing a restaurant wrote the following:

College students are always looking for a great place to eat and still have money to have fun with on the weekend. They need look no farther than about a mile down Route 93 from the Hazleton Penn State campus to find the Yong Hao Buffet, conveniently located in Valmont Plaza. Their buffet of diverse Chinese classics can make any mouth water. The service is extraordinary, and it is as clean as a grandmother's bathroom. Best of all, it will not leave a college student broke.

—Eric S. Reich

Having established the main idea—that students need to find good, inexpensive places to eat—at the beginning, this writer spends the rest of the paragraph describing a Chinese restaurant that actually exceeds these criteria.

If the topic sentence is at the beginning of the triangle-shaped paragraph, where do you think the topic sentence would be in the inverted triangle-shaped paragraph? If you said, "at the bottom," that's correct. In this paragraph the details come first and lead up to the main idea.

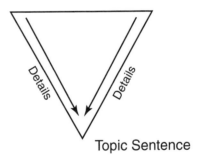

One example of this type of paragraph would be a description used to make a point, such as the following:

Imagine staying in a hotel with another person you do not know. Imagine the room that you are staying in is only about eight to ten feet long and so narrow that you can spread your arms and touch both walls. To many people, this is not a hotel; it is their home. When I was a junior in high school, we took a trip to Rahway [New Jersey] State Prison to ask the prisoners questions about prison life. I think every student should visit a prison at least once to make him/her think twice about breaking the law.

—Andy Stankovich

Here the writer describes something that most people are familiar with—a small room (perhaps a closet) barely wide enough to spread one's arms in—and compares it to a situation most people are unfamiliar with—spending every day in such a room with a stranger. Having raised the reader's curiosity, he makes his main point: A student might be less likely to break a law if he or she knew what living in a prison cell was like.

By now you should have a good idea of where the topic sentence will appear in the hourglass-shaped paragraph—in the center. In this type of paragraph, the details lead up to, and away from, the main idea.

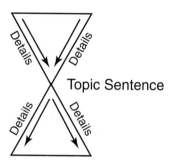

Here is an example:

> At the Mountain Lake Biological Station in Virginia's Allegheny Mountains, the roadsides are dotted with white campion (*Silene alba*), a weedy invader from Europe. Botanist Janis Antonovics had spotted the gangly plant on visits to the station and recognized it from his childhood in England. He also knew why many of its white, three-quarter-inch flowers sported smutty black centers instead of the usual yellow ones. These plants were infected by *Ustilago violacea*, a fungus, or smut, that also plagues white campion in Europe. This smut essentially commandeers the plants, forcing both male and female flowers to produce fungal spores instead of pollen or ovules.
>
> Yvonne Baskin, "Birds, Bees, and STDs," *Natural History* 108 (Feb. 1999): 53.

The main idea of this paragraph is that the fungus, *Ustilago violacea*, attacks plants in Europe and the United States. The writer starts out with a discussion of where the campion plants can be found. Then she says that the center of its white flowers are usually yellow, but that the botanist Janis Antonovics noted that the ones at the Mountain Lake Biological Station in Virginia had "smutty black centers." Now the reader's curiosity is aroused—what would change the centers from yellow to a smutty black? The writer answers this question very clearly in what becomes the topic sentence of the paragraph, "These plants were infected by *Ustilago violacea*, a fungus, or smut, that also plagues white campion in Europe." The rest of the paragraph goes on to describe how the fungus attacks plants.

You should have in mind the "shape" of what you are writing. It will help you decide how to organize what you want to convey to your reader.

EXERCISE 5.1   IDENTIFYING PARAGRAPH SHAPES

Read the following paragraphs and determine how they are organized. Underline the topic sentence or sentences. Then decide which pattern the paragraph most closely resembles: the triangle (*T*), the inverted triangle (*IT*), or the hourglass (*H*). Mark *T*, *IT*, or *H* in the space after the paragraph.

1.   In Maya Angelou's essay, "Graduation," she describes her class's preparations, attitudes, and letdowns during their graduation. In her neighborhood, graduation was a grand event, and everybody got involved in the ceremonies. Maya and the rest of her graduating class of 1940 had many dreams about being successful, but their spirits were dampened by Mr. Donleavy's (a white politician) speech. Once again, Maya, her classmates, and the Black community had to come together and bounce back from discrimination.

—*Eric S. Reich*

Paragraph Pattern: _____

2.   The house lights blink, dim, and finally go out. Somewhere in the faint light visible under the front of the stage, the orchestra begins to play the overture. The people settle down, make their final, whispered comments to the people next to them, and get comfortable in their seats as the curtain rises. You can feel the anticipation in the air. The performance of a long-awaited show has begun.

Paragraph Pattern: _____

3.   Last summer I took a very big step and moved to the shore for three months. The house and my job had been taken care of prior to the summer. The months of December through May I spent dreaming of the fun that lay ahead of me: the days I would spend basking in the sun, the afternoons working, and the nights out with my friends. I couldn't wait to get there. June finally arrived, and I was headed for the sunny shores of Rehobeth, Delaware. The night of June 15th I packed the car and was off. I was about to learn a major lesson in life. As I got closer to the beach, it started to rain, and it rained and rained, just the way to start off my "sunny" summer. As I entered Rehobeth, I realized that I had left the key to my apartment at home. I had to find my roommate and use hers. She was at work so I had to track her down. By this point it was raining so hard that I got soaked just running from the car to the restaurant. She was so busy that I waited an hour for the key.

Then I was off to my home away from home. After unpacking I was ready for the fun I'd been dreaming of for the past six months. It was nowhere to be found. I spent my first night at the shore alone, in my damp apartment, listening to the radio. Some exciting day!

Paragraph Pattern: _____

4.   Most people do not know how much valuable information you can acquire at a gym. You can get the type of input that can make your life a lot less stressful. The next time you go to a gym, open your ears and listen to your fellow weight lifters' advice. When you become a regular at your local gym, you can obtain some noteworthy suggestions. For example, some people start talking about how they wished they could have changed things in the past and done them differently. A twenty-six-year-old man once told me how he got his girlfriend pregnant when he was nineteen years old, got married at twenty, and never got a chance to go to college. He had to get a job in a factory and will probably have to work there for the rest of his life. After hearing that story I became more cautious because I didn't want to end up like him. You can get opinions on all types of problems. People can tell you how to fix that knocking noise your car makes, install your new computer, or even how to break up with a psycho girlfriend. So when you cannot find your answer in a book or computer, go ask your friends at the gym.

—Eric S. Reich

Paragraph Pattern: _____

CREATING COHERENCE AND UNITY IN A PARAGRAPH

In addition to a clear topic sentence that tells the reader what the paragraph will be about, other devices can be used to create unity or *coherence*. To *cohere* means to hold together in a logical way. If the ideas in your paragraph do not hold together logically, it is very hard, perhaps impossible, for your readers to understand what you are trying to tell them.

In Chapter 4 we talked about connecting ideas and sentences with conjunctions. These and other words that make it possible to connect ideas and go smoothly from one idea to another are generally called *transitional words.*

Transitions are similar to road signs, which help you find your way when you are driving. In writing, transitions tell the reader what to expect:

- **Add an idea:** *in addition (to), similarly, also, furthermore*
- **Give an example:** *for example, for instance, to illustrate*
- **Show change or comparison:** *however, in contrast, but, yet, on the other hand, though, even though, although, on the contrary*
- **Show result:** *therefore, thus, as a result*
- **Summarize or conclude:** *in short, to summarize, to sum up, in conclusion, to conclude*
- **Enumerate:** *first, in the first place, second*
- **Show time:** *finally, later, after a while, before, then, next, after that, eventually*
- **Show emphasis:** *indeed, in fact*

Note: Other words may be used to indicate transitions; these are only the most commonly used ones.

EXERCISE 5.2   **USING TRANSITIONS FOR COHERENCE**

Read aloud the following paragraph, written by a young musician. You will find that the sentences are very choppy and the ideas do not flow smoothly. Rewrite the paragraph, combining sentences and adding transitional words as necessary to improve the coherence and unity of this paragraph. Note that there is one sentence that doesn't seem to belong at all. Identify and delete that one.

After moving in with John last spring I began looking for a gig. I called talent agencies and hung out at the local music stores and bars. In a couple of weeks I had set up a few auditions. I found an apartment and moved out of John's place. I auditioned for several bands, and they seemed interested in me. I started going to local jam sessions to play and socialize with other musicians. They seemed to be in a clique. I got a call from a band in just a week. They needed me to fill in. I had some gigs with them and things were going well. My career went into a lull after those freelance gigs. The bands I had auditioned for had decided on someone else. No other groups needed players. I needed money. I looked for a day job to support myself until I could find work in a band. The regular jobs were as hard to find as the musical jobs. I was very depressed.

Another way of creating unity in a paragraph is by using pronouns that refer back to your subject.

| EXERCISE 5.3 | USING PRONOUNS TO UNIFY IDEAS |

Read the following paragraph. Note the highlighted pronouns. Determine what they refer to and be able to discuss how they contribute to the unity of the paragraph by tying ideas together.

> Every morning the mailman [he was a "man"] came into the office where I worked. He always had a smile on his face, regardless of the weather. Even when it was snowing or raining, he was cheerful and always had a joke for me. He made my day brighter all year around.

Yet another way to create unity is to repeat the main idea, ideally using synonyms or different phrases that express the same idea so that you are not just being repetitious. At the same time, you can remind your reader of what you're talking about.

| EXERCISE 5.4 | USING REPETITION TO UNIFY IDEAS |

Underline the ideas that have been repeated in the following paragraph. Then determine why the writer repeated these phrases. What effect does the repetition have on the paragraph? Be able to discuss your answers to these questions.

> One day while I was driving home I noticed all the trash on the sides of the freeway. I thought about how people throw their empty cans, bottles, and bags all over the roadways. Drivers who pitch garbage out of their cars have no respect for the environment. If everyone would just care for this world, beautiful landscapes could be preserved, but instead litter covers roadsides and fields. If people would just clean up after themselves instead of tossing stuff out as they drive along, the world would be a much prettier and healthier place.

APPLYING WHAT YOU'VE LEARNED

1. Write a triangle-shaped paragraph with the topic sentence at the beginning. Use one of your brainstorming lists from Chapter 3 to get an idea for the topic. Usually this sort of paragraph works well when you want to state an opinion at the beginning and support that idea in the rest of the paragraph. For example, "Whenever I eat at a fast food restaurant, I can't help but notice that many customers waste their money and don't even realize

it." The writer then goes on to explain how people fail to take advantage of free refills on drinks, buy a big cup when they could save by buying a smaller one, and the like.

2. Write an inverted-triangle-shaped paragraph with the topic sentence at the end. Check your brainstorming lists for a topic or brainstorm a new list. As we have discussed before, this sort of paragraph works well when you want to describe something or tell an anecdote (short story) to illustrate your point and pique the reader's interest before you state your main idea. For example, a writer might describe the hours, location, and salary offered for a certain position and then come to the conclusion that this is the perfect job for him or her.

3. Write an hourglass-shaped paragraph with the topic sentence in the middle. Brainstorm an idea or check your lists from Chapter 3. You could start with background material or a description of your topic, state your main idea, and then either agree or disagree with it. For example, you could highlight the main features of a popular restaurant or describe a mouthwatering meal you had there, state that it is an excellent place to eat (topic sentence), and then elaborate on why it deserves its good reputation.

4. Supply the missing transitional words in the following paragraph. Use words that fit logically into the meaning of the sentences. (See the list of transitional words on page 55.)

During my freshman year in high school, I wanted to play on the girls' volleyball team. _____ the tryouts, I learned that six other girls and I had made the final cut. Practicing volleyball two hours a day _____ being together for trips and games drew us together. We all became friends, and it showed when we played. _____, we ended the season with an overall record of 15-1. Going into our sophomore year, we decided to play _____. _____ tryouts, three new sophomores and one new freshman were added to the reserve roster. _____ two of our starting players were injured that year, we had enough talent to make up for their loss, and _____ we had an outstanding season.

CHAPTER 6

How Do I Tell the Difference Between a Topic and a Thesis?

It is important to understand how a topic and a thesis differ. A topic is an area or subject that you might like to write about. You should start with a topic that interests you and narrow it down to an aspect of this topic that you can form an opinion about. Only then do you have a thesis. For example, the environment is a topic, but a specific statement about how people can save the environment is a thesis. As a writer, you must be able to make a distinction between these terms.

In the same way that you took your ideas gathered from freewriting and narrowed them down to a topic sentence or main idea, you narrow down your ideas for a longer paper to a main or controlling idea called a *thesis*. A topic sentence is the controlling idea for a paragraph, and a thesis is the controlling idea for an essay, which is a series of related paragraphs on the same topic. (See Chapter 5 for more information on topic sentences.)

DEFINING TOPIC AND THESIS

Thesis is a word taken directly from the Greek and means "position," as in taking a position. The *Random House Dictionary of the English Language* defines a thesis as "a proposition stated or put forward for consideration, one to be discussed and proved." So when your instructor asks you to formulate a thesis for your paper, you need to think about a statement that expresses your opinion or that takes a position on a certain subject or topic.

For example, the statement, "The sky is cloudy today" is a statement of fact, but it's not a thesis because it does not express an opinion or take a position on the subject of the weather. On the other hand, "Cloudy days tend to make people feel sleepy" expresses an opinion, an idea, a position that needs to be explained or defended.

A simple way to test the effectiveness of a thesis is to use the "so what?" response. If the reaction to your thesis could be "so what?" you have just stated a fact, perhaps an obvious one at that, and no further thought or support is needed.

Checklist: Five Tips for Evaluating a Possible Thesis

A workable thesis should be

1. Stated as an opinion
2. Limited to one main idea
3. Stated in clear, concise terms
4. Expressed as a statement, not a question
5. Able to be proved (be logical)

EXERCISE 6.1   **DETERMINING TOPIC AND THESIS**

Keeping these ideas in mind, and using the checklist, evaluate the following statements. Which is a topic, and which is a thesis?

1. The time I was in trouble with my boss

_____

2. A memory that shaped me was my encounter with another vehicle

_____

3. The person that changed my life

_____

4. Getting a job

_____

5. The birth of my son

_____

6. When my grandfather died

_____

7. Moving taught me life lessons

_____

8. One of my best friends from elementary school got arrested at age 12 for accessory to murder

_____

9. Having another brother has changed my life in a lot of different ways

_____

10. About three months ago I made a decision that changed my life forever

_____

11. How my niece and nephew influenced my decision not to have children

_____

12. Meeting my girlfriend/wife changed the way I view life

_____

CREATING A WELL-FOCUSED THESIS

You could think of a thesis as sort of a contract with your audience. You are promising to talk about one limited subject, and not cover too much ground. In other words, your audience can expect that you will discuss the stated subject, not something else.

A common problem is that writers try to develop a thesis that is too broad; it covers too much material. For example, a writer who starts with a statement such as "Computers are a necessary aid to learning in high schools, colleges, universities, and even elementary schools" is headed for disaster because the topic is much too broad to cover in the usual 500- to 600-word paper.

| EXERCISE 6.2 | **REFINING YOUR THESIS** |

Look back at Exercise 6.1. Even the statements that meet the criteria for being a thesis could be worded more effectively. Revise these, using the checklist.

Number 9, for example, is fairly good, but *a lot of* is an overused expression, and *different ways* could be stated more explicitly.

Number 10 should be much more specific. The writer should say what changed in his or her life.

_____

_____

_____

_____

_____

_____

_____

THE "I THINK THAT" TEST

Another test of a thesis is to put the words "I think that" in front of it. If what you have said completes this thought, you may have a working thesis; just completing the thought does not guarantee that you have a logical thesis, however.

For example, "I think that getting a job" does not work as a thesis because it is not complete. It lacks an opinion. "I think that getting a job" what? Provides a valuable learning experience for a teenager? teaches a young person responsibility? Either of these endings works to balance your thesis by providing an opinion.

You can think of "I think that" as being similar to the training wheels you may have had on your bicycle when you were learning to ride. When you have learned how to balance yourself on your bike or how to write a balanced thesis (a focused statement expressing a single opinion), you can remove the training wheels. When your thesis says, "Getting a job teaches a young person responsibility," you can omit "I think that" because your opinion is now clear.

It may take awhile to write a thesis that states your opinion concisely and makes it clear to your audience exactly what you will be talking about, but it is absolutely essential to do this before you go on. If you don't have a workable thesis, it is impossible to develop the rest of the paper in an effective, logical manner. Therefore, it is worth devoting some time at the beginning in order to save time as you go along.

APPLYING WHAT YOU'VE LEARNED

1. Read the following sentences and decide whether each would or would not make a workable thesis. (Could you write a logical, clear paper starting with this thesis?) Apply the criteria discussed in this chapter (includes an opinion, is limited, clear, concise, provable, and stated as a sentence). Write a *W* (workable) or a *U* (unworkable) on the line beside each possible thesis; if you decide that the statement is not workable, revise and improve it.

   _____ (a) Today, the news media have too much influence over the outcome of elections.

   _____ (b) The Electoral College is an old, stupid system which should be abolished.

   _____ (c) Do we need campaign finance reform?

   _____ (d) It costs so much to run for office that only millionaires can consider public service.

   _____ (e) People get the government they deserve.

   _____ (f) Many young people do not bother to vote.

   _____ (g) A third party is necessary because voters have absolutely no choice with the Democrats and Republicans.

   _____ (h) With millions of people participating in elections, one person's vote doesn't count, so you might as well not vote.

   _____ (i) Election reform is needed at the city, state, and national levels.

   _____ (j) Responsible voters read up on the issues and candidates before they go to the polls.

2. Read the first paragraph in this chapter and decide what the main idea is. How does the rest of the paragraph relate to the main idea and support it?

3. Write a thesis for each of the five following topics. Keep in mind the guidelines for a good thesis, discussed in this chapter.

   (a) Online course scheduling

   (b) Peer tutoring services

   (c) Required courses

   (d) University restrictions on smoking in campus buildings

   (e) Parking on campus

   (f) Food in campus cafeterias

   (g) Gun control legislation

   (h) Political campaign finance reform

   (i) Alternative medicine such as herbal supplements

4. The following statements may be too broad or too simple to work as a thesis. Think about each idea, discuss it with your peers if possible, and revise it into a thesis statement that you could develop into a 400- to 500-word essay. Determine an audience for each thesis.

(a) Violence on television leads to violence on the streets and in our homes.

Revised thesis: _____

Audience: _____

(b) A college education is necessary for a good job.

Revised thesis: _____

Audience: _____

(c) We live in a materialistic culture.

Revised thesis: _____

Audience: _____

(d) Transportation on campus needs to be upgraded.

Revised thesis: _____

Audience: _____

(e) Gun control is a controversial issue in our society.

Revised thesis: _____

Audience: _____

(f) Most college students do not eat healthy foods.

Revised thesis: _____

Audience: _____

(g) Campus housing needs major improvements.

Revised thesis: _____

Audience: _____

(h) People should be able to download music free from the Internet.

Revised thesis: _____

Audience: _____

(i) Universities should provide free child care for students.

Revised thesis: _____

Audience: _____

(j) Public schools do not prepare students for college.

Revised thesis: _____

Audience: _____

How Do I Write a Rough Draft?

You've brainstormed some ideas, chosen a topic, perhaps done some research on it, written a workable thesis, and gathered your information into logical groupings. Now what do you do?

When asked to actually write an essay, many college students just sit down and start writing. We have already talked about how to generate ideas and come up with a topic and a thesis. Now we need to think about how we are going to organize our ideas. Here are some suggestions.

THE BLUEPRINT APPROACH

When a contractor builds a house, he or she usually follows a blueprint. The blueprint is an architect's drawing of what the structure should look like, with specifications for how to construct it. In essence, it is an outline for building the house. What do you think would happen if the contractor did not have a blueprint to go by? The result would be a very funny looking house, no doubt with one side higher than the other, windows and doors that don't fit, odd-shaped rooms, and other irregularities. In other words, the parts would not fit together to make a unified, useful structure. The same thing happens when a writer does not have a blueprint for what he or she wants to say, except that in this case the essay is disorganized and ultimately meaningless.

While builders rarely if ever build a serious structure without plans, writers attempt to "build" their essays without plans all the time. While it is easier to revise an essay than it is to remodel a building, making major revisions can be difficult. It is much easier to organize your ideas on paper *before* you start writing a rough draft.

How you organize your paper is up to you, or your instructor may specify that you write an outline. Unless you are required to write a formal outline, use a style that works for you. (See Appendix A for a sample outline.)

You may want to put your ideas in boxes or clusters of related information. Or you could write an informal outline, keeping in mind that you have to develop major headings or "umbrellas" to put related ideas under, and if something does not fit under the "umbrella," you either have to discard it or create a new heading for it.

A conventional college essay, for example, usually has five or six paragraphs: an introduction (one paragraph); a body (three to four paragraphs), and a conclusion (one paragraph).

The *introduction* generally consists of one paragraph and is used to establish your thesis or main idea. It also should create some interest on the part of the reader so that he or she will want to read the rest of your paper.

The *body* can consist of as many paragraphs as you need to convey to your reader what you want to say. The body contains examples, facts, and illustrations that support your thesis or develop your main idea.

The *conclusion* summarizes your ideas and ties up the ideas in the rest of the paper. It can also restate the main idea. It should leave the reader feeling comfortable that the paper has been wrapped up in a satisfactory way and not merely ended.

Let's see how this would look if you made the basic structure for that blueprint we talked about:

Introduction (usually including a thesis)

Body Paragraph One (First topic sentence)

Body Paragraph Two (Second topic sentence)

Body Paragraph Three (Third topic sentence)

Conclusion

GETTING STARTED

Getting started on a rough draft is the hardest part of writing. Some writers have the idea that their sentences will be cast in stone, and each sentence must be perfect. This is far from what actually happens when most people write.

Don't strive for perfection in the first draft, because you will undoubtedly make many changes before you get to your final version. Keep in mind that you can and should make changes. So get something on paper (or your computer screen) to get started.

Checklist: Eleven Tips to Help You Write That First Draft

1. Don't worry about perfecting the introduction; you will probably change it later anyway.

2. Write on notebook or colored paper to remind yourself that this is a rough draft, or print this draft on different paper from what you will use for the final draft. Use scrap paper if it is clean on one side.

3. If you don't use a word processor, you can still move sections around by cutting and pasting them onto another piece of paper.

4. Write your draft on one side of the paper only; it is easier to read, and you can cut and paste if necessary. Always write or print final drafts on just one side.

5. Write your thesis, but be aware that it may change. If it does, remember that writing a first draft is a process of exploring what you want to say. Don't limit yourself to your original idea if you feel that it isn't working. Your change may be for the better.

6. If you really feel that you can't get started, you may have what is called writer's block. One way to deal with writer's block is to use a tape recorder to capture your ideas. You can then listen to what you have said and make notes. Use these notes as the basis for writing your rough draft.

7. Take a break if necessary. After you have a preliminary draft done, get away from it for a day or so. When you go back to it, you will have a fresh perspective on what you have written. You will see where, for example, an idea needs to be clarified, where something needs to be added or taken out, and how material might be organized differently or expressed more clearly.

8. Don't worry about what your first draft looks like. You can correct spelling, word choice, and punctuation later on. This is the time to get your ideas down. First drafts are, by definition, messy. They should be.

9. Remember, above all, that a first draft is not meant to be a finished product. It is a process of finding out what you want to say.

10. Be aware that good writers seldom, if ever, are satisfied with their first drafts.

11. Keep in mind that a handwritten page (depending on your penmanship) will be only about two-thirds as long once it is typed. Of course, you will still have the same number of words.

You have probably heard or read the opening words of the Declaration of Independence. They sound as though they had come to Thomas Jefferson and

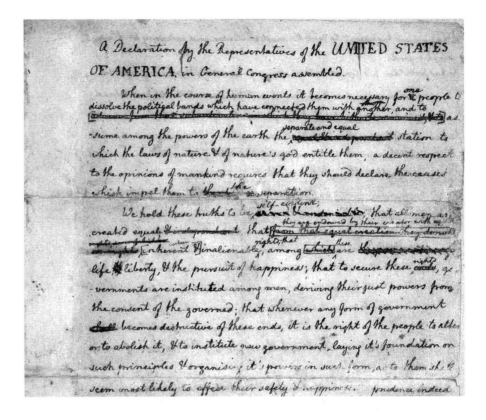

the other writers unchanged and in perfect order, perhaps through some divine intervention.

However, you may be surprised to see what the rough draft of this document looks like. Fortunately, a copy of it is preserved in the Library of Congress and is reprinted here along with a transcription so that the two versions can easily be compared.

When in the course of human events, it becomes necessary for ~~a~~ *one* people to ~~advance from that subordination in which they have hitherto remained,~~ *dissolve the political bands which have connected them with another,* and to assume among the powers of the earth, the ~~the equal & independant~~ *separate and equal* station to which the laws of nature and of nature's god entitle them, a decent respect to the opinions of mankind requires that they should declare the causes which impel them to the ~~change~~ *separation.*

We hold these truths to be ~~sacred & undeniable~~ *self-evident,* that all men are created equal ~~& independant~~, that ~~from that equal creation they derive rights~~ *they are endowed by their Creator with* ~~rights which include~~ certain & inalienable *rights, that* among ~~which~~ *these* are ~~the preservation of~~ life, & liberty and the pursuit of happiness; that to secure these ~~ends~~ *rights,* governments are instituted among men, deriving their just powers from the consent of the governed . . .

You can see that many words have been crossed out and replaced with terms that more clearly and accurately convey the meaning that the authors intended. For example, the phrase "for a people to advance from that subordination in which they have hitherto remained," which is dense writing even considering eighteenth-century style, has been revised to read "for one people to dissolve the political bands which have connected them with another." This phrase expresses much more clearly what had to be done—the colonies had to break the "political bands" which tied them to England.

Also, the words "We hold these truths to be self-evident, that all men are created equal" may sound familiar and "right" to us. Little did we know that the original said: "We hold these truths to be sacred and undeniable . . ."

So, as you can see, even the writers of the Declaration of Independence with all their wisdom had to revise what they wrote. It seems safe to say that they considered their first effort a rough draft and knew that they would have to make changes in it.

In terms of the actual process of writing, not much has changed over the last two centuries. We have advanced technologically; Jefferson, who had to write everything by hand, would be amazed by a manual typewriter, not to mention a modern word processor. But the procedure by which you get your initial ideas down in order to revise and improve them is basically the same as it was in the 1700s. Take a look at the original draft of this chapter below. You can see that many changes were made.

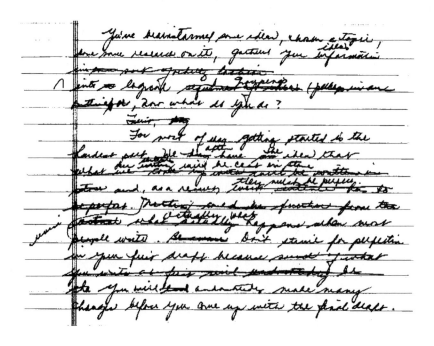

Experienced writers know that good writing involves rewriting. They write at first to get their ideas on paper, so that they can see what they want to say. Then they think about how it could be improved. They are not afraid to get started because they know they can always make changes later.

APPLYING WHAT YOU'VE LEARNED

1. Write a rough draft for the next writing assignment in your class or at work, whether or not you are required to hand one in.

2. Try writing a rough draft by hand. This will enforce the idea in your mind that this is not the final version of your paper. Just the act of having to type up the handwritten draft gives you the opportunity to make changes which will improve your paper. It forces you to take a close look at what you have written and decide if this is the best way to say what you have in mind.

3. Tape record the ideas for your paper. Then listen to what you have said and write your rough draft from the tape, adding or omitting material as you go along.

4. Read the following introductions. Then decide which one is the rough draft and which is the revision. What makes the revision better? See Chapters 9 and 10 for a more thorough discussion of introductions and revisions.

   (a) Every student has reports to write for at least one of his or her classes, but many of them have trouble getting access to a computer to type them. Not all students have computers in their dorms or homes, so they need to use the computer lab to type their reports. There are only 45 computers available for all 1,310 students on campus. Therefore, the ratio of students to computers is approximately 30 to 1. Every student should have a computer available when he or she needs one.

   (b) How do you feel when you go to the theater and find that the movie you wanted to see is sold out? Or how does it feel to arrive at your favorite store only to find it closed? Well, this is how the typical student on this campus feels on a daily basis in the computer lab. Rarely are there any computers available for students to use, since the ratio of students to computers is about 30 to 1. This is unfortunate because computers play a major role in a student's life, both academically and socially. Although not everyone can afford to own a personal computer, every student should have access to a computer when he or she needs one.

   —Jamie Tarone

CHAPTER 8

How Do I Organize My Paragraphs?

In Chapter 7, we talked about the blueprint approach to organizing your writing. Just as builders use a plan or blueprint to build a house, successful writers plan what they are going to say before they start writing. Builders have a choice of different styles for houses, such as Colonial, Victorian, ranch, bi-level, or farmhouse. The style of house which a contractor builds depends on the tastes, lifestyle, resources, and size of the family that will occupy it, as well as the shape and characteristics of the lot on which it is constructed. Similarly, you can choose modes or styles in which to express your ideas, depending on your subject, audience, and purpose, the three factors that we have emphasized all along. Some of the common ways to organize essays are the following:

- Comparison/Contrast
- Narration (telling a story)
- Description
- Example
- Process ("how-to")
- Argument/persuasion

If you are trying to point out the differences between two cars (or two periods in history), you should use comparison/contrast as your mode of organization. You may be comparing those two cars in order to persuade your reader that one is the better vehicle to buy. In the same paper you may give examples of why one car is superior. You may also narrate an experience you or someone you know had with the vehicle being considered, in order to point out an advantage or disadvantage of owning this car.

Be aware that more than one mode can be used in the same paper and usually is. For instance, a basically persuasive paper might use examples in order to get its point across. You should choose one mode as the dominant way of organizing your paper, however. This provides the blueprint or framework on which to arrange your ideas.

In this chapter, we look at the characteristics of these modes and give you examples of papers written in the various styles, along with their assignments. Keep in mind that any mode is used as a *means of organizing your ideas, not an end in itself.* Keep your thesis and purpose in mind. You control the mode; don't let it control you.

COMPARISON/CONTRAST

Comparing and contrasting is a widely used way of organizing ideas. For example, essay questions often ask you to compare two writers, two schools of thought, two historical figures or times, two political parties, and the like. When using comparison/contrast, however, keep the following points in mind:

- Choose subjects to compare that are basically similar. Don't try to compare Japan and your hometown.

- Know enough about your subjects that you can discuss both of them intelligently. Again, don't try to compare something unknown or exotic with something very familiar to you.

- Give both subjects equal time. Don't devote most of the paper to one item and barely discuss the other (this can be avoided by talking about two things with which you are equally familiar).

- Discuss the same characteristics of both subjects. For example, if you discuss the prices, hours of operation, choice, and quality of food in one restaurant, then you have to cover the same criteria for the other eating place.

- Compare and contrast for a reason: use the mode to develop and support your main idea. You don't want to end up with two lists of characteristics just for the sake of analyzing the two things.

- Organize your comparison/contrast paper according to an A+B pattern, an A/B pattern, or a combination of the two.

In the A+B pattern, you discuss one subject (A) thoroughly and then go on to discuss the other subject (B). The disadvantage of this pattern is that you force your reader to draw the comparisons after he or she reaches the end of the second paragraph. This may work for limited comparisons, though.

In the A/B pattern, you talk about both subjects in terms of their characteristics, which are the criteria or standards by which you are judging them. You would devote a paragraph to each standard. For example, you could discuss the prices at two restaurants in one paragraph, then use another paragraph to discuss the menu. The advantage of this approach is that the reader does not have to hop from paragraph to paragraph to make and understand the comparisons: they are right in front of the reader.

In some cases, a combination of the approaches is useful. You could start a paper by giving the historical background or a brief description of two establishments using the A+B pattern. Once the reader has become familiar with the two businesses being compared, you can use the A/B pattern to discuss the characteristics of the two establishments.

Provide an adequate conclusion for your comparison/contrast paper that restates your purpose for writing. You may want to conclude that one item or establishment is superior to the other, that you prefer one over the other, or whatever it is that you set out to discuss.

Comparison/Contrast Assignment: "Consumer Reports"

Choose two products, services, establishments, or sports teams (not individuals) and compare and contrast them using criteria that you have chosen according to the nature of your subject. Examples of products might be cars, computers, sports equipment, household appliances, hobby items such as different kinds of kits for the same project, stereo systems, house paints, or anything else purchased by consumers. Services and establishments may include banks, restaurants (fast food, upscale, ethnic, family, pizza places—don't mix types), Internet providers, car repair shops, department stores, discount stores, music stores, day care centers, video rental places, and supermarkets, among others.

Pick goods or services that you have used and are familiar with. You may want to do some research regarding prices and details, such as specifications, for example, but you should already have some of the information in your head.

The purpose of this comparison/contrast paper will be to show that, in your opinion, one of these products, services, or teams is superior to the other. Throughout the paper you must provide evidence that will support your conclusion. Be specific. This paper should have a clear thesis that indicates at the start which item you prefer, using the criteria you have established.

Organize your discussions of the criteria by starting with the least important and moving to the most important or vice versa, whichever approach seems to suit your subject.

You may want to use the A+B method, the A/B method, or a combination of the two.

Be sure to give both subjects equal time; pay attention to proportion when you are writing. Provide clear transitions such as "on the other hand" or "however" when you are introducing contrasts.

This paper should be about 500 words in length, so pick a subject that will give you enough to talk about.

Sample Paper: Here is an example of a comparison/contrast paper. It compares two utility vehicles. The criteria for comparison are highlighted.

Battle of the Utility Vehicles

Big people need big cars. That's just a fact of life. Of course, not all people drive big cars because they need the size. Some drive them because they need the hauling room or the safety that comes from driving a large vehicle. The cars that will best suit the needs of both types of people are the Chevy Tahoe and the Ford Expedition.

These beasts can be compared using the criteria of performance, style, seating, safety, and price. Both of these vehicles will be base trim (that means without all the bells and whistles).

The performance is important because it coincides with the fact that these are utility vehicles, not *sports* utility vehicles. For example, the Tahoe boasts a 5.7 liter engine. The Expedition comes with a base 4.6 liter, but you can opt for a 5.4 liter engine. The Tahoe would have a definite advantage in the trailer-pulling category, but it also gets worse gas mileage. Still, the Expedition can develop more torque than the Tahoe, so they end up very close in the performance tests.

Style and seating are also very important when choosing a vehicle. Style includes color combos and seat material. Both cars come in similar color packages, but only the Tahoe offers the two-tone color option. As for the interior, both have the option for cloth or leather seats. The major difference is that the Expedition can haul nine people, not five like the Tahoe. Still, when the third row of seats is in place, much of the trunk space is lost. That is a big loss for the Expedition.

As with any vehicle, safety is of utmost importance. Both are equipped with driver and passenger airbags and passed federal crash tests with flying colors. You can drive at ease with either of these vehicles.

The last issue to compare these two trucks is the big one: **price**! The Tahoe starts at $23,585. That is not a bad price for a truck that has that much to offer. The Expedition, on the other hand, starts at a high $29,370. I feel that is a little too much to ask for a car that does not offer that much in return.

In conclusion, it is apparent when comparing these two that they are very close in all areas. But I feel that the Tahoe is the better of the two utility vehicles. My opinion is based on the fact that the Tahoe has a bigger engine and more room for the passengers and any objects that you choose to store in the rear. The Expedition is way overpriced for what it offers. Both are excellent vehicles, but the Tahoe gives you more truck for your buck!

—Matthew E. DeWire

EXERCISE 8.1   **EVALUATING THE COMPARISON/CONTRAST PAPER**

Read the paper carefully and be able to discuss the answers to these questions.

1. Are the criteria chosen to compare these vehicles appropriate? What other criteria could be used to judge cars?

    _____

    _____

2. Identify the transitional words used in this essay. Are they effective? What other words could have been used?

    _____

    _____

3. Are you convinced that the Tahoe is best? Is there anything else you would have wanted to know?

    _____

    _____

4. In what order are the criteria discussed? What other order could have been used? What would be the effect of discussing them in another sequence?

    _____

    _____

NARRATION

In order to illustrate an idea or clarify a point, a writer often tells a story or narrates an event. Generally, this is an event that the writer or a close friend has experienced firsthand. The point is not just to tell the story but to use the story to show why the main idea of the writing is true.

When using narration, keep the following points in mind:

- You know the story, but your reader doesn't, so include all the details that your audience will need in order to understand and appreciate what you are saying.

- Be sure to relate the significance of the story; don't just narrate what happened without linking it to your main idea.

- Make sure that you have established your main idea or thesis clearly.

- Check proportion. Narrating what happened should take up no more than two-thirds of your paper. Use the other third to discuss the significance of the event and relate it to your thesis.

Narration Assignment: "A Shaping Experience"

Choose an event in your life that has changed the way you think or the way you look at life. Relate this personal experience in a way that your audience can appreciate what happened as well as *why* and *how* it changed your thinking. Make sure that your audience can see the significance of the event. This should not be merely a narrative or story.

Think back over the events of your life to find an event that was important to you. It could be happy—an award, a win, a new friend, the birth of a child, or unhappy—a fight, a loss, a divorce, a firing, a frightening experience, a discovery of prejudice. Consider only an event that had a very strong influence on you. If this happening truly mattered to you, you may find it easier to relate its significance to your readers. Try not to be sentimental about this; for this reason, a death may be a poor choice.

This paper should be approximately 500 words in length. Therefore, you should pick an event that can be told in a relatively short paper such as this. Events that took more than an hour or so to happen probably won't work, although the lead-up to the event may have taken longer.

Give a little background information at the beginning of the paper to orient your reader, and some information at the end to tell briefly what happened following the event, but spend the major part of the narrative relating a single event that developed quickly.

Remember, you want your audience to understand how this experience changed your approach to life or your thinking; you want to make your audience feel just what you felt, insofar as this is possible.

Sample Paper: Here is an example of a "Shaping Experience" paper. Note how the author develops his ideas by telling a story about his adventure.

The Myth

Not far from my hone is a small, very old, one-lane covered bridge. It is located right outside Washington's Crossing State Park, in the middle of Bucks County, Pennsylvania, and is a very popular hangout for teenagers. The bridge is said to be haunted by the ghost of a baby that was drowned in the creek below the bridge, early in the eighteenth century. The parents of the baby were said to have held the poor child's head under the water because they could not love the child, who had been born deformed.

The myth associated with the drowning is as follows: On a cold, dark night when a car is parked on the bridge with the engine and the lights turned off, the cry of the baby can be heard. After that, the story becomes fuzzy. Some say death is soon to follow, while others say a curse will follow, and some stories even involve the idea of being chased away by a white pickup truck.

My first experience with Crybaby Bridge occurred on a cool fall evening, two years ago. I had heard the stories and wondered if the myth were true. It was pitch dark as my friend and I approached the old, somewhat dilapidated bridge. No houses or signs of life for that matter could be seen in the distance. Amy, my friend who had driven me to the bridge, had visited there many times and wanted to test the myth that night. I was frightened and persuaded her not to. I promised her that the next time we visited the bridge I would try it with her; fortunately, that opportunity never came with her.

I visited the bridge many times after that, occasionally with girls who tended to become frightened very easily. I toyed with the idea of testing out the myth many times, but never actually did until one cold, dark night in November of the following year.

It was somewhere around one o'clock in the morning when we arrived at the bridge. My friend Joe was driving, and another friend, Mike, was also in the car. The three of us decided this would be the night that we would test the validity of the myth.

My friend drove over the old bridge and did a U-turn on the other side of the bridge in case something did happen. Then at least the car would be pointed in the direction that we had come from, allowing us to make a fast exit.

We parked on the bridge, and following the procedures dictated by the myth, we turned off the lights and shut off the engine. After a few seconds, Mike could be heard muttering, "This is stupid. Nothing is happening." But before he could finish his sentence, headlights appeared less than 100 yards from the small, one-lane bridge, approaching extremely fast. Joe saw them, quickly turned on the engine, and floored it.

For at least ten minutes, the vehicle, that appeared to be a white pickup truck, chased us down the long, winding road. Our car's speedometer was rapidly approaching 70 miles per hour, and the pickup still appeared to be right behind us. It soon became apparent to me why the speed limit on the road was 15 miles per hour after several near head-on collisions with some large trees.

The end of the road was near, and Joe didn't appear to be slowing down as we approached the stop sign. The tires squealed as he slammed on the brakes, and we rounded a sharp corner. The back end spun around but eventually caught up with the rest of the car, and again Joe pressed down firmly on the gas pedal. The strangest thing happened when I peered back to check the position of the vehicle that had almost chased us off the road. It was gone without a trace. It appeared that the truck had vanished.

That visit to Crybaby Bridge is one I will not soon forget. None of us dared to try the myth again, and I haven't been back to the bridge since. Was the vehicle chasing us part of the myth, or was it an attempt (and a very good one) to frighten us away from visiting the bridge? I don't know the answer. In my mind the myth is true, and I will think twice before testing another myth with such dangerous overtones.

—Robert Riegen

Robert Riegen, "The Myth," *The Best of Four* (The Pennsylvania State University) 1999:18.

EXERCISE 8.2　EVALUATING THE NARRATION PAPER

Read the paper carefully and be able to discuss the answers to these questions.

1. What is the author's purpose for telling the story of his visit to the bridge?

    _____

    _____

2. What did the author learn from this experience?

    _____

    _____

3. Have you ever tried something that you had been told was very dangerous, but you wanted to find out for yourself? What was the result?

    _____

    _____

4. Do you know any other myths or urban legends about spots where teens tend to hang out?

_____

_____

5. Why do people continue to believe myths and legends such as this?

_____

_____

Description

You may use description in order to enable the reader to experience a place or thing in the same way (as nearly as possible) that you perceived it. Vivid description is an effective way to convey your feelings and reactions to your subject.

The key to successful description is to:

- Use colorful, meaningful words rather than trite, overused terms to describe your subject. Compare the following two descriptions. Which one grabs your attention and gives you an accurate picture of how this situation appeared to the writer?

  A. The heavyset, hardworking owner leaned up against a dirty counter in the pizza place.

  B. A fat, sweaty Italian man bent over a not-too-clean, green marble counter in the local pizzeria.

- Be honest: "Tell it the way it is." The second description may not be complimentary, but we think you would agree that it gives you a much clearer picture of what the scene actually looked like. In fact, this is what effective description does—it paints _word pictures,_ words that recreate the original image in the reader's mind. The more vivid and accurate the writer is, the more likely the reader will be able to see things the way the writer did.

- Put yourself as a writer in the reader's shoes—what does he or she need to know in order to see the scene the way you saw it?

Description Assignment: "A Worthwhile Place"

Describe a place that is worth your reader's trouble to visit. You might talk about a place where you go to entertain yourself, to relax, to get away from the responsibilities of everyday life, to learn something, to experience a different culture, to enliven a dull weekend, and the like. Your aim will be to describe the place in such a way that you can persuade your reader that it is worth visiting.

In any case, you need to provide basic information: who, what, where, when, how. More importantly, though, you want to provide an insider's view of this place. What does it feel like to be there? What are some of the typical sights, sounds, smells, sensations, and tastes? What personalities might you meet there? Remember the observation assignment when we discussed brainstorming ideas? Here is a good time to put that to use—as you are brainstorming and developing a topic for your favorite place.

Ask yourself what makes this a worthwhile place to visit and spend time? Why is it more worthwhile than the usual spot that your readers might visit?

This paper should be about 500 words long, so pick a topic that gives you enough to talk about, but not one that is so complex that you can't cover it in a paper of this length.

Put yourself in the position of a reader who knows nothing about this place. Describe it adequately so that the reader can appreciate and experience for him or herself why this is such a special locale.

Sample Paper: Here is an example of a paper describing a "worthwhile place." Note that the author uses description as the major mode of persuading the reader that this place is indeed worth checking out.

Dreamland

In the heart of the Fingerlakes region of New York state, nestled between the hills, lies the small village of Watkins Glen. This quaint town possesses the same attractions as most of New York's waterfront villages, but it also features a truly magnificent glen. Tucked away in the mountain, the glen is unknown to many, keeping its mystique alive.

As you enter the unassuming parking lot, the attendant directs you to the entrance of the glen. You begin your journey by twisting your way through a stone corridor.

Observing the constant flickering of the guide lamps and the nonstop sound of water trickling, your mind begins to wander to a new state. These sights and sounds prepare you for the realm you are entering.

Upon leaving the corridor, you are greeted by a beautiful waterfall that eases your mind into a relaxed state. As your eyes wander, they observe a magnificent setting filled with waterfalls, berry bushes, and an unaltered gorge. As you wander through these sites, you understand what the corridor was preparing you for: a world filled with beauty that brings relaxation to all who visit.

After observing your location, you begin to trek up the paths of your choice. The paths take you under and over dozens of waterfalls, ranging from five to almost one hundred feet high. The trails allow you to experience the true force of the water while exposing you to most of the sheer rock sides of the glen. Throughout your journey you can stop and view the ever-lasting rainbow from the constant mist of the falls, or rest for a bit on one of the benches overlooking the winding path of the river. The feelings you experience allow you to bounce in and out of reality like a child in Disney World.

Once at the top, you can enjoy a cold beverage or an ice cream cone to prepare you for your jaunt back. While descending through the glen you can choose to take many different routes. You may want to skim the upper ledge or continue back down the way you came. No matter which path you choose you will not be disappointed, for all of the routes bestow the splendor of the glen. The glen has so much to offer you could probably spend several days there without grasping the entire mystique of this remarkable setting.

Watkins Glen delivers a sense of new discovery that leaves you with an appreciation of what our world has to offer. It adds something to your personality and alters your perception, all the while allowing you to unwind from the tortures of your daily life. You may never revisit the glen, but your mind will drift back often to experience all of its glory. From start to finish, Watkins Glen delivers an atmosphere where perfect harmony reigns.

—Matt Ciprich

EXERCISE 8.3   **EVALUATING THE DESCRIPTION PAPER**

Read the paper carefully and be able to discuss the answers to these questions.

1. What sensory observations does the writer use to recreate his experience of the glen in the reader's mind? Are they effective?

    _____

    _____

2. Is there anything else you would have liked to know about the glen?

    _____

    _____

3. Is this a place you would like to visit after reading this? Why or why not?

    _____

    _____

EXAMPLE

Using examples is one of the best and most common ways of illustrating your ideas and helping a reader to understand the point that you are trying to make. How many times have you heard a person say, "For example . . ." and then go on to relate an incidence of what he or she is talking about. We do this all the time. In this way, we relate the unfamiliar to the familiar and let the reader or listener in on our train of thought.

When using example as a major mode of developing a paper, keep in mind the following points:

- Use one major example or several smaller ones to illustrate your main idea. Whether you choose one or several depends on what it is you are trying to show and how powerful and/or complex the examples are.

- Use examples that you can reasonably expect your audience to be familiar with. The point will be lost if the reader does not understand the example or if it is not adequately explained.

- Give enough details in the examples so that the reader can understand them. Don't assume that the reader can fill in what may be missing.

- Choose examples carefully to make sure they are relevant to the point you are trying to make and relate them clearly to your main idea. Don't force the reader to make the connection, because he or she may make the wrong one.

Example Assignment: "It's True/Not True Because . . ."

Take a proverb (a statement of folk advice) such as "Haste makes waste" and illustrate that the proverb *is* or *is not* true by using several examples or one major example. Be selective in your choice of examples and make sure that they illustrate your point of view clearly. Don't get sentimental or mushy. You are dealing with an abstract idea, so you need concrete examples to explain it. For example, a phrase such as "the best things in life are free" will probably lead to a lightweight essay about blue skies and sunshine. Avoid this sort of approach by using solid examples.

You may use one extended example or several shorter ones, whichever technique fits your proverb and your experience with it. Pick a proverb that relates to you personally. Be sure to show how the examples relate to the truth or falsity of the proverb: this should not be just a narrative.

Please use *one* of the following proverbs:

All that glitters is not gold.
A fool and his/her money are soon parted.
The grass is always greener on the other side.
The squeaky wheel gets the grease.
Quit while you're ahead.
Father (or mother) knows best.
Opportunity only knocks once.
Look before you leap.

Sample Paper: Here is a paper that uses example as its predominant mode. Note that the author uses one major example to persuade her audience that sometimes people should heed their parents' advice.

Father Knows Best

Despite several words of caution, do you remember doing something anyway? Can you relate to a situation that could have been prevented by listening to advice? Most likely these questions could be answered positively if you were ever skeptical of something your parents warned you about (and who wasn't?).

Even though many young people believe that they know everything there is to know about life and all of its complications, they are mistaken. Children think that through time their parents lose intelligence and therefore are ignorant. In actuality, parents have learned from their mistakes through experience, so they try to prevent their offspring from making wrong decisions that could lead to a potentially dangerous situation.

One wintry night in December a few years ago the weather outside was frightful, but the fire was not delightful for me. I desired to be anywhere but home, so I pleaded with my father to let me see my boyfriend Brian that evening. My dad reminded me of the unfavorable weather forecast and the unreliable condition of my car, but his warnings were not enough to convince me. I persisted and finally persuaded my father to let me go, even though he was not fully supportive of his changed decision.

Without considering the possible consequences, I disregarded the advice given by my father. I was oblivious to the warning light on my dashboard that read "service engine soon," and I proceeded to Brian's house.

I arrived safely and believed that my return home would be without incident, but I was wrong. As I ventured home around midnight, I prepared myself mentally to drive on the snow-covered roads. The trip was a bit risky because I was not used to driving in the snow, especially with bald tires.

I carefully worked my way down the road until I slid off the side into a small ditch. After regaining my pulse, I traveled a little farther. All of a sudden, the speedometer fluctuated between 20 mph and 80 mph. The windshield wipers, headlights, radio and heater stopped working simultaneously: my battery was dead!

I was only half a mile from Brian's house, so I walked back and rang the doorbell. He came out and tried to help me with the car. When he realized that there was nothing he could do, we went back to get help from his father.

After standing out in the snow for at least two hours, we were getting desperate to start my car. It needed to be moved off the road since it was in the way of the snow plow.

Finally, with no other alternatives, Brian's father went back to his house and returned with a battery from his older truck. The battery fit like a glove, and the car started instantly.

Father knows best can be depicted from this personal experience as well as others in my life. If I had listened to my father in the first place, I could have saved a lot of time and frustration. I could have saved other people a great deal of trouble too. I was fortunate that I was near a familiar area where I was able to receive help.

I now realize how much my father knows, and I trust what he recommends. People should think twice before they overlook advice from their parents. They generally know what is best, and through their wisdom they try to lead you in the right direction to prevent undesirable consequences.

—*Debi Snyder*

| EXERCISE 8.4 | **EVALUATING THE EXAMPLE PAPER** |

Read the paper carefully and be able to discuss the answers to these questions.

1. How well does the writer's example illustrate the proverb that she is trying to prove?

    _____

    _____

2. Could this example have been used to prove another of the proverbs which were suggested as topics? If so, which one(s)?

    _____

    _____

3. Was the writer's technique of using one major example (rather than several short ones) effective here? Why or why not?

    _____

    _____

4. What advantage does using one proverb have over using several?

_____

_____

PROCESS ("HOW-TO")

People are often asked to explain how to do something. You may be asked to put these instructions in writing. A paper that tells how to do a task is organized according to the process mode. Being able to give clear directions is a useful skill. Have you ever bought something such as a child's toy or a piece of furniture that you had to assemble after you got it home? Have you tried to follow the directions and ended up with a tricycle that had the wheels sticking out of the top? Most of us can relate to what happens when the piece of paper that came with the item was no help at all. Many people know how to do something, but they are at a loss when asked to explain the process to someone else. So knowing how to write directions clearly can be beneficial, both in the classroom and on the job.

The instructions can be given for an *observer*. For example, if you were explaining how to change a tire on a car, the instructions would be expressed this way: "First the car is parked on level ground and chocks are put behind the wheels so that it will not roll."

More commonly, however, instructions are given for the *doer*. In this case, the person is told what to do in straightforward commands: "Park the car on level ground; then place chocks behind the wheels to keep the car from rolling." Here we are going to discuss how to write a process paper for the doer.

When writing instructions for the person who will be performing the process, keep the following points in mind:

- Provide a list of equipment and/or material that will be needed.

- Indicate the purpose, the why of the task, and give the doer an idea of the scope of it. (Will it take half an hour? two days? a week?)

- Write the directions in the *active* voice: "*Turn off* the electricity, *collect* the tools you'll need . . ."

- Explain the steps in a logical sequence: what comes first, second, etc. (Don't tell a diver who's already underwater, for example, that he or she needs a partner to perform this act.)

- Provide needed transitions between steps: *then you, after that, next,* etc.

- Put yourself in the place of the person doing this for the first time. Include all the steps as well as hints for how to handle problems that may arise and "tricks of the trade" (ways to make the job easier).

- If you have to use special terms or jargon, be sure to explain it. For example, a banquet waitress may refer to perishable food such as butter and cream that is put on the table before the main meal as "lives." Each profession has its own particular terms that may be unfamiliar to newcomers.

- If you use graphics such as pictures or diagrams, they should supplement the text but not take the place of written explanation.

- Choose a process that can logically be covered in a paper of about 500 words. If the task is complex, explain one specific part of it.

- Remember: your reader should be able to perform this process after studying your instructions; be complete in every detail.

Process Assignment: "How-To"

Choose something that you know how to do from *firsthand experience*. Explain to someone with little or no knowledge of this task how to perform it. Assume that your audience is reasonably intelligent.

Do not try to describe something that you have never done. This is not primarily a research paper, although you can use outside sources if you wish. Also, *do not use recipes:* do not just copy something out of a cookbook.

Begin your paper by giving the reader a reason for doing this. What is the advantage of being able to do this—economic? emotional? professional? Also, assure your reader that it is possible to learn this skill.

Include a list of materials/tools the reader would need to accomplish this task (if applicable).

Be sure that you include *all* the steps involved. Refer to the other suggestions for writing a successful process paper.

The ultimate criterion (the "bottom line") is that a reader of average intelligence should be able to perform this task by reading your paper and following the steps you have outlined. Try to put yourself in the position of a person who has never done this: what, specifically, would this person need to know?

Sample Paper: Here is a paper that uses the process mode to explain how to get the most out of study time.

How to Make Better Use of Study Time

In order to succeed in college you have to have disciplined study habits. Studying in college is different than studying in high school, because in high school if you failed a test you always had homework grades to bring up your overall grade. In college, most classes do not offer graded homework assignments; therefore, your exam grades account for almost your entire overall grade. The most important parts of studying are allowing yourself the necessary time to study, comprehending what you read, keeping a time schedule, and spending an appropriate amount of time on each subject. This essay will explain some common mistakes made by college freshmen and offer some helpful solutions to overcome these problems.

Allowing yourself enough time to complete each assignment is key. According to Walter Pauk, the director of the Reading Research Center at Cornell University, "For each task, set a deadline that will be difficult to meet, and then strive to meet that deadline" (39). Pauk also suggests that, "If you complete the assignment, reward yourself with some small but pleasant activity." He also suggests that, "If you fail, don't punish yourself. Just hold back your reward and set another goal" (39). Different subjects will require different amounts of study time. One way you might go about setting a reasonable deadline would be to time yourself doing a comparable assignment. Or, for example, it may take three hours to write an English paper that is due in two days. Your friends asked you to go out the night before the paper is due; a reasonable goal would be to strive to complete the paper before you go out so you can reward yourself by going out and having fun.

Comprehending what you read is another major factor in your success at college. In most of your readings there are underlying suggestions, descriptions, and ideas that do not jump out at you when you skim over the reading. A solution to this problem might be to read a paragraph or two and then write down a brief summary of the paragraphs in your own words. This helps you put the information that you read into words and meanings you can understand.

Keeping a time schedule helps you plan out what absolutely has to be done for the day, what should be done if you have time, and what you would like to do if you accomplish everything else that needs to be done. As Pauk states, "A time schedule is a game plan, a written strategy that spells out exactly what you hope to accomplish for a day, a week, or even the entire term— and how you plan to do it" (41).

How much time you spend on each subject will determine your grade for that class. Ronald Blue, from Lehigh Community College, offers this chart as an approximate study time per week for each exam given every three to four weeks. This chart is based on his extensive observation of student performances on college tests. Keep in mind that your study time may be more or less depending on your personal strengths and weaknesses. Subjects which give you more difficulty may take six hours or more of study time, while subjects that come easier to you may only take three hours of studying per week to reach your desired grade.

Total Hours	**Hours per Week**
22 hours for an A	6 hours per week
16 hours for a B	4 hours per week
14 hours for a C	3.5 hours per week
10 hours for a D	2.5 hours per week
0 hours for an F	0 hours per week

Thomas F. Staton, Ph.D., is the author of "How to Study." In his book he offers another interesting method for improving studying. He has developed a method called the PQRST method. It stands for: Preview, Question, Read, State and Test. This method is very useful for students that have trouble comprehending what they read. He suggests that, "You preview the material to be studied and as you are previewing the material ask questions about what you are reading. Reading effectively causes you to have a reaction to what is being said. State in your own words what you have just read and test yourself on the information you have learned" (26). This will help you review the information that you read, making you think about the information from a variety of different ways.

In conclusion, there are many ways to study to achieve your personal goals. There are no set of standard rules for studying that will work for everyone. You have to decide which way works the best for you. Ronald Blue put it best when he said, "You cannot have multiple goals. Everything comes in its own season. There is a time to learn, a time to play, and a time to work. Failure begins in an excuse, a shortcut. There is no royal road to learning or achieving excellence" (1996). You control your own destiny. What are you going to do with it?

—*Reagyn Slocum*

Works Cited

Blue, Ronald C. "How to Study." (12 Aug 1996) http://www.indiana.edu/~iuepsyc/Study.html (13 Sept. 2001).

Pauk, Walter. *How to Study in College.* Boston: Houghton Mifflin, 1993.

Staton, Thomas F. *How to Study.* Nashville, Tennessee: "How to Study," P.O. Box 40273, Nashville, TN 37204, 1982.

EXERCISE 8.5 **EVALUATING THE PROCESS PAPER**

Read the paper carefully and be able to discuss the answers to these questions.

1. Do you think you would be able to improve your study habits by following these instructions?

2. What else (if anything) would you need to know in order to do this
    task?

    _____

    _____

3. Could you follow these instructions in the order they are given?

    _____

    _____

4. What, according to the author, would be the motivation for learning how
    to do this?

    _____

    _____

5. Identify the transitional phrases the writer has provided and discuss
    whether or not they are sufficient to help the reader move logically from
    one step to the next.

    _____

    _____

6. Are the instructions clearly stated, or could they be revised? Which ones
    might you have trouble following?

    _____

    _____

PERSUASION

Much of the writing you do will be aimed at convincing other people that
what you believe is true, and that they should agree with you or at least tolerate
your beliefs. This is called *persuasion*—getting someone to see things from your
point of view and perhaps act on this vision of things.

In order to achieve your goal, you have to use your powers of persuasion.
You have to make the reader agree with you and do whatever it is that you
think he or she should do. Writing that ranges from begging one's family for
money to legislation that changes the way you live involves persuasion.

Being able to write persuasively is of great importance in our society. As
the saying goes, "The pen is mightier than the sword." In an earlier day, you

might have been able to get what you wanted by beating someone with a club and taking or doing what you intended to, but today you are much more likely to "beat" someone into submission with words.

When writing persuasively, keep the following points in mind:

- Know, consider, and respect the other person's point of view.

- Make concessions when necessary; people are more likely to agree with you if they can see that you agree with at least some of their ideas.

- Provide logical arguments for your case; don't fall into the traps of faulty reasoning such as broad generalizations, misuse of terminology, arguing in circles, attacking the other person's beliefs unnecessarily, using false comparisons, and failing to see several sides of an issue.

Persuasion Assignment: "The Death of a Stereotype"

Many different groups are misunderstood and stereotyped by others. For instance, cheerleaders, athletes, models, actors, and musicians may find that others think their work involves nothing but glamour and fun. Housewives, members of the military, truck drivers, and others find that people underestimate the intelligence needed to do their jobs. And prejudices based on gender, ethnic origin, and religion still affect many people.

Sometime in your life you may have found yourself the subject of a stereotype or prejudice. This may have involved a group that you associated with, the way you looked, the clothes you wore or products you used, or even your ethnic background or religious preference.

In this paper, you should address one stereotype that has been applied to you or someone close to you. Your purpose is to convince the people who hold this belief that it is not factually accurate. Your audience should be the intelligent but ignorant people who hold this stereotype but who have never seriously examined the facts behind it.

You should write tactfully, though. Put yourself in the place of your audience: How did this stereotype get started? Why would an otherwise intelligent person believe it?

Write persuasively, using examples of why this stereotype is not true. Don't attack the people who hold it, but show the facts that you have observed that would let the reader see the other side of the stereotype.

This paper should be about 500 words long, so develop your topic accordingly.

Sample Paper: Here is an example of a paper that uses persuasion as its dominant mode. Note that the author uses concrete examples to persuade her audience that farmers are knowledgeable and hard working.

Farmers Are Not Hicks

There seems to be a misconception that a farmer is a "hick" or a lazy country person with no education. Farming has come a long way from milking by hand and using horses to plant crops. It is hard work and takes much more dedication than most people have.

Believe it or not, the farmers' work is never done. They are up at the crack of dawn to milk the cows and feed the animals. Then it is off to the fields. Around four or five in the evening they must milk the cows and feed the animals once again. Upon completing all of this, it is time to take a break and eat. After eating they must go back out to do repairs on tractors, buildings, and machinery to keep the farm in the best possible running order. Once they have accomplished enough work for the day, they try to get a few winks of sleep before starting another day. Vacations are not part of a farmer's job description because their job requires their presence twenty-four hours a day, seven days a week, fifty-two weeks a year.

Even though farmers put in many hours of work, they still manage to find time to keep up with the new technology. Today, many farmers have college degrees. It takes considerable knowledge to keep a farm operating efficiently. For example, the rotation of crops planted in the fields is scientifically based so not all the nutrients are taken out of the soil. Farmers spend much time researching newly developed seeds and machinery to see what will increase the productivity of the farm. A "hick" could not be a farmer for the simple reason that he/she is not educated enough to survive among the competition.

Sometimes we take farmers for granted and do not think of them as an important aspect of society. But, what would the world be like without farmers? Well, there would be a great decline in the amount of food on store shelves. This would include foods such as bread, butter, milk, cheese, ice cream, fruits, meat, and vegetables. Too many of us do not think about where food comes from or how it is made. We should learn to appreciate the hard work farmers put in so we can have these items.

Although people have already characterized me as a "hick" because I grew up on a farm, I have learned the outstanding role of farmers and how to defend them. So, the next time you meet a farmer, do not prejudge that person as a "hick"; look at him or her as a well-rounded individual who knows what hard work is.

—Crystal Hauck

| EXERCISE 8.6 | **EVALUATING THE PERSUASION PAPER** |

Read the paper carefully and be able to discuss the answers to these questions.

1. Where do you think the stereotype of the "hick" came from?

    _____

    _____

2. Why do we continue to hold these outdated beliefs?

    _____

    _____

3. Why is this writer especially qualified to write about her subject?

    _____

    _____

4. Has she convinced you that farmers are not hicks? If not, what else would you want to know?

    _____

    _____

5. How well do the writer's examples work to prove her point? What other examples could she have used?

    _____

    _____

APPLYING WHAT YOU'VE LEARNED

1. Compare two products, services, or other items, and write a list of suitable criteria for judging these things.

    Write a comparison/contrast paper that discusses the two items you have chosen and shows that one is superior to the other.

2. Make a list of situations in your life that have influenced you to the extent of changing your behavior and/or your way of thinking about something. Note why these situations were so meaningful to you.

Write a narrative explaining why this situation changed your thinking and shaped your behavior.

3. Brainstorm a list of your favorite places and jot down why each one would be worth a visit.

   Write a paper describing your favorite place and explaining why it would be worth visiting.

4. Think of a proverb that relates to an experience in your life. Write some notes telling how a real-life situation either proves or disproves the proverb.

   Write a paper giving one large or several examples of why, in your experience, the chosen proverb is true or not. (Don't try to argue both sides.)

5. Think of something that you know how to do well. Make some notes on the steps involved in accomplishing this task.

   Write a process paper in which you teach someone else how to do this task that is familiar to you.

6. Think of some stereotypes that have been applied to you or to people that you know. Write these down and make notes on how you think they got started and why they are not true.

   Choose one of these stereotypes and write a persuasive paper that explains why the stereotype is not true.

CHAPTER 9

How Do I Write Introductions and Conclusions?

Writing teachers may instruct students to let their readers know what they are going to tell them, tell them, and then tell them what they have already told them. While this sounds repetitive, there is some value in this approach. You need to establish your main idea clearly, develop it fully, and then summarize or conclude your paper in a way that is satisfying to the reader. In other words, the reader must be able to feel that the paper is satisfactorily concluded, not just abandoned.

WRITING AN INTRODUCTION

The three basic sections to your paper are the **introduction**, the **body**, and the **conclusion**.

In general, the introduction consists of the first one or two paragraphs of your paper and serves the following purposes:

- States the main idea of your paper (tells the reader what you are going to talk about)
- Gives the reader background on your topic so that he or she can understand what will follow

- Creates enough interest in your topic that your reader will want to continue reading.

- May suggest the organization of the paper. For example, "The three main reasons for lack of participation in politics are . . ."

- May present a story or anecdote that illustrates what the paper will discuss

Let's look at two introductions that were written for a process ("how-to") paper.

1. Securing a Corporate Sponsor for Your Racing Team

There are two different types of corporate sponsors: publicly held corporations and privately held companies. Any team telling you they walked into a company and gave their proposal, and came out with a check all in the same day, is either lying or just plain lucky. Securing sponsor monies is a must if your racing team wants to operate for a full season. Since every team needs money, competition for sponsors is stiff. Therefore, you should decide on the best approach and make no mistakes in your presentation.

2. Buying an Electric Guitar

Buying the "right" guitar has become an increasingly difficult task for the uninformed buyer. Hundreds of different guitars have been introduced in the last few years, making the knowledge of guitar basics a necessity for anyone wanting to buy one. A little research and knowledge of the basics presented here will probably make your choice a better, easier one.

Reviewing the purposes of an introduction, which seems better? Let's analyze the first introduction:

- Does it tell you what the paper will be about? Well, sort of, but what kind of team are we talking about here? Presumably, it's an auto racing team. But it doesn't say that anywhere, so we may be wrong. It could be a greyhound racing team, for example.

- Does it give the reader enough background? It tries to, but it confuses the issue by bringing up publicly and privately held companies and not explaining them (though that could be done in the body).

- Does it suggest the organization of the paper? No.

- Is the introduction itself clearly organized? No: if the paper is to be about getting money from sponsors, that should come first.

In short, the reader is left with a number of unanswered questions. Remember, just because you have in mind what you want to say, that doesn't mean that you have made it clear to your reader. Readers should not have to be mind readers.

Let's analyze the second introduction:

- What is the main idea here? This seems fairly clear: since so many different types of guitars are on the market now, it is more difficult for a person without basic knowledge of guitars to buy one that will suit him or her.

- Does it give the reader enough background? It says that "hundreds of different guitars have been introduced in the last few years," so a buyer has to be more informed than before.

- Does it suggest the organization of the paper? Yes: it says that the "basics" of buying a guitar will be presented.

- Is the introduction itself clearly organized? Yes: it states its topic, gives a reason for discussing it, and suggests how the reader may benefit from knowing about the topic.

Clearly written paragraphs are seldom, if ever, done quickly. No doubt the author of the second introduction wrote and rewrote it until it seemed to say what he or she intended. The writer had *subject, purpose,* and *audience* in mind while writing.

EXERCISE 9.1   WRITING AN EFFECTIVE INTRODUCTION

The following essay lacks an introduction. Write an appropriate introductory paragraph on a separate piece of paper that clearly tells the reader what the paper is about. If you need to, refer to the list of purposes for an introduction.

(Write an Introduction)

The special feature of my backyard was the small creek that ran through it. I used to be the only person in my grade school that had any sort of water in their yard, and that fact made me Miss Popular for about a week. When our old wooden bridge was washed away in the Flood of 1989, I used stepping stones to cross the small creek, which was no small accomplishment considering the creek was like an ocean to me at the age of six.

A willow tree created a curtain of leaves between the back of our property and the start of the neighbor's property. On rainy summer days, that yard became a rain forest, where enchanted creatures, fairies and elves, would romp and play. I'd pull out one of my "play dresses" from its tattered hamper and proceed to saunter around the trees and the creek, pretending I was Titania, the fairy queen herself.

In the side yard was another willow tree, but the tree had grown so high that none of the willow branches hung down low enough for curtains. I took the dead branches and made them my scepter, and the shorter ones I'd use for a crown. Also in the side yard was a spring house with a pond that was always full of water, dead leaves, and heaven knows what else. Frogs lived in the spring house, and occasionally I saw them leaping around the yard.

I was a solitary child, and I never had any friends who lived next door that I could invite over. My yard in the spring, summer, and fall became my world, where I could find solace from the reality of life.

When I was in junior high, my family moved to the house I am currently living in, a gray colonial in a development. Being at the cynical age of thirteen, I didn't realize the loss of my enchanted forest until long after we had moved. As I look out the window onto our flat backyard with a few decorative trees here and there, the memory of that shaded green forest returns to me. It returns to me with its lilac trees, its purple ground ivy, and the musical creek that would lull me to sleep on warm summer nights.

Oh, there are some beautiful things about having a flat backyard. The sunsets are gorgeous, and the sky looks huge. The wind blows around our house, shaking the eaves and whistling under the shingles. It blows through the grain in the nearby fields, creating a pattern of waves like the ocean. But there is nothing here that reminds me of my old backyard, nothing at all. And I still miss it.

—*Liz Ellis*

EXERCISE 9.2   **WRITING YOUR OWN INTRODUCTION**

Refer back to the lists of possible writing topics that you brainstormed in Chapter 3. Choose a topic from one of the lists—observations, memories, unexpected happenings—and write an introduction to a paper based on this topic on a separate piece of paper.

The body can consist of as many paragraphs as you need to convey to your reader what you want to say. The body contains examples, facts, and illustrations that support your thesis or develop your main idea. A college essay, for example, usually has five or six paragraphs—an introduction (one paragraph), a body (three to four paragraphs), and a conclusion (one paragraph).

WRITING A CONCLUSION

The function of the conclusion is to wrap up your ideas and leave the reader feeling satisfied. You cannot merely stop at the end of your last idea and leave the reader hanging.

In general, the conclusion consists of one paragraph and serves one or more of the following purposes:

- Summarizes the main ideas of your paper.
- Makes a call for change (persuasive paper).
- Suggests the future of your topic.
- Restates or emphasizes the thesis of your paper.

A conclusion may consist of an apt quotation, but do not waste time looking for just the right one if you can't think of it fairly quickly. You will need some sort of summary to go with it in most cases anyway.

Let's look at a conclusion that was written for a position paper on the topic of whether mentally challenged people should be institutionalized or put in community housing:

> I realize that there are many moral reasons against putting mentally retarded people in institutions. But, I also know that it is important to keep them open for the people who cannot be served in the community. As of 1995, the number of mentally retarded people in this country who were institutionalized was less than 10 percent (Erb, "Continuing," 403). Institutions are not necessary evils, but they are necessary.
>
> —*Amanda Kvedrowicz*

> Robert G. Erb, "Continuing the Search for a Shoe That Fits: Rejoinder," *Mental Retardation* 33.12 (1995): 403–405.

The student who wrote this conclusion is an experienced worker in a facility for the mentally challenged. Therefore, she knows what she's talking about. The topic of this paper was whether or not governments should continue to provide institutionalized care for mentally challenged people. The trend is toward community dwellings, but the author feels that institutions are still necessary for those people who need them and explains in the body of the paper why this is so. In this conclusion, she points out that less than 10 percent of mentally retarded people were actually institutionalized, according to statistics compiled in 1995. This means, of course, that 90 percent of mentally challenged people were able to live in other settings such as community housing. She comes to the conclusion, though, that institutions should be maintained for those people who really need them. This is a satisfying way to wrap up the argument that she has presented and remind the reader once again of her position on the issue.

EXERCISE 9.3   **WRITING A SATISFYING CONCLUSION**

The following essay lacks a conclusion. On a separate piece of paper, write an appropriate ending that would satisfy the reader and tie up the ideas developed in the paper. If you need to, refer to the list of purposes while developing your conclusion.

The proverb, "The grass is always greener on the other side" implies that something always looks better than what one has at the current time. In many instances, once you get to the other side, you will find that the grass is not any greener than it was where you were in the first place. Yet people are always looking for something better, and a lot of things are more attractive from a distance, which is why most people are disappointed when they reach the other side, as I've learned the hard way.

A year ago, I was living in a small, untidy bedroom. I never had any place to put my clothes, shoes, books, etc. My single bed made me feel like an oversized child. My cubbyhole of a room made me feel claustrophobic. Eventually I became so depressed that I couldn't stand the sight of it.

About that time, the neighbors who lived in the other half of our double house decided to move. My parents, who own the house, didn't know what they were going to do with it. They did know that they weren't going to rent it again.

I realized that this was the perfect opportunity for me. I came to the conclusion that I could be the new resident. I wanted to live in the attic. I discussed my plan with my parents, but they didn't want to pay for the upkeep of the house. However, with a lot of effort on my part, I eventually persuaded them to let me live there.

The attic had a special quality for me. When I was younger, I would go next door to visit my neighbor, and we would sit in her attic and just talk. Her room was what I envisioned heaven to be like, perhaps because everything in it was white.

The day came when it was time for me to move next door. We carried my things over, and eventually I personalized the room to my liking. When I was finished decorating, I sat down and admired my work. It was absolutely perfect.

As the days passed, I spent all of my free time in my new room. I enjoyed the peace of mind that it gave me. It became my personal sanctuary. However, it wasn't perfect all the time. I was always a bit nervous because my deceased grandparents had lived in the house, and I thought their spirits would come back and visit me. I suppose I was being superstitious.

As I got used to the room, it became less and less special, probably because the newness was wearing off. It was still my getaway spot, but for some reason, it wasn't the same. In the beginning, my younger sister would always come to visit me. She would tell me how lucky I was to have such a nice room. Now, not only does she not tell me how lucky I am, but she doesn't even come over and visit. The only time she does come over is when she wants something. Also, my double bed has turned out to be a nightmare. It is just too big for one person. I'm constantly turning and tossing, and I can never get a good nght's sleep.

(Write a Conclusion)

—Julianne Slavick

EXERCISE 9.4   WRITING YOUR OWN CONCLUSION

Write a conclusion for a paper on a separate piece of paper based on one of your brainstorming topics. (See Exercise 9.2.)

WRITING ON THE JOB

Sharon Hess

Director of Community Affairs

Sharon Hess is Director of Community Affairs and Senior Circle Advisor at Berwick Hospital Center, Berwick, Pennsylvania. She was born in Wilkes-Barre, grew up in Mountaintop, and currently lives in Berwick, all in Pennsylvania.

Sharon's first job was in the composing room of the *Berwick Enterprise* (currently the *Press-Enterprise*) newspaper. In this job, she was responsible for writing advertising copy, composing classified ads, and doing a great deal of proofreading. She says that this job taught her to meet deadlines and to be exact. The written material had to be error free and on time. She worked at this job for eight years before coming to Berwick Hospital.

At the hospital, Sharon has held progressively responsible positions during the last 21 years. She started as a Personnel Secretary and was promoted to Personnel Assistant, Ombudsman for Employees, Employee Benefits Coordinator, Director of Personnel, and Vice President, Personnel.

After holding all of these positions in Personnel, Sharon became Director of Community Affairs. This job includes serving as a liaison between the Auxiliary and the Administration, directing volunteers, and coordinating community events such as the "Downtown Days" in Berwick when free health screenings are provided for the public.

Since November, 1999, she has also headed Senior Circle, an organization which now has over 1,500 local members age 50 and above. Senior Circle is a national program sponsored by 50 hospitals that belong to Community Health Systems. It "promotes health, wellness and lifestyle opportunities for Seniors." Benefits include room upgrades if they are hospitalized, use of an office, and monthly meetings and events, among others.

As you can see, Sharon is a very busy lady. She has worn many "hats" at the hospital and continues to do so. She says that in all of her endeavors, effective communication has been crucial. Her past and present writing includes:

- the Senior Circle newsletter
- the Auxiliary newsletter
- letters and flyers to the community
- brochures describing services and events
- plans for her programs
- monthly reports to the headquarters of Senior Circle

- patient booklets (proofreading)
- thank-you notes and acknowledgements
- daily e-mail to the hospital staff
- reports to the chief executive officer and assistant CEO of the hospital
- minutes of meetings

In her previous positions, Sharon also had many writing assignments, including personnel policy statements, benefit programs, staff evaluations and recommendations, a community health publication, and newsletters.

Sharon says that she is writing more now than ever before. She has some advice for writers:

- Always have a plan, no matter what you are writing.
- Get your thoughts down on paper; you can make changes later.
- Keep your communications clear and simple.
- Give your writing to someone else to critique; you may be thinking in one direction and they in another, so get some feedback.
- Date everything.
- Pay attention to the details; they're important.
- Meet all deadlines (that is, hand things in on time).
- Keep a calendar and make daily notes on it.
- Set priorities for what you need to do.

Although you may think that you will never use what you are learning in your writing classroom, Sharon says, "I have news for students: they need to retain that knowledge because they will need it."

Sharon clearly enjoys what she is doing and puts a great deal of effort into it. Perhaps that is why she was recently named Woman of the Year by the Berwick Business and Professional Women's Club.

Her final statement on writing? In the words of Francis Bacon, "Writing maketh an exact man" [or woman!]. ✍

EXERCISE 9.5   **RESPONDING TO WRITING ON THE JOB**

1. Sharon Hess closes her interview with these words from Francis Bacon, "Writing maketh an exact man." What do you think this quote means? What does being an "exact man" (or woman) mean, and how does writing make one an exact person?

_____

_____

2. Sharon gives several pieces of advice to writers. Which one(s) do you find most useful? why?

_____

_____

APPLYING WHAT YOU'VE LEARNED

Introductions

1. Analyze the following introductions. As you think about them, consider these questions.

   - Do they clearly establish the writer's main idea?
   - Do they give you enough background so that you can understand where the writer is coming from?
   - Has the writer basically kept him- or herself out of the discussion (no "skeletons" of previous topics or statements such as "In this paper I am going to. . .")?

a. I came to college completely undecided. I saw a lot of people around me who thought they knew where they were going and were sure that was not going to change. I did not take that approach. Instead I took as many required courses as possible, so that I could find out what might interest me in the future.

—*Don Smith*

b. Anyone who is familiar with mental retardation is well aware of the raging debate over institutionalizing people with this affliction. Almost every affiliated organization such as The Association for Retarded Citizens (ARC) proposes that no one should be placed in an institution. On the other hand, some recognize the need to keep this option available. In our local area, The Relatives and Friends Association of White Haven Center has been fighting to keep White Haven Center open. On the larger scale, The Voice of the Retarded (VOR) states that they are the only national organization that supports keeping institutionalization as an available option (Voice of the Retarded. "Speaking Out for Choices." 2000 <http://www.vor.net/about.html>).

—*Amanda Kvedrowicz*

c. Big people need big cars! That's just a fact of life. Of course not all people drive big cars because they need the size. Some drive them because they need the hauling room or the safety that comes from driving a large car. The cars that will best suit the needs of both types of people are the Chevy Tahoe and the Ford Expedition.

—Matthew E. DeWire

d. St. Thomas is an island paradise. It is the largest of the three islands, which include St. John and St. Croix. They make up the island chain known as the U.S. Virgin Islands. St. Thomas includes Charlotte Amalie, the capital of the Virgin Islands, and Crown Mountain, the highest point in the islands. However, St. Thomas's greatest feature is Megan's Bay. It is one of the most magnificent beaches in the world, because of its picturesque views, rustic bar and restaurant, and its beautiful sunsets.

—Seth Hueter

e. Over the summer I went to Wildwood, New Jersey, with my boyfriend Mike and my friends Jessica and Frank. Most people would say that they had the best time at the beach, but I had more fun at the arcade.

—Wendy Witkowski

f. If you are a roller coaster fanatic, then Six Flags Great Adventure is the place for you. Located in New Jersey, this thrilling theme park offers eight exciting roller coasters. Each has a special feature which distinguishes it from the rest. For example, Skull Mountain is unique because it is an in-the-dark adventure. Except for the Train, a small coaster designed for children, after every ride you will be in a state of awe.

—Jamie Tarone

g. Violence in today's society is at its all-time high. In fact, America seems to be exposed to violence more so than before. Americans, however, especially parents should not react to this problem so nonchalantly. Violence needs to be addressed with responsibility.

—Peter C.

Conclusions

2. Analyze the conclusions in exercises 1 through 7 (which, you will notice, go with the introductions above). As you think about these, ask yourself the following questions:

- Do they effectively tie up the ideas?
- As a reader, do you feel satisfied that this is a logical ending?
- Are the details appropriate for an ending, or should some of this material be in the body of the paper? (Some summarizing may be justified.)

a. I recently ended up with the major that I am in now. I avoided this major because of all the work associated with it. But I knew that I enjoyed all the studying and work that I had done in the past for this major, which is criminology. Either I will go on to law school or I will go into federal law enforcement. Opportunities are everywhere, and I will just see what happens as I go along.

b. In conclusion, I hope I have been able to help clarify this issue. I realize that there are many moral reasons people are against putting mentally retarded people in institutions. But, I also know that it is important to keep them open for the people who cannot be served in the community. Institutions are not necessary evils, but they are necessary.

c. In conclusion, it is apparent that the two [Tahoe and Expedition] are very close in all areas. But I feel that the Tahoe is the better of the two utility vehicles. My opinion is based on the fact that the Tahoe has a bigger engine and more room for the passengers and any objects that you choose to store in the rear. The Expedition is way overpriced for what it offers. Both are excellent vehicles, but the Tahoe gives you more truck for your buck!

d. The sunset at Megan's Bay was the most breathtaking one I have ever seen. As the sun set over the horizon, I could hear the waves crash into the beach in perfect unison with our laughter. It was the greatest feeling on earth. I would definitely recommend Megan's Bay in St. Thomas as a vacation spot to anyone. I had the time of my life.

e. If you are looking to get away for the weekend, I recommend that you go to Wildwood [New Jersey]. As you are lying on the beach, swimming in the ocean, or playing the games, you will forget all of your troubles and worries. If you have a chance, watch the sky as the sun goes down with its bright blue, pink, purple, and white colors scattered through the sky. Stop by, play some games, have some food, and have the time of your life. It's an experience you will never forget.

f. The Chiller is one of the fastest roller coasters you will ever experience! I still can't believe how fast it actually goes. It is crazy! It is definitely the scariest roller coaster at Six Flags Adventure. Thunder Mountain, Medusa, Viper, Batman, Skull Mountain, Scream Machine, and the Train are the rest of the roller coasters. A true roller coaster fanatic will hit this park at least once in his or her lifetime and ride all of them!

g. The negative effect of TV violence on our society needs to be addressed by concerned Americans, especially parents. What can they lose? Apparently, they can only gain from teaching their children right from wrong. Therefore, I suggest that if parents take the initiative to fight for a cutback in the amount of violence airing on television something can be done. Once the public comes together and enforces the issue maybe there will be a change in the entertainment industry. Then maybe there will be appropriate programming for a general audience.

Writing Conclusions

Read the following essay and write a conclusion that follows logically from what has been said.

Rock Climbing

Rock climbing exhilarates the people who have enough courage to try it. It will frighten even the biggest daredevil. Venturing up the rock, the climber receives an ultimate high. My first climb was very thrilling. It helped me learn to trust other people and taught me that determination is very important when trying to reach a goal.

Securely fastened in my harness, I was ready to begin my first climb. As I stood at the base of the rock, I gazed straight up to the top. From this perspective, the climb ahead of me looked almost impossible—I had to climb about seventy feet in order to reach the top! Not knowing what to expect, I felt a little queasy and scared. After taking a deep breath and chalking my hands, I approached the rock.

First, I extended my right arm above my head in order to feel for a decent handhold. I explored each crevice and crack with my fingers as well as my toes. As I probed the coarse, rigid surface of the rock, I found a spot that I felt comfortable gripping. I then raised my leg and slowly pulled myself off the ground. With each advancing step I felt the abrupt tug of the rope on my harness. As I looked up to see how far I was from the top, my eyes became irritated by the grainy dust particles falling from above. My bare feet scraped uncomfortably against the rigid rock surface; however, I fought the unpleasant feeling. The constant lifting of my arms made me distinctly aware of the potent stench coming from my armpits. Throughout my journey I heard the occasional plummeting of rocks to the ground along with the muffled yells of my cohorts below. I took several rests in order to regain my concentration and courage along the way.

Keeping a brisk pace, I continued toward the top. As I neared the final stretch of the climb, I began to feel very tired and weak. My muscles felt tight, and my fingers began to ache. I came to a standstill and started to tremble. I could taste the saltiness of the sweat running into my mouth as it slithered down my face. After a long, hard struggle, I lost my grip. As I fell backwards, I clenched the rope with my fists and extended my legs so that I wouldn't smash my head against the rock. As I was falling, a feeling of bottomlessness assaulted the pit of my stomach.

After stretching quite a bit, the rope suddenly jerked and I was swinging in midair. My feet dangled lifelessly in space.

(Write a Conclusion)

—*Bree Black*

Writing Introductions

Read the following essay and write an introduction that clearly states what the paper will be about:

My Special Class in Day Care

(Write an Introduction)

I was very excited on the first day. I couldn't wait to help out with the five-year-old kindergarten class. As soon as I walked through the door, I knew I would like it. The room was filled with a great group of happy, inquisitive children.

Every day we went over subjects such as math, reading, and art. Also, we had playtime and lunchtime. Math was a fun subject to teach. I felt like a real teacher because I got to write on the chalkboard. The children made me so proud by getting a right answer or doing something well. This was the first time I thought about becoming a teacher. Their enthusiasm and motivation led me to this idea.

Reading was my favorite part of the day. During this period, we went over how to spell words such as *the, one, dog, cat*. Then we had the children form a circle around me, and I would read a story to them. Once again, the children impressed me. Their cooperation was wonderful, and they were very interested in the stories. This was evident through their posture and facial expressions. Even though I was the teacher, the kids were teaching me a lot.

Art was one of the class's favorite subjects. It was a time of self-expression through drawing, coloring, painting, gluing, etc. I'll never forget when a girl named Kelly handed me a piece of paper and said, "This is for you." Colored hearts and flowers filled the paper. I was so touched! I never knew a piece of paper could mean so much to me.

In conclusion, I really did learn a lot that summer. Overall, teaching is an extremely enjoyable job with many rewards. These rewards are not material things such as cars, clothing, or compact discs. They are the feelings you experience when a child does something to make you proud, like learning a new word, sharing items, answering questions correctly, etc. The child's accomplishments become your accomplishments. Every day I felt like a better person inside, because I knew I was making a difference in someone's life. If I had not taken that position over the summer, perhaps I would still want to help animals instead of children.

—Jamie Tarone

PART III

Refining Your Writing

CHAPTER 10

How Do I Share My Rough Draft with Peer Writers?

Once you have your rough draft written it is a good idea to share it with others in order to get some feedback. Some instructors allow you to work with peers during class time, but others may not. If class time isn't available, you should try to find a fellow student to share your work with, preferably someone from your class who knows the assignment and the instructor for whom you are both writing.

YOUR ROLE AS A WRITER

When participating in a peer editing session, you need to get your rough draft done *on time*. The system does not work if you scribble a couple of paragraphs before the editing session and really don't have any idea what you wanted to say. If you don't know, your editor won't know either. Your instructor may deduct points if your draft is not completed on time or may simply refuse to take the finished paper without an edited rough draft.

In order to get the most out of these peer-editing sessions, you have to take a positive attitude toward them. You should see this as an opportunity to get valuable, honest responses from people who are in the same boat as you are. So you should keep your mind open to what they have to say. It is human nature to be defensive about something you have done or created. You don't want people to criticize it. In some cases, you may feel that your work is very good, and you don't want anyone questioning it. In other cases, you know it's lousy, and you don't want anyone to see it. The trick is to get past both of these extreme attitudes and see collaborative editing as a chance to clean up your writing when it doesn't "cost" you anything (that is, *before* the paper is graded).

Once you have the comments from your editor, *use them*. This does not mean that you have to change every single thing that your editor has marked. It is possible that he or she has misinterpreted something you said. However, in most cases, editors tend to be right, so you should consider their comments carefully and perhaps make the suggested changes.

If you ignore your editor's comments, you may do so at your own expense. When grading papers, instructors often find that they are commenting on the same mistakes that the editor has already noted. For example, an editor might point out that a paper does not have an adequate conclusion, but the writer ignores the comment and hands in the paper as is. When the instructor grades the paper, he or she deducts points because it lacks a proper ending. Reading over the editing sheet, the instructor sees that the editor noted the problem, but the writer did nothing about it. So the writer missed an opportunity to improve the paper prior to handing it in. So take an objective attitude and heed your peer editor's advice; in most cases, it will be to your advantage.

YOUR ROLE AS A PEER EDITOR

As an editor, you need to take your role seriously. You need to read the draft carefully and not be afraid to point out mistakes or make suggestions when you see something that you think could be changed. Far too many editors, no doubt not wanting to hurt the writer's feelings, fail to point out problems when they see them. Keep in mind that you are not doing a peer a favor by failing to comment accurately on his or her paper; eventually the instructor will note the problems and assign a grade to the paper accordingly. It is far better to make suggestions and help the writer correct problems *before* the paper is handed in.

Remember, editing time is also not the time to just socialize with your peers. Sometimes editing is done in groups; resist the temptation to talk about other topics and stick to the business at hand—editing.

What would you actually look for when you are editing? The following checklists and explanation will give you some guidelines.

General Checklist: Peer Editing

In evaluating your own papers and those of your peers, you should consider the following. You will notice that we are looking at the big picture first and then working down to the details.

Appropriateness for the Assignment—is this the "house" you or your peer wanted to build?

__ Does the paper do what was asked for on the assignment sheet?

__ Does the paper follow the pattern of organization that may have been assigned for the paper?

The Overall Structure—the blueprint

__ Does the paper have an identifiable introduction, body, and conclusion?

__ In terms of the "blueprint," does this house have a foundation, walls, and a roof?

Organization, Development, and Coherence—bricks and boards in order

__ Is the thesis stated clearly?

__ Does each paragraph have a topic sentence that indicates its major idea?

__ Are the paragraphs fully developed?

__ Are the generalizations in the topic sentence supported with specific examples?

__ Are there clear-cut transitions between paragraphs and between ideas within paragraphs?

__ Is there a consistent point of view (for example, if you started out writing from a *you* point of view, don't switch to *I, we*).

Sentences—the major building blocks

__ Do all the sentences express a complete idea? (No fragments)

__ Is the sentence structure varied, or are they all constructed the same way?

__ Is the passive voice generally avoided? (For example, "The star player failed the final exam" is better than "The final exam was failed by the star player.")

__ Are the sentences parallel? Do they balance?

__ Are there misplaced or dangling modifiers?

__ Do the parts of the sentence fit together so that they make sense?

__ Do the sentences seem choppy and childish? (inadequate subordination, ideas not adequately combined)

Word Choice—the raw material for the building blocks

__ Are the words specific, unambiguous, precise, not redundant?

__ Are the words appropriate in their context? Are they the "right" words for the idea?

__ Are the words slangy or trite?

__ Is the tone of the paper consistent? (no jokes in the middle of a serious paper)

__ Is the writing wordy?

Punctuation, Grammar, and Spelling—the finishing touches

__ Are commas, semicolons, and other punctuation marks used properly?

__ Is punctuation overused or missing?

__ Are there agreement problems? (subject-verb or noun-pronoun)

__ Is tense used consistently? (no switching from present to past and back)

__ Are words misspelled? Run your spell checker.

Strongest and Weakest Points—weathering the storms

__ What are the strongest points of this paper? (What makes it especially attractive and sturdy?)

__ What are the weaknesses of this paper? (Where do we need a few more nails or supporting beams?)

Focusing on Mode Checklists: Peer Editing

Process Checklist: How-to

CONTENT AND ORGANIZATION

What, in your own words, is the writer trying to teach you how to do?

Does the introduction clearly state what the paper is about? If yes, how? If no, what is wrong with it?

List the materials and/or tools that you need to perform this process, according to the author:

Is there anything, in your opinion, that is missing? If so, list it (them).

If the tools/materials are unusual, does this paper tell you where you could get them?

List briefly the steps in the process that is being described. If any are out of order, indicate to the writer where you think they should go.

1.

2.

3.

4.

5.

etc.

Does the conclusion provide a fitting end for this paper?

MECHANICS

Mark mechanical errors—spelling, punctuation, and so on.

List errors in sentence structure.

OVERALL EVALUATION

Do you think that, after reading this paper, you could perform this task? Why? Why not? Be specific.

Strengths:

Weaknesses:

Suggestions for improvement:

Description Checklist: A Worthwhile Place

CONTENT AND ORGANIZATION

Briefly, what is the place?

Has the writer narrowed his/her topic so that this is a definite place (not a whole city, or just any quiet spot)?

What does this paper tell you about the place that you might not have known before?

What is one thing about the place that you would like to know more about?

What is one specific thing the author said that would make you interested in this place?

Is the conclusion satisfying, or does the paper just stop?

MECHANICS

Mark mechanical errors—spelling, punctuation, wrong verb tenses.

Mark errors in sentence structure.

OVERALL EVALUATION

After reading this paper, would you want to visit this place? Why or why not?

Strengths:

Weaknesses:

Suggestions for improvement:

Comparison/Contrast Checklist: Consumer Reports

CONTENT AND ORGANIZATION

Are the items to be compared or contrasted clearly described?

Briefly, what do you understand them to be?

What are the criteria being used to evaluate these items?

Are these criteria suitable for the subjects being discussed?

If not, make suggestions for improvement in criteria.

Are the criteria established applied equally to both subjects? If not, make suggestions for improvement.

Are the subjects discussed in the same order throughout the paper? If not, where does the order break down?

Is the order A+B , A/B, or both? Does the order make it clear what the author is comparing and contrasting? If not, where does the order need work?

Are both sides given "equal time"? If not, suggest change. (It is very important that they get equal time—writers tend to pick one thing that they know about and another that they know next to nothing about and don't want to research—the result is a very unfair, lopsided paper)

Is there a final evaluation or recommendation at the end?

Is one item clearly shown to be preferable to the other, or does the author "waffle"? (If one item is not clearly superior, a well-reasoned explanation of their respective benefits may be acceptable.)

MECHANICS

Mark mechanical errors; spelling, punctuation, verb tenses.

Mark errors in sentence structure.

OVERALL EVALUATION

After reading this paper, can you judge for yourself the superiority of one item over the other?

Strengths:

Weaknesses:

Suggestions for improvement:

Narration Checklist: A Shaping Experience

CONTENT

What do you understand this event to be? (Describe briefly.)

What do you think the significance of this event is (according to the author)?

Does the introduction state clearly what the paper is about? If yes, how? If not, what would you suggest as an improvement?

Are there adequate transitions between paragraphs and between ideas? Mark places where a transition may be necessary.

Is there a clearly identifiable conclusion, or does the paper just stop? Are you satisfied, as a reader, with this conclusion? Make suggestions if you think additional material is needed.

ORGANIZATION

What parts of the paper (if any) need to be rearranged? Mark places where you cannot follow the writer's ideas easily.

Is the narrative part of the paper in proportion to the significance part? In other words, do they get more or less "equal time"? If not, suggest where more information (or less) is needed. (Remember, the paper should not be nearly all narrative with just a couple of significance sentences tacked on at the end.)

Make suggestions for improvement. For example, are there places where the writing could have been more interesting? Other ideas?

MECHANICS

Mark mechanical errors—spelling, punctuation, verb tenses.

Mark errors in sentence structure.

OVERALL EVALUATION

Do you understand what this event involved and why it changed the writer's attitude and behavior?

Major strengths:

Weaknesses:

Suggestions for improvement:

Example Checklist: Proving or Disproving a Proverb

What, in your own words, is the thesis of this paper?

Do you think that the thesis suits this paper?

Does the introduction state clearly what the paper is about? If yes, how? If no, what is missing?

What examples does the writer use to develop his/her thesis? List them briefly.

1.

2.

3.

Are these examples relevant to the writer's thesis? If not, why not?

Alternatively, does the author use one big extended example?

What is this example?

Is it appropriate for the thesis? If not, why not?

Has each example (or one big example) been fully and adequately developed, or are you asking questions about the example? ("I don't understand. . . . Tell us more.") Mark the example(s) that may need more work.

MECHANICS

Mark mechanical errors—spelling, punctuation, verb tenses.

Mark errors in sentence structure.

OVERALL EVALUATION

After reading this paper, are you convinced of the writer's point of view? If not, what else would you need to know?

Strengths:

Weaknesses:

Suggestions for improvement:

Persuasion Checklist: The Death of a Stereotype

CONTENT

What judgment or false image (stereotype) did this paper challenge?

Is the paper focused on just *one specific* stereotype?

Is this a stereotype that the author knows firsthand? Has he or she (or someone very close to the writer) been stereotyped this way?

How did this stereotype get started?

Why would people believe this stereotype?

In what way(s) does the writer show that the stereotype or false image is *not* accurate? What evidence does the writer give to show that the stereotype is not true?

Indicate places (if any) where you think the writer should be more tactful. (The writer needs to avoid being labeled as biased also.)

ORGANIZATION

Mark any places where the ideas are not presented in a logical sequence.

MECHANICS

Mark mechanical errors—spelling, punctuation, verb tenses.

Mark errors in sentence structure.

OVERALL EVALUATION

Do you feel persuaded that the stereotype is false?

If not, what additional proof would you need in order to be convinced that it's not true?

APPLYING WHAT YOU'VE LEARNED

Evaluating a Peer's Work Using the Editing Checklists

1. Evaluate a paper written by one of your peers, using the appropriate Editing Checklist (depending on the mode of the paper) and the General Checklist given in this chapter.

2. Choose one of the sample student essays in Chapter 8. Choose the appropriate Editing Checklist, depending on the mode of the paper. Using this and the General Checklist, edit the paper.

CHAPTER 11

How Do I Revise My Rough Draft?

Now that you have shared your rough draft with a peer editor, you have an idea of how you could improve it. You may also have some feedback from your instructor that you can use. Do ask your instructor for advice on how to make your paper better. This is not cheating or asking for extra help. Most instructors are available during editing days and before or after (even during) class to answer questions you may have about whether you're on the right track and how best to write a final draft of your paper. They will be glad to help you with the revising process.

It has been said that anything worth writing once is worth writing again. In fact, good writing almost always involves rewriting.

Toni Morrison, the author of *Beloved,* among other works, has said, "I used to worry considerably about my writing. . . . Now, though, I have enormous confidence because I know that I can always rewrite it."

In Chapter 3, we talked about getting started with ideas and a rough draft. Here we are going to discuss how to revise that rough draft or first draft that you have already written.

Revisions can be done efficiently if you follow these few steps:

Start with the content (paying special attention to remarks your editors and instructor have made).

Make sure that your paper does what the assignment asked you to do.

Clarify your subject, purpose, and audience.

1. Read the introduction.
    - Does it provide the necessary background so that your audience can understand what follows?
    - Does it state the main idea or thesis of your paper?
    - Does it set a tone for the rest of the paper?

2. Read the first paragraph.
    - Does it have a topic sentence?
    - Is the topic sentence related to the thesis?
    - Do the rest of the sentences support the topic sentence? (If not, revise or eliminate.)

3. Read the rest of the body paragraphs, analyzing them the way you did the first paragraph.
    - Are each of the body paragraphs related to each other with transitional sentences?

4. Read the conclusion.
    - Does it reflect or restate the main idea?
    - Does it summarize or tie up the ideas stated in the paper in a way that provides closure or satisfaction for the reader?

5. Read the entire paper again *out loud*.
    - Does it flow smoothly?
    - Do any parts sound awkward or unclear?
    - Are there any unnecessary words or sentences? (If so, weed them out.)
    - Does each word say what you meant? (Not vague or trite)
    - Are the ideas presented in a logical, definite order (chronological, spatial, by category)?

Make necessary changes.

REVISING FOR GRAMMAR AND MECHANICS

Now, revise the mechanics and grammar. Start reading at the end and go back to the beginning. (This way you can concentrate on the words rather than the ideas.) Pay attention to comments made by your editor and instructor.

1. Does each sentence express a complete thought?
2. Are there any fragments or run-ons?

3.   Do subjects agree with their verbs, and pronouns with the words they refer to?

4.   Are there any dangling or misplaced modifiers?

5.   Is punctuation used correctly? (Not enough commas? Too many?)

6.   Are all words spelled correctly? Run your spell checker.

Make necessary changes.

Put it away (preferably overnight). **Let it "jell."**

Proofread it again.

Make changes; proofread.

Make last changes. Retype it if necessary.

SAMPLE PAPER BEFORE REVISION

Let's see how the revising process can work. Here is the original paper that a student produced in response to an assignment to write an extended definition. He chose to define *socialization*.

Socialization

When someone hears the word *socialization,* one's mind is usually very limited as to what the word really means. If someone was to ask a common person—with no in-depth knowledge of the word—what socialization means, they would most likely give an answer somewhere along the lines of talking or hanging out with friends, neighbors, acquaintances, store clerks, etc. However, there are many different types of socialization and many different types of socializers to go along with the types of socialization. It is probably important for people to know about these different types of socialization so they know how much socializing goes on every day. Socialization has many more meanings than just talking to different types of people.

Usually, the people who have a great deal to do with a child's social learning are parents or guardians. They are obviously not solely responsible for how a child interacts with society, but they usually try to teach their child right from wrong. Parents can also be classified as learners, watchers, and helpers of a child's social learning, but cannot always be held responsible for outside influences.

A simple, basic definition of socialization is "what you have been taught your whole life and how you interact with different types of socializers." To generalize socialization, it could be broken down into two categories. The first category being formal socialization and the second category being informal socialization (Roskin 139).

A good example for both formal and informal socialization would be school. The formal socialization part of school would be interaction between the individual and friends and the individual and teachers. During interaction with friends, socialization occurs through discussion, supportiveness, and the reinforcement of an individual's ideas. Interaction between an individual and a teacher results in the teacher working to better the individual's knowledge of the subject at hand and to help the individual within reason. Informal socialization is different from formal socialization, but both are related when speaking on the category of schooling. A few examples of the informal type in a school would be class elections, kids sitting together in study hall, or people gathering in a cafeteria for lunch.

Socialization may also occur from political or nonpolitical activities (Roskin 167). Through these two types of socialization, the media is probably the most popular and has the biggest influence. However, most people do not recognize or do not even bother to think of the media as a major socializer. One would be wrong not to recognize that the media is probably the biggest socializer today—it connects people and gives them something to socialize about. Anyone who pays attention to current events or recent news will always have something to converse about whether they are at a mall, at the gas station, or sitting in a bar. In the sense of the media, they could be classified as both formal and informal types of socialization. The media covers all aspects of a highly socialized culture.

The definition of socialization is important for anyone in the social science field to know because they should recognize how and when they are socializing. One cannot become a psychologist or a politician if they have no knowledge in the area of socialization. In this day and age, the world is becoming smaller. People are socializing everywhere, all the time. With technology such as the Intermet, television, and e-mail, most people are socializing all of their waking day.

Michael G. Roskin, *Countries and Concepts* (New York: Prentice Hall, 1998).

—*Sean Grove*

The instructor commented on this paper:

> *Your audience and focus are not clear. This seems to be a collection of rather unrelated generalizations. You need to establish a framework and a purpose for this paper. Remember—subject, purpose, and audience. Also, correct the mechanical errors noted. Please see me.*

Discussing the paper with his instructor, the student discovered that, in addition to a lack of focus, the paper had a number of stylistic and mechanical errors.

For example, looking at the first paragraph, a critical reader would see that the writer used the phrase "different types" four times in three sentences.

Reading the paper aloud would help the writer detect this sort of problem. Also, the second sentence has an agreement error—"If someone was to ask a common person . . . what socialization means, *they* would most likely give an answer. . . ." In paragraph four, the phrase "individual and teachers" is used twice, and "individual" is again used twice (in the same sentence). In paragraph six, other agreement problems (anyone/they; one/they) as well as the trite phrase "day and age" detract from the effectiveness of the writing.

The instructor asked the student what he really wanted to focus on in his paper. The student said he wanted to define socialization by discussing the various types of social learning which children are exposed to.

Next the student had to decide what his subject, purpose, and audience were. He came up with this:

Subject: socialization in our culture

Purpose: to define socialization by discussing the ways in which children (and adults) in our culture learn social behaviors

Audience: people interested in social science

The instructor suggested that he write a "blueprint" so he wrote this:

Socialization—a learned behavior (acquired in childhood)

Types of socialization:

    formal

    informal

Examples: parents' values (informal)

        schools (teachers/formal; friends/informal)

           media—TV, magazines, online sources (formal and informal)

World becoming smaller; importance of having social skills

Conclusion: social scientists need to have a clear understanding of socializing in order to interact with different types of people.

SAMPLE PAPER AFTER REVISION

The student then wrote this revised version of the paper.

Socialization

When someone is questioned about socialization, the most common answer or perception the person would give would be somewhere along the lines of talking or hanging out with friends, neighbors, acquaintances, store clerks, etc. However, the actual definition of the words is much more in-depth. A simple, basic definition of socialization is what you have been taught your whole life and how you interact with different types of socializers. What most people don't realize about socializing is that it is a learned behavior and that there are many contributing factors to social learning.

The term *socialization* can be broken down into two categories—formal and informal. These two categories are what makes up someone's social behavior (Roskin, p. 139). Parents or guardians, for instance, would be part of someone's informal socialization. Parents are obviously not solely responsible for someone's social behavior, but they usually try to teach the child right from wrong depending on a family's values. Even though parents help to begin their child's social behavior, they cannot always be held responsible for outside influences.

An excellent example for both formal and informal socialization is school. Formal socializing within a school occurs between a child and a teacher. This interaction results in the teacher working to better the student's knowledge of the subject at hand and helping out with other kinds of problems the student may be facing. Informal socialization in a school, however, occurs between peers. Socializing among peers is probably one of the biggest factors when speaking of someone's social behavior. People learn a great variety of social behavior from their peers such as how to speak, what to wear, how to act, etc. They basically teach each other what is and is not socially acceptable.

The biggest, most popular type of socialization that has the ability to integrate everyone is the media. However, most people do not even acknowledge the media as a socializing tool that connects everybody. Anything from television to magazines to computers is a link of the media and they all give something for people to socialize about. Anyone who pays attention to current events or recent news will always have something to converse about whether they are at a mall, in a gas station, or in a bar. The media is another excellent example of formal and informal socialization that covers all aspects of a highly socialized culture.

Today, the world is becoming smaller. With technology such as the Internet, television, and e-mail, people are socializing most of their waking day. It is important for people in the social science field to have an understanding about socialization because in this line of work they will most likely spend most of their time interacting with different types of people. If someone were to have problems in the area of socializing and he or she had an understanding of the word, then that person might be able to acquire the skills that are lacking. Furthermore, the more social skills someone acquires, the more adept he or she will be in socializing with other cultures, which will be necessary for some people in their respective field.

Michael G. Roskin, *Countries and Concepts* (New York: Prentice Hall, 1998).
—*Sean Grove*

The revised paper is not perfect (if, indeed, perfect papers exist), but it is much more clearly focused and organized. The reader has fewer questions about what the writer was trying to say.

APPLYING WHAT YOU'VE LEARNED

1. Which of the following editor's comments would be more helpful to the writer in terms of revising and improving the paper? Why?

    (a) I really like your paper; you've done a good job. Sometimes it's a little hard to follow, but otherwise it's great. Maybe you could check your punctuation.

    (b) Overall I can see that you have put a lot of thought into your paper. However, it's hard for your reader to follow your thoughts because the paper lacks a clear thesis. Try to rethink your thesis and state it clearly, keeping in mind that your reader (audience) doesn't have the background knowledge of the subject that you do. Then carry through your support in a logical sequence—first reason, second, and so on.

    The sentences would also be easier to read if they weren't so long and, in some cases, strung together. Avoid those comma splices and start a new sentence when you are stating the next thought. Reading your paper out loud might help you find these places.

2. Read and analyze the following two sets of paragraphs. Which is the original and which is the revision? How can you tell? What makes the revision better? (Be specific.)

Set One

    (a) When you are driving down the road, you may see a sign that says "Blasting Ahead" on a highway that is under construction. And to turn off two-way radios. So, as you are driving down the road, you expect signs saying, "Slow Down" and also traffic will be slowing down. As you approach the site there is absolutely nothing at all going on. So—if there is no blasting going on, they should take down the signs.

    (b) Have you ever driven down a highway under construction and seen a sign that says "Blasting Ahead"? What do you expect to see in the next mile or so? If you are like most drivers, you expect to see another sign that says "Slow Down." You may also notice that traffic will be going more slowly in the area. However, more often than not, you approach the site and find that there is absolutely nothing at all going on. So—if there is no blasting at the time, the workers should take down the signs.

Set Two

(a) Ever since I was little, I have loved thunderstorms. They let me escape from the problems of my life for a little while. As I lie in bed, I hear the first drops of rain on my window. Soon, they become a sustained drizzle, running down the pane. Then that drizzle becomes a roar of rain pounding down. Then lightning flashes through the sky. Answering the lightning, the thunder roars back, blowing out the lightning like a candle. Suddenly, my room turns black. We've lost the power! As I grope for a flashlight, the lights blink back on. Settling back down, I sense that the storm is letting up. Soon it will be over, and I will be back to the worries of my life.

(b) As I lie here in my cozy bed, a sense of anxiety comes over me. The first few drops of a thunderstorm hit my window. Soon, the drops turn into a steadier rain. I begin to relax. My worries seem to fade into the night. Then the sprinkle becomes a pounding rain. The wind hits my window, and lightning fills the sky. As if to answer the lightning, the thunder roars back, blowing out the lightning like a candle. Suddenly my room is black. We've lost the power! Just as I start to move, the dark blanket is lifted, and the power is back. As I settle down, my worries return.

CHAPTER 12

How Should My Paper Look?

The way your paper looks says a great deal about your attitude toward writing and about your own sense of responsibility. Sloppy, poorly typed or handwritten papers generally give the impression that you don't really care what your work looks like. And while instructors make every effort to grade papers objectively, it's no secret that a neatly typed, clearly printed paper already has an advantage over a paper that is hard to read. This doesn't mean that neatness will make up for having nothing to say, but it does mean that a good paper is likely to make an even more favorable impression if the instructor can read it easily. This could be especially important in large classes where the instructor may not know the students personally and has nothing to judge them on except the work they hand in.

FORMATTING

Most instructors will give specific instructions as to how they want papers to look. For example, some written assignments, such as laboratory reports may have specific formats, which will be explained by the instructor. But certain standards apply to all papers. Use the following checklist before you hand in an assignment.

Checklist: Formatting

__ Double-space all lines.

__ Leave a one-inch margin on all sides of the paper.

__ If you are not using a cover sheet, type the following information in the top, right-hand corner of the first sheet:

Your Name

Title and number of the course

Title of the assignment

Date

Some instructors will ask you to add their names to this endorsement. In this case, the text would start approximately two inches from the top of the first sheet.

__ Number each page after the title page in the upper right-hand corner.

__ If you are using footnotes, leave at least two inches at the bottom of each page on which they will be typed.

__ Type references or sources on a separate page at the end of the paper.

__ Print on good quality, 8½-by-11-inch paper.

__ Staple or paperclip pages together. Never hand in loose sheets, which can be lost or rearranged.

__ Provide a cover or folder only if the teacher requires one.

Note: never turn in a handwritten paper unless the instructor has specifically said it is okay to do so.

PROOFREADING

Proofreading your paper is the crucial last step you should take before handing it in. Proofreading is not just a matter of running a spell checker, although that is a good place to start. Proofreading is also not editing or revising, and it should be done as a separate step. Most instructors will accept a few handwritten corrections if you notice a mistake in a typed paper when you are handing it in. The goal should be to catch mistakes beforehand, however, so that your reader doesn't have to guess what you meant and your meaning is not misinterpreted.

Checklist: Proofreading

Careful proofreading includes the following steps:

__ Read your paper aloud to check for missing words.

__ Read your paper from the end to the beginning so that you can concentrate on the words rather than the meaning.

__ Check to see if you have used the wrong word altogether; for example, you used *too* for *to.*

__ Look for extra spaces or missing spaces as well as general mistakes in typing.

__ Check for proper margins.

__ Look for reversed or transposed letters; for example, you typed *form* when you meant *from.*

__ Check capitalization in names, titles, and the first word of each sentence.

__ Never begin a typed sentence with a mark of punctuation that belonged at the end of the previous line. For example, don't start a line with a comma.

__ If you are not using a word processor, make sure that words are divided properly at the ends of lines. For example, type *ther-a-pist* rather than *the-rapist.* Make sure you have not distorted your intended meaning. Check a dictionary if you are unsure about how to divide a word.

Note: see Appendix B for a list of proofreading symbols.

EXERCISE 12.1   **PROOFREADING**

Proofread the following paragraph. Use the symbols in Appendix B to mark mistakes.

Everyone agrees that the porpoise of taking a shower is to clense oneself. It occured to me resently that as soon as we get done with our showers we begin to cover our bodys with allsorts of unnatural substances. Guys tend too keep it simple with deodorant, colon, hiar spray and may be soom foot powder if they had been working hard that day. Wimmen, on the other hand, have cover theirselves with deodorant, perfum, hair die, loshun, lip stick, eye shadow, liner and others. It seens to me that the porpoise of taking a shower is not too get cleen but to get a new layer of chemikals.

WRITING ON THE JOB

Maribeth Shea-Hosler

Student

Maribeth Shea-Hosler is a junior at Penn State, Schuylkill, majoring in Criminal Justice. In contrast to many other undergraduates, Maribeth has three children and a wealth of on-the-job experience. She was born in Moravia, New York, and attended school there until she became a teenage mother. The birth of her son did not stop her from taking her GED and ranking fourth out of 400 people taking the exam. She also took some business courses at a local community college.

Maribeth held a number of jobs before returning to college. All of them, she says, required that she be able to communicate clearly and at a level that her readers could readily understand.

As a waitress, Maribeth had to communicate effectively with the public and get the orders straight. She says, "You need to adapt to the situation you're in and the people you're working with." You have to be able to communicate with people who have varying levels of education.

Later, Maribeth was hired as one of the few line women working for a cable company in Pennsylvania. This position entailed much more writing than one might think. As she says, "It was not just a matter of stringing a wire from one place to another." On this job she wrote:

- a daily log of her activities
- a technical, accurate, dated description of each customer's installation
- a detailed inventory of tools and supplies

She emphasizes that you were held accountable for what you did on this job, and accurate, articulate written reports were essential. If something went wrong, your records had better be right.

After she was laid off from the cable company, she became the manager of a bar and pizza restaurant. On this job, her writing included:

- detailed instructions to the people she supervised
- daily task assignments
- employee evaluations
- summations of interviews

- monthly reports
- marketing plans

At age 30, Maribeth said to herself, "This is not where I want to be," and decided to return to college. There she found that her writing skills needed to be honed and that she would be writing nearly every day. Her history professor taught her how to write essay exams, and her composition classes gave her the skills to write "articulately, precisely, and quickly."

Maribeth has some advice for student writers:

- Do not assume that because you know something about the topic you can just start writing.
- Start your research process early.
- Weed through the material. [Choose what is relevant to your topic.]
- Make an outline.
- Write a basic rough draft.
- Go back to your research and make sure you're correct; be specific.
- Organize your paper so that people can understand it.
- Get some feedback from peers, family, and others. "You may not see something that someone else can."
- Write it, put it away, go back to it, revise it.
- Write the final draft and proofread it.
- Above all, "Don't just knock off a paper."

Maribeth says that her college papers take anywhere from six to eight hours for a simple assignment to several weeks for a more complicated research paper. She also advises people to keep all their papers. "Nine times out of ten what you may see as just a paper will be useful to you in the future."

Writing accurately is especially important in Maribeth's field, which is probation and parole. She emphasizes that reports on clients have to be accurate, factual, and unbiased. She notes, "You had better know what you're talking about because people's lives depend on what you say." She also explains that the reports are based on fact, but they ask for opinion (based on fact) at the end. The point here is that you have to be careful to separate fact from opinion.

Maribeth feels that it is especially important for women to empower themselves by becoming knowledgeable and by being excellent communicators. Only in this way can they become advocates for themselves and the causes they believe in.

When she is at home, Maribeth finds herself writing detailed notes to her family, so that they can't say, "But you didn't tell me that." Doing this eliminates a great deal of confusion in everyday life, and enables her to excel at her studies. Just for the record, she has a 4.00 grade point average.

As you can see, Maribeth has found being able to communicate well vital in all phases of her life. She sums it up this way, "Good communication skills apply in all workplaces." ✍

EXERCISE 12.2   **RESPONDING TO WRITING ON THE JOB**

1. Maribeth Shea-Hosler says, "Nine times out of ten what you may see as just a paper will be useful to you in the future." What do you think she means by this? Choose a paper that you have written or are in the process of writing and on a separate piece of paper write a paragraph explaining specifically how this paper could be of further use to you (for example, in your career).

2. Write a paragraph on a separate piece of paper in which you agree or disagree with Maribeth Shea-Hosler's comment that "Good communication skills apply in all workplaces." Use examples to support your position.

APPLYING WHAT YOU'VE LEARNED

1. Proofread the following paragraph. Mark all mistakes, including misspellings, incorrect or missing punctuation, incorrect word choice, and wrong verb tenses. There are at least 20 errors.

Revenge

Last summer I learned that revenge is not always sweet. My senior prom was terribel, the girl I was going out with at the dumped me as soon as the prom was over. I was humiliated and hurt about and I wanted to even up the score with her. The night after the forth of July my frieds, Joe and Rick and I decided to get even. We decided too knock over my girlfriends mailbox. We all jumped into a car around midnight and head to her house. Joe, who was driving, pulled the car up to her mailbox, knockt it over, and we went home. Two weeks later the cops came to visit me, they new I was responible. My too friends told to many people about are activity and the word got back to the police.

I omitted to the crime and had to pay a hundred and twenty-five dollars in fines. I also had to apologized to my ex and her family. My parents growned me for a month and still worry even time I leave the house. I got my revenge, but it wasnt very sweet. It just maid life a little harder for me.

CHAPTER 13

Why Should I Worry about Punctuation?

Many students ask, why should I worry about punctuation? It's just an English teacher's hangup, right?

Punctuation, believe it or not, has a real purpose. It can clarify or emphasize what you want to say. It can even change the meaning of your sentence, sometimes drastically. Read this sentence and think about how you could punctuate it:

Jack said the teacher is a bore.

Here is one possibility:

Jack said, "The teacher is a bore."

You may have thought of this option first. However, there is another perfectly acceptable way to punctuate this sentence:

"Jack," said the teacher, "is a bore."

Note that we have not changed the wording of the sentence, but we have completely changed the meaning by moving around the commas and the quotation marks. The meaning of what you write can be crucial to you. Even lawsuits are interpreted according to the written law, and punctuation helps to determine the meaning of the law. The bottom line is that punctuation makes it easier for a reader to understand what you have written and reduces the possibility that the reader will misinterpret your thoughts.

OBSERVING PUNCTUATION

Read the first two paragraphs of the following essay (written in response to an assignment that asked students to discuss an experience that changed their way of thinking) and add or correct punctuation as necessary in the highlighted sentences. Think about how the punctuation (or lack of it) changes or obscures the meaning of the sentences.

The Material World Is Not Enough

Sometimes in life we value objects more than we value our own life. We all fall victim to this at one point in our life, I know I did. Every teenager wants to have his or her own car, that gives the teen some sense of control or independence. Having my first car meant freedom and independence to me but more importantly it was my first real responsibility. When I bought my first car it felt like I had achieved a very important goal.

I always wanted my own car and when I got it I made sure it looked nice. I had a stereo system installed that consisted of two $5\frac{1}{2}$" speakers in the front two 6 x 9 speakers in the back and two 10" woofers in the trunk along with a 600-watt amplifier. After I had my car system put in I had new tires with "K" star rims put on. Now my car looked and sounded the way I wanted it to.

My mother really never approved of the car at first because it was a clutch (manual). She felt it was too much for a young driver and she would have felt better if I had bought an automatic but I practiced driving my car every chance I got. And within a few months I had it down pat, I overcame the doubt and worries about my driving the car. I thought I was Mr. Big-Shot driving around showing off my car, all I wanted to do was to be with my car. I was beginning to spend more and more time with the car, even my mother had to tell me that a few times. But my showing off days would come to an end.

It was the night before Christmas Eve, and I was planning to drive to school the next day, because it was the last day before Christmas break and I wanted to show off my car. That night I had gone to a friends house to watch a movie and hang out. I left early because I wanted to get home and call my girl-friend. My friends house was about five minutes from my house but while I was driving I realized that I forgot to put my seat belt on. I put it on and continued to drive, within a blink of an eye a deer darted out of the woods, I hit the deer and lost control of the car and swerved into a tree. I must have blacked out because when I came to a car had pulled over to help me and I had a headache from my head whipping forward and snapping back. Luckily the man in the car was nice enough to let me call my mom and a tow truck. What if I never put my seat belt on? What could've been the result? I didn't want to know I was just happy to walk away.

Well the car was totalled and there was nothing I could do to fix it. I was upset that my car was gone, there went my independence, my freedom and I felt helpless. I was not even upset that I could have been seriously hurt. But later on that night when I was trying to sleep, it hit me that it was just a car and I could buy another one, but my mom couldn't buy another me (so to speak).

My mom bought me a new car and I appreciate this one more than my first car. Before my mom handed me the keys to the new car she made me understand that being materialistic about things you have is selfish. I respected the fact that she told me that and I like my car but I don't idolize it. This situation has made me humble and made me value my life a lot more than material things.

—*Shawn Manderson*

ANALYZING PUNCTUATION

The first paragraph of this essay contains three very common errors that writers make. First, look at this sentence:

We all fall victim to this at one point in our life , I know I did.

This is a classic example of the error called a comma splice, which we discussed in Chapter 4. (See also the Hub, pages 240–241, for more information on comma splices.) Two sentences are incorrectly held together with a comma rather than separated by a period or semicolon (;). There are two complete ideas here, so hooking them together with a comma is not an option. Try the following solutions to avoid a run-on sentence:

We all fall victim to this at one point in our lives . I know I did. (Two independent sentences separated with a period)

We all fall victim to this at one point in our lives ; I know I did. (two independent sentences separated with a semicolon)

The next sentence is another example of the same problem, but here the solution could be slightly different:

Every teenager wants to have his or her own car, **that gives the teen some sense of control or independence.**

Try this solution:

Every teenager wants to have his or her own car, because **that gives the teenager some sense of control or independence.**

Here we have added the word *because* to connect the thoughts and show a causal relationship between the first idea and the second.

When deciding how to punctuate two sentences, you should first determine what relationship between them you want to convey to the reader. For example, a period makes a definite break between the two ideas. The reader has to stop and start over. A semicolon makes slightly less of a break and shows a closer relationship between the ideas. A word such as *because* or *since* indicates the closest relationship. This is true even if you are using words to show contrast such as *but* or *however*. (See Chapter 5 for a list of words you can use to connect ideas.)

Now, let's analyze this sentence:

Having my first car meant freedom and independence to me but more importantly it was my first real responsibility.

It is hard to tell how many sentences we have here because there is no punctuation. The writer has used the word *but* to connect two groups of ideas: that having a car meant freedom and that it meant responsibility. In this case, we need a comma before *but* to indicate that there are two separate sentences, one on each side of the connector.

Having my first car meant freedom and independence to me, but more importantly it was my first real responsibility.

Inserting the comma makes it easier for the reader to get the meaning of the sentence the first time he or she looks at it.

Now look at this sentence:

When I bought my first car it felt like I had achieved a very important goal.

Because this sentence has no punctuation except the final period, it is hard for the reader to interpret what the writer meant. It would have been considerably easier to read if the writer had put a comma after *car:*

> **When I bought my first car, it felt like I had achieved a very important goal.**

The first part of the sentence is a phrase introducing the main idea. Words such as *if, when, because, since, although,* and *even though* indicate dependent clusters of words; that is, the thought is dependent on the main idea. The comma tells the reader where the dependent idea stops and the main idea begins. Without the comma, the reader has to guess where the break comes, and sometimes that guess can be wrong, obscuring the intended meaning of the sentence.

In the second paragraph we find another common problem—the punctuation of words or phrases in a series. (See the Hub, pages 214–216, for more information on how to punctuate words in series.) Think about how to punctuate this sentence:

> **I had a stereo system installed that consisted of two 5½" speakers in the front two 6 x 9 speakers in the back and two 10" sub woofers in the trunk along with a 600-watt amplifier.**

In this sentence the writer is listing a number of items that he had installed in his car. The specifications (numbers and sizes) make this a potentially difficult sentence for the reader to comprehend, especially on first reading. In order to minimize confusion, he needs to add commas after *front*, after *back*, and after *trunk:*

> **I had a stereo system installed that consisted of two 5½" speakers in the front, two 6 x 9 speakers in the back, and two 10" sub woofers in the trunk, along with a 600-watt amplifier.**

EXERCISE 13.1   CORRECTING PUNCTUATION IN "THE MATERIAL WORLD IS NOT ENOUGH"

Read the rest of the essay, and supply commas and other marks of punctuation as needed. For example, the writer talks about going to his "friends house" but neglects to put in the apostrophe to show possession. Also correct any marks that have been used improperly.

APPLYING WHAT YOU'VE LEARNED

Provide all necessary punctuation in the following pararaph, including capital letters at the beginning of sentences. Then read the paragraph aloud to make sure that the sentences make sense with the punctuation you have supplied.

Our natural heritage is our country's most valuable possession we have a large variety of different types of lands from the rocky Grand Canyon to the swampy Everglades to the rocky shores of Maine there are so many sights to see but unfortunately they are disappearing our land is now being forested drained built upon and farmed the acreage of land that is protected by the government is very small it seems like every town is experiencing the building of new developments and shopping centers the land that was once occupied by animals is now home to buildings and parking lots since their homes are now gone the animals must find new places to live for example in some parts of the country the animals that are losing their habitats are endangered species in the Pacific Northwest the northern spotted owl is losing its home the woods they live in are being forested a controversy began when the northern spotted owl was put on the threatened species list in 1990 the logging of the owls habitat then came to a halt however out of jobs the loggers were furious[*]

—*Lisa Olson*

[*]This paragraph is the introduction to a position paper entitled "Loggers Might Not Give a Hoot, but Environmentalists Do."

CHAPTER 14

How Do I Revise My Paper Now That It Has Been Graded?

The first thing you should do when you get a graded paper back is read the instructor's comments and corrections carefully. This may seem the obvious thing to do, but some students don't bother to read and "digest" the remarks that have been made on their papers. In most cases, your writing instructor has taken time to analyze your paper carefully and make suggestions to help you improve your writing. Therefore, it is definitely to your advantage to take the time to read, understand, and act on the comments on your paper.

This is not the time to let your pride stand in the way. Grit your teeth and read what the teacher has said. Perhaps, in place of lengthy comments, the instructor has asked you to make an appointment to speak with him or her. In that case, do it. The instructor may feel that it would be more helpful to you to discuss, face-to-face, ways to improve your writing. Sometimes there is just too much to be said to make all the comments in writing. In any case, you need to take advantage of the help that is being offered. After all, you are paying for this course, so get everything out of it that you can.

If the teacher has not specifically asked you to get in touch, you can still ask for clarification of the comments that were made and for further suggestions for revision and improvement. Don't be afraid to ask the instructor to clarify a comment if you can't read his or her writing. (It happens!) Better you should ask than just ignore the comment.

Another option is that the instructor may refer you to your school's writing assistance center (most colleges have them). Typically, the service is free, nonthreatening, and available at convenient hours. Here again, you should take advantage of this extra help. Interestingly, the best students do!

REVISING A GRADED PAPER

Whatever route you take to get help, you are now faced with a graded paper that you have to revise. If you complete the following steps, you will no doubt come up with a much improved paper.

1. Read the instructor's comments carefully.
2. If you don't understand them, ask for clarification.
3. Think in terms of global revisions rather than band-aid solutions. Just correcting the spelling errors will not be sufficient.
4. Decide whether you are generally on the right track or whether you will have to rethink your thesis and the overall structure of your paper. If necessary, do so. Perhaps your paper is just not responsive to the assignment: you haven't done what the assignment asked you to do.
5. If the thesis of your paper is workable and the general organization is okay, what does need work? Determine this from the instructor's comments. For example, the paper may need more development, a tighter organization, more examples, a more consistent point of view, more support for your thesis, a clearer introduction and/or conclusion, and so on.
6. After you understand what needs to be done, try to write the paper over without being a slave to the original. You may be using the same ideas, but you don't have to be hampered by the shortcomings of the original paper. Don't be afraid to set the original paper aside and, using the same ideas (if they worked the first time), rewrite the paper; just avoid the problems found in the original.
7. When you have written and retyped your revision, follow the usual suggestions for proofreading and double checking before you hand it in.
8. If the instructor requires that you hand in the original graded paper with the revision, please do so. (Yours may be one of 75 or 100 papers that the grader read two weeks ago. He or she cannot remember each original comment.)

A SAMPLE GRADED PAPER

Read the following paper that was written in response to an assignment that asked the student to write about a place that has special meaning to him. The object is to make it meaningful to his readers as well. Analyze the original paper, paying attention to the instructor's remarks.

A Worthwhile Place

You can see and smell it a mile away, but there is no place like it. This mys- *wordy* terious place is a farm ~~that is~~ located in the beautiful rolling hills of the Poconos. This working farm has livestock ranging from cows to chickens and crops from corn to soybeans. When most people hear the word *farm* they think of a boring smelly place, but you will see otherwise.

On entering the farm you will see a quaint little farmhouse on the left. This house is *Extraordinarily (adverb)* nestled between two extraordinar~~y~~ tall hemlock trees. Scattered on the outside of the dwelling are hex signs, which originate from the Pennsylvania Dutch. Hex signs have all different floral designs and sayings such as "Wilkum." *Wilkum* is the word for welcome in Pennsylvania Dutch. As a border around the building you notice kaleidoscopic perennials and ravishing annuals.

About one hundred feet past the residence, the meat market stands. This *Wordy* is a one-floor building ~~that is~~ split into a store and preparing room for the meat. The shop is located on the left; as you walk in the smell of beef and pork *Wordy* fill your nostrils. In front of you is a ~~meat~~ case ~~that is~~ filled with a variety of styles of meat. On the counter behind the case, an old-fashioned cash register *Find a synonym (purchases? products?)* is still in use. Also the meat slicer is there with the paper for wrapping meat. *Try: In the next room the meat is ... (wordy)* The next room ~~is where~~ the meat is prepared for sale. As you walk in you can faintly hear the sound of Garth Brooks on the radio. Such tools as knives, *"chopping blocks" are not "tools."* saws and chopping blocks are placed haphazardly around the room. Making sausage and cutting steaks on the band saw are chores that are done in this part of the structure. At lunchtime all the farm workers congregate here for a delicious country-style meal. "Gram," who owns the farm with her husband, *Wordy* prepares the meals ~~around the farm~~.

The adjoining room is where the livestock is killed and skinned; it is known as the "kill room" for obvious reasons. This is the only morbid part of the farm, but it is a necessity. The only tools in this horrible room are the hoist and the *We lost "you" in this paragraph.* hose. The room right beyond the kill room is the meat locker. This is where carcasses, finished products, and general food items are kept. There is always a keg of beer on tap in the cooler, which is another name for the meat locker.

Calves are held in the first stable outside of the market. Cows between the ages of one and two are kept here. About this time the smell of the manure *, however,* might get to some people. After a couple of seconds ^ you will forget about the *at* odor because you will be looking ^ a dozen big cute calves. In the stable corn *PROOFREAD* stalks are used for bedding so that they cows do not get cold or wet. Other types of bedding that are used are sawdust and straw. Hay is not used because cows eat hay. There are two doors in the stable, used for feeding and cleaning purposes. Windows are scattered on the walls for ventilation in the summer.

The next fabrication is the shed. All the bags of feed for the different animals are kept here. Also in the left corner, there is a small machine shop that is used to fix the equipment. The tractors are kept here in the winter so they are easier to start. Throughout this building there are tons of old-fashioned tools *Clarify time reference--was lived when?* that remind you of how this type of life was lived. On top of this shed is a hayloft that can hold up to five thousand bales of hay. This is just a fraction of the hay that is baled in a summer.

Pigs are held in the stable next to the shed. This is split into three parts: one for piglets, one for adolescent pigs, and one for adult pigs. The stable is set up like this because if pigs are not the same age they beat each other up. Connected to this is the chicken coop. Here there are about three hundred egg-producing chickens. Eggs are produced during the day and overnight so eggs *Run-on sentence   Comma splice* get collected twice a day. Chickens need warmer temperatures, hence the coops do not have many windows.

Beyond the chicken coop and pig stables are the fields. All together there is *AGR (there are) Try to avoid there is/there are.* over one hundred acres of farmland that the Haydts use for crops. The Haydts *Who? Tell us the name of the owners sooner (ORG)* are the owners of the farm. Every year there is something planted at a different spot. This is so that the ground does not get totally stripped of one nutrient. Each different crop uses different nutrients. Wheat, oats, soybeans, corn, and hay are examples of the different crops that are sowed and harvested each year. All of the products from the crops are used right on the farm or sold to other farmers.

P (comma)

As you leave the farm ^ you look at how simple and enjoyable this life is. The farm symbolizes an escape for a lot of people because you are not hassled by the fast-paced lifestyle of a job. Any farm will be an escape for you ^ *P (comma)* but this farm is definitely a worthwhile place. You will not believe it until you see it.

Instructor's Comments:

You obviously know what you're talking about. The description here is excellently detailed, but we lose track of the visitor--the "you." If you are going to use this approach, you have to be consistent.

Make sure you have a logical sequence of events. Check punctuation, especially commas.

I'd like to see a revision.

A WORTHWHILE PLACE (REVISED)

Now read the revision and notice what changes the writer made in order to create the improved, revised version.

A Worthwhile Place

You can see and smell it a mile away, but there is no place like it. This mysterious place is a farm located in the beautiful rolling hills of the Poconos. The Haydts, "Gram" and "Pap," have farmed this location for over forty years. This working farm has livestock ranging from cows to chickens and crops from corn to soybeans. When most people hear the word *farm*, they think of a boring smelly place, but you will see otherwise.

On entering the farm you will see a quaint little farmhouse on the left. This house is nestled between two extraordinarily tall hemlock trees. Scattered on the outside of the dwelling are hex signs, which originate from the Pennsylvania Dutch. Hex signs have all different floral designs and sayings such as "Wllkum." *Wilkum* is the word for welcome in Pennsylvania Dutch. As a border around the building you notice kaleidoscopic perennials and ravishing annuals.

About one hundred feet past the residence, the meat market stands. This is a one-floor building split into a store and preparing room for the meat. The shop is located on the left; as you walk in, the smell of beef and pork fills your nostrils. In front of you is a case filled with a variety of styles of meat. On the counter behind the case, an old-fashioned cash register is still in use. Also the meat slicer is there with the paper for wrapping the finished products.

In the next room, the meat is prepared for sale. As you walk in you can faintly hear the sound of Garth Brooks on the radio. Such tools as knives, saws and sausage presses are placed haphazardly around the room. Making sausage and cutting steaks on the band saw are chores that are done in this part of the structure. At lunchtime all the farm workers congregate here for a delicious country-style meal. "Gram" prepares meals.

The adjoining room is where the livestock are killed and skinned; it is known as the "kill room" for obvious reasons. This is the only morbid part of the farm, but it is a necessity. You probably will not want to stay in this room too long. The only tools in this horrible room are the hoist and the hose. The room right beyond the kill room is the meat locker. You see this is where carcasses, finished products, and general food items are kept. There is always a keg of beer on tap in the cooler, which is another name for the meat locker.

Calves are held in the first stable outside of the market. Cows between the ages of one and two are kept here. About this time the smell of the manure might get to you. After a couple of seconds, however, you will forget about the odor because you will be looking at a dozen big, cute calves. In the stable corn stalks are used for bedding so that the cows do not get cold or wet. Other types of bedding that are used are sawdust and straw. Hay is not used because cows eat hay. There are two doors in the stable, used for feeding and cleaning purposes. Windows are scattered on the walls for ventilation in the summer.

The shed is the next fabrication you gaze upon. All the bags of feed for the different animals are kept here. Also, in the left corner, there is a small machine shop that is used to fix the equipment. The tractors are kept here in the winter so they are easier to start. Throughout this building tons of old-fashioned tools remind you of how this type of life used to be. On top of this shed is a hayloft that can hold up to five thousand bales of hay. This is just a fraction of the hay that is baled in a summer.

Your next stop is the pig stable. This is split into three parts: one for piglets, one for adolescent pigs, and one for adult pigs. The stable is set up like this because if pigs are not the same age they beat each other up. Connected to this is the chicken coop. You see close to three hundred egg-producing chickens. Eggs are produced during the day and overnight, so eggs get collected twice a day. Chickens need warmer temperatures; hence the coops do not have many windows.

Beyond the chicken coop and pig stables are the fields. Altogether the Haydts use over one hundred acres for crops. The fields stretch out as far as your eye can see. Every year there is something planted at a different spot. This is done so the ground does not get totally stripped of one nutrient. Each crop uses different nutrients. Wheat, oats, soybeans, corn, and hay are examples of the various crops that are sowed and harvested each year. All of the products from the crops are used right on the farm or sold to other farmers.

As you leave the farm, you look at how simple and enjoyable this life is. This life is simple by being self-sufficient. Little contact with the fast-paced, outside world is needed. The farm symbolizes an escape for a lot of people because you are not hassled by the fast-paced lifestyle of a job. Any farm will be an escape for you, but this farm is definitely a worthwhile place. You will not believe it until you see it.

—Walter Kowalski

Note that this revised version has the visitor looking at various things, smelling odors, making stops at various places. We are seeing the farm through the eyes of the visitor.

Instructor's comment: This is a great revision—we keep track of the "observer" much more easily.

EXERCISE 14.1   **ANALYZING THE REVISION**

The first few changes to "A Worthwhile Place" have been discussed; now you need to find the rest. First identify what changes the student writer made. Then determine which comments the changes are in reference to. Finally, evaluate what the overall benefits are for each change.

_____

_____

_____

_____

_____

_____

APPLYING WHAT YOU'VE LEARNED

1. Revise a graded paper that has been returned to you, using the suggestions and examples given in this chapter.

2. Use the comments on a graded paper to avoid making the same mistakes in a new piece of writing. For example, if several run-on sentences (comma splices) are marked, be sure you don't have any run-ons in the paper you are currently writing.

3. Make a list of the mistakes that are repeatedly marked on your papers in order to avoid making them in future papers. For example, spelling errors or comma splices may be common problems for you.

4. Read and digest the comments on a graded paper. Then rewrite the paper *without looking at the original.*

CHAPTER 15

How Do I Take an Essay Test?

Reading all the assigned material, taking complete notes on class lectures, and paying attention to the material that the instructor emphasizes are wise ways to prepare throughout the semester for tests.

Just before a test date, the instructor may tell you exactly what the test will cover. He or she may even give you sample questions to research and write the answers to. If an instructor does give you some questions beforehand, prepare all of them, even though you know that only some of them will be on the test. By knowing the answers to all of the questions, you will be ready, no matter what appears on the actual test. You will also feel much more confident, knowing that you can answer whatever question is asked. Pay particular attention when the instructor is preparing your class for the exam, and take notes on the instructions he or she gives you.

UNDERSTANDING WHY INSTRUCTORS GIVE TESTS

You should also think about why the instructor is testing you. There are three main reasons for giving tests:

1. To see if you have absorbed and understood the subject matter of the class

2. To see if you can think about this material and relate it to your own ideas and other reading
3. To see if you can apply what you have learned in the class to a specific situation or issue

Most instructors do not want you to simply give them back the class notes without some indication that you understand concepts as well as facts and can also apply them.

EXERCISE 15.1   **THINKING OF REASONS FOR TESTS**

Write down other reasons that instructors might give tests. Think about why you might be tested in the courses you are currently taking.

_____

_____

FORMING A STUDY GROUP

Form a study group to work with before the next essay test. If study questions are provided, assign each group member a question (or questions) to answer. Then set a firm date, well before the exam, to meet and share answers. Note: if your group is like most, some people will be more prepared than others. Therefore, it's a good idea to do at least an outline of an answer to *each* question yourself. This way you can judge the accuracy and completeness of the members' responses to the test questions.

If study sheets or possible test questions are not provided beforehand, use group time to go over lecture notes and reading assignments to determine what the questions are likely to be. For example, what has the instructor emphasized in class? What seems important from the readings? (You can also do this by yourself, of course.)

TESTING YOURSELF

While you are reading your textbooks, ask yourself study questions about the material. These will help you focus on the major ideas. Predicting what will be asked on the test is crucial, especially if the instructor does not give out specific study questions before the test.

REVIEWING YOUR PREVIOUS TESTS

When a graded test is returned to you, go over the instructor's comments carefully. *Never* just throw away a test without reading the comments on it; instead, try to determine why you received the grade you did. If you do not know the reason for your grade, make an appointment with your instructor to discuss the test and have the grade explained to you. You should not be contesting the grade but seeking constructive information so that you can improve your performance on the next exam.

The day of the test arrives, and you are sitting at your desk in the classroom. What do you do now? Here are some suggestions that have worked for other students.

Checklist: Ten Tips for Writing Successful Answers to Essay Tests

1. Read all the questions before you decide which ones to do.
2. Read the directions carefully.
3. Plan your time carefully.
4. Have a general plan for your answer before you begin writing.
5. Determine the organization of your answer by the way the question is worded. For example, if the question says, "Give three reasons for," form your answer into three parts.
6. Avoid vagueness and generalizations.
7. Don't moralize or give your own opinion unless you are asked to do so.
8. Make sure the points in your answer follow a logical sequence.
9. End your answer with a concluding sentence.
10. Proofread!

ANALYZING TIPS TO SUCCESSFUL ANSWERS

1. Read all the questions before you decide which ones to answer. Don't try to do the hardest one (for you) if you have a choice. There is nothing wrong with choosing the ones you think you can handle easily. Your instructor will not be impressed when you mess up the "hard" one.

2. Read the directions carefully.
   a. Make sure you understand the main *instructions.*

Example: If you are asked to write on two out of three questions, don't answer all the questions. Most instructors will read only the required answers in numerical order and disregard the rest.

b. Pay attention to the *verbs*.

Examples: If you are asked to *compare* the written and filmed versions of a novel or short story, don't merely summarize the plot. Also, give equal time to both versions. Don't spend three paragraphs on the film and only briefly mention the written text.

If you are asked to *define* a term such as *states' rights,* be sure to tell what it means, giving examples if applicable. Don't merely discuss the term in general.

If you are asked to *analyze* the plot of a story or novel do not merely summarize it. The person testing you already knows the basic plot.

c. Pay attention to the *nouns*.

Examples: If you are asked to give the *causes* of the Civil War, don't list the *effects*.

If you are asked to give the *effects* or *consequences* of the Civil War, don't just describe the event.

d. Pay attention to the *number* of things asked for.

Example: If you are asked to discuss *three* reasons for the South's secession from the Union, don't give two (or four!). Too many can be as undesirable as too few.

Sometimes the number is indicated in a more subtle way. If the question says that the Civil War had social, political, and economic effects, you know that you must discuss these three elements in your answer.

e. Pay attention to *descriptors*.

Examples: If the question asks "What is the *historical* significance of Grant and Lee's meeting at the Appomattox Court House?" don't emphasize the military aspect of it.

If the question asks, "What were the *major* issues dividing the North and the South?" decide what the most important issues were and describe them in detail. Concentrate on the main issues only.

f. Pay attention to *qualifying* or *restricting* phrases.

Example: If the question asks, "What were the main goals of the South *after 1865,* don't discuss what happened *before 1865.*

3. Plan your time carefully. Look at the number of questions you have to do and allot the time you have accordingly. If one question is worth

more points than the others, be sure to plan extra time for it. You don't want to find yourself with an entire question to answer and only five minutes to do it.

4. Think about your answer and have a general plan for it before you write. Make a few notes if you have time. You won't have time to do much (or any) rewriting. Jotting down a topic sentence can help you stay on the track and write a unified answer. Don't just begin to write and hope the answer will turn into something relevant, clear, and coherent.

5. Decide how to organize your answer from the way the question is worded:
   Example: If the question asks:
   > Compare and contrast the leadership styles of Ulysses S. Grant and Robert E. Lee.

   A possible topic sentence might be:
   > Although Grant and Lee came from very different backgrounds which influenced their military actions, their leadership styles were similar.

   Example: If the question asks:
   > What were the three main reasons for the defeat of the South?

   You know you have to organize your answer into three parts, which discuss the reasons.

6. Avoid vagueness and generalizations. Support your answer with detailed examples and illustrations, and facts. Be specific. Don't pad! Quality rather than quantity is what counts.

7. Don't moralize or give your own opinion unless you are asked to do so. For example, don't discuss historical events from the point of view of your own religious convictions.

8. Make sure the points in your answer follow in a logical sequence. Provide transitions where necessary, so that your reader can follow what you're saying easily (*after that, next, third, as a result, in contrast, nevertheless, however, in addition, furthermore,* etc.).

9. End your answer with a concluding sentence that ties up and/or summarizes what you have said.

10. Leave some time at the end to look over your answers and make minor revisions or additions if necessary. Proofread! During this step you will find those sneaky little errors such as writing 1965 when you meant to write 1695.

EXERCISE 15.2   **ANALYZING THE STEPS FOR SUCCESS**

Think about an essay test you have taken and apply the steps for success to see how you could have improved your performance on this test. If you have an old essay test or a sample test, go over it and apply these steps to familiarize yourself with the process. Then the next time you take an essay test, you should feel more confident about how to approach it.

EVALUATING A SAMPLE ESSAY QUESTION AND ITS ANSWER

Let's take a look at a typical essay question asked in a literature class and the an-swer that a student wrote.

Question

The theme of this course is Loony Ladies and the Men Who Loved Them. In *A Streetcar Named Desire,* Mitch says to Blanche, "Are you boxed out of your mind?" In *A Doll's House,* Helmer says to Nora, "You are out of your mind! I won't allow it! I forbid you [to leave me]!" And in *Hedda Gabler,* Judge Brack says, "People don't do such things." [Hedda has shot herself.]

To what extent are these women victims of their circumstances and to what extent may they be "out of their minds" (at least in the eyes of their con-temporaries)? Be specific in discussing their circumstances and actions. Con-sider the time in which they lived.

Answer

In each of the three plays, time played a very important role. Hedda, Blanche, and Nora each lived in an era where women were viewed as possessions and inferior to men. They were not permitted to have an opinion. If they did, they were either being emotional or it was dismissed. When they all came to their end, they acted hastily or irrationally. This made them appear "crazy" to the people surrounding them.

Nora was extremely oppressed by the time she lived in [late 1800's] and by her husband. She tried to fool herself into believing she was happy in her marriage. She continually played the part of the good, submissive wife she thought she should be. But, slowly, things started coming together in her mind. She started questioning the reasons why she shouldn't be able to take out a loan to help her family, and wondered if the laws were really right. She realized she had had no thoughts or opinions she could call her own. They had all been her father's or Torvald's [her husband]. Fed up with her sham of a marriage, she left to find herself. At that time, it was unheard of for a woman to leave her husband. It would have been viewed as a "crazy" thing to do. But it was necessary for Nora to keep her sanity.

Blanche's descent into her crazy world began after the suicide of her young husband. She felt the need to be with someone and searched for love with many other men, including one of her own students. But, because of the shame she felt and the damage it would cause to her image, she created a false identity. She became a manipulative liar, and tried to trick Mitch into marrying her so she wouldn't be alone.

Hedda was in a marriage very similar to Nora's. She also had many other factors that drove her to suicide. She had become pregnant although she did not want children, her ex-beau had killed himself, and Judge Brack was looking for an "arrangement" with her. She took her life because she felt she had come to a dead end with no hope of coming back.

All three of these characters acted in the only way they saw possible. They each felt trapped in their own lives, and they thought the only way out was to do what they did.

Analysis of Answer

In analyzing this answer, which is quite good overall, we see that the student gave the most complete answer to the character whom she discussed first (Nora). No doubt assuming that some of the basic ideas would be automatically applied to the other two characters, she was not as thorough in her analysis of Blanche. For example, readers familiar with this play would note that Blanche really does lose her mind as a result of several traumatic events in her life—the death of her relatives, the loss of her ancestral home, and being raped by her brother-in-law, as well as the suicide of her husband, which is mentioned. As the play ends, she is being admitted to an insane asylum.

The discussion of Hedda is more complete; however, since Nora and Hedda both lived in the late nineteenth century, and Blanche lived in the mid-twentieth century, it might have made more sense to arrange the answer chronologically, leaving Blanche until last. Then the point could have been made that while attitudes toward marriage and women in general had improved somewhat in 60 years or so, repression was still very much in evidence.

Another option would have been to discuss the protagonists in the order mentioned in the question. In this case, Blanche would have come first. Since her play is set in the 1940s, a reflection back to earlier times could have provided a transition into Nora and Hedda (1890s).

The answer is basically sound, though, because it does discuss the times in which these women lived and how their circumstances affected, even determined their actions.

Also, the answer is clearly organized (with the exception noted above). It has an introductory sentence that reflects the question: it emphasizes the role of time and establishes the status of women. Only after the student has clarified this situation does she start to talk about how the women behaved. In addition, after analyzing the three characters, she sums up their situations by saying, "They each felt trapped in their own lives, and they thought the only way out was to do what they did." This is an excellent conclusion to the analysis. She doesn't merely stop at the end of her comments about the characters.

Considering the limitation of time, and that she had no chance to revise what she had written, this student gave quite an adequate answer to the question, one that showed that she had read and understood the material and was able to apply it to the question asked.

APPLYING WHAT YOU'VE LEARNED

1. Go over a graded essay test that has been returned to you. Read the comments carefully; try to determine why you lost or gained points for a certain answer.

2. Discuss the idea of forming a study group with your friends. Ask them what their experience has been with groups of this sort. What were the advantages? disadvantages? How could your particular group make this work?

3. Ask your professor to provide you with samples of what he or she considers a complete answer to a typical test question (not one which will be on the actual test, of course).

4. Ask your professor for copies of old exams to study. Be aware, though, that providing these exams may not be universal policy.

Students Talk about Writing the Basics

Compiled and edited by Cheryl Reed, Ph.D.

SECTION 1: Things Your Spell Checker Never Told You

Sometimes words that mean different things sound just like each other. When we write, we spell these words differently to show the reader what we really mean. This can give you problems if you can't remember which spelling to use with the meaning you want. Here are some clues to help you remember which spelling to use with the words that most often give writers trouble.

1.1 Writers Write: SPELL CHECKER CONFUSION

Joe Rosengarten

One time my computer had a broken shift key and other problems. I relied on an evil grammar and spell checker, and missed this sentence in one of my papers:

He stranger in dressed in a white suit.

The reader could think many things about this sentence and the author, but the truth is that *all the words are spelled correctly*. The problem is, they don't make sense as a sentence. Here's what I thought I typed:

The stranger is dressed in a white suit.

My software couldn't catch these mistakes, but *I* did when I read through the paper later.

1.2 The wily apostrophe

With pronouns like *she's*, *he's*, *it's*, *you're*, and *they're*, the apostrophe is your signal that two words have been *contracted* (combined to save space). Part of the verb "is" or "are" has been left out. The apostrophe acts like a hinge between the pronoun and what's left of the verb.

■ **your / you're**

Your, which shows you own something (*your* book, *your* car) has the word *our* in it, which also shows ownership (*our* house).

You're has the wily apostrophe in it, a dead giveaway that you're looking at two words hooked together: *you are.*

- **they're / their / there**

  Their, which shows ownership (*their* house, *their* family), has the word *heir* in it. Your *heir* takes over ownership of your property after you die.

  There, which talks about where something is, has the word *here* in it. If you see *here*, you know this word is talking about location, location, location.

  They're, which is actually two words (*they* **are**) packed neatly together, has an interruption in it, the wily apostrophe. This is a clue that *something's been left out!* The apostrophe signals you've combined two words to make a **contraction**.

- **could of / would of / should of**

  In conversation, we all blend one sound into another to save time and to help our sentences have a pleasing rhythm and tone. Mistakes like *could of, would of,* and *should of* happen when we spell words or phrases the way they sound. What we're really doing when we use these words is making a contraction of two verbs. *Could've, would've,* and *should've* are short versions of *could* **have**, *would* **have**, and *should* **have**.

1.3   Writers Write: THE REBEL WORD *IT*

Kristen Kolbe

Understanding *its — it's*

Many writers run into trouble when they use the pronouns *its* (possessive) and *it's* (contraction). Which sentence makes sense:

The cat licked it's paws.   or   The cat licked its paws.

The only difference between the two is one tiny mark, the apostrophe. But this is a big difference! The first sentence says:

The cat licked **it is** paws.   IT's (contraction)

This, of course, doesn't make much sense. Can we avoid using *its* altogether? Let's see:

The cat licked the paws at the end of the legs attached to itself.

I guess you can see why we have to come up with another way to tell when to use *it's* and *its*. Let's try that again:

The cat licked ***its*** paws.   ITS (possessive)

That makes more sense! Now I'll tell you why we have such confusion over which form of *it* to use: **It doesn't follow the rules.** The very rules you use to make a noun possessive (show ownership) make pronouns into contractions (combinations of a subject and a verb)! Here's what happens when you follow the rule to add apostrophe plus *s* to a word to show possession:

it's   it is

he's   he is

she's   she is

Is *it* a rebel, a troublemaker, a word to watch out for? Maybe not. Maybe it just follows its own rules. Another way to think about *its* and *it's* is that pronouns are very precise about what they say. Adding apostrophe plus *s* to a noun (for example, someone's name) can show ownership, like this:

Bob's cat ran away.

Or the apostrophe plus *s* can make the noun a contraction:

Bob's sad.

The same word

Bob's   Bob + apostrophe + s

means completely different things in these two sentences. The first sentence tells you who owned the cat:

The cat that Bob owned ran away.

The second tells you how Bob feels (what a grammar book would call his "state of being"):

Bob is sad.

Pronouns make a more precise distinction between contractions and possessives. Without the apostrophe, the pronoun *owns* or *possesses* something:

Its paw was covered with mud.

The paw that belonged to **it** [the cat] was **muddy**.

With the apostrophe plus *s*, the pronoun has been combined with another word, the verb "is":

It's shedding all over my new sweater.

It [the cat] **is** shedding.

With nouns, you have to understand the whole sentence to know what an apostrophe is trying to tell you. With pronouns, you always know that the apostrophe is telling you you're looking at two words: a pronoun and the short version of a verb. If you don't want to signal a subject and a verb, don't use an apostrophe with a pronoun!

ACTIVITY 1.3: ITS/IT'S

Part 1. Use either *its* or *it's* to fill in each blank so that the paragraph below makes sense.

_____ a well-known fact that a dog will chase _____ tail. _____ neighbor the cat is, of course, much too cool for such silliness. If _____ a good laugh you want, thinks the cat, get a dog. If you want intelligence, beauty, and charm, the cat seems to be saying, _____ me you want. What do you think?

Part 2. In at least five of the following sentences, *it's* or *its* has been used incorrectly. Identify and correct each error.

1. Its been terribly busy at the restaurant!

2. Its popularity is obvious.

3. People are drawn to it's atmosphere.

4. It's food is pretty decent, too.

5. It's in a convenient location.

6. Everyone loves its reasonable prices.

7. Also, its open most nights until midnight.

8. It's a fun place to work, if you don't mind working hard.

9. What's it's owner's name?

10. It's Mama, of course!

Part 3. Read the following paragraph. Add an apostrophe to turn *its* into *it's* wherever necessary.

As I entered my dark apartment after watching the horror film, I thought, *Well, if its my time to go, so be it.* Before I could reach a light switch, I saw it. Its eyes seemed to glow in the dark. *Its here, its really here,* I thought to myself. I was afraid to move, afraid its heat sensors or night vision would find me. Finally, I couldn't bear its terrifying gaze a minute longer. I ran for the light switch, yelling, "You'll never get me!" How foolish I felt! "Its only the light on the thermostat," I breathed out, both relieved and embarrassed.

I hoped my neighbors would never know that my frightening visitor lived out its days stuck to the wall, measuring the temperature. *Its a good thing these walls can't talk,* I thought.

1.4   Spelling tricks

Sometimes, the way a word is spelled gives you (unintentional) clues about its meaning. Here are some tricks of spelling that you can use to remember which sound-alike to use.

- **where / wear**

  Where, which talks about location, has the word *here* in it. Ask yourself, **"Where is it? Here!"**

  Wear, which means to put on clothing or jewelry, contains the word *ear* (a place you'd wear jewelry).

- **than / then**

  Then, which has to do with what time a certain thing happened, is spelled with an *e* like the time word, *when*. An easy way to remember this is to ask yourself, **"When? Then!"**

  Than has nothing to do with time. It compares things:

  We were more worried *than* you were about the exam.

- **wander / wonder**

  There are several ways to remember how to spell **wonder**, which means to question, to think deeply, or to feel amazement about something. First, *wonder* comes from the same word that gives us *wonderful* (astonishing, amazing, awesome, startling, or stunning). You *wonder* (question or think) about *wonderful* (amazing) things. Second, *wonder* is spelled with an *o*, just like *ponder*, which also means to think deeply about something.

  The best memory cue we've found to remember the difference between these sound-alikes is Langston Hughes's title, *I Wonder as I Wander.* The poet *wonders* (feels awe, or thinks deeply about things) as he **wanders** (roams).

- **to / two / too**

  Here, we have a preposition **(to)**, a number **(two)**, and an adverb **(too)**. They each have different functions in a sentence and mean quite different things, but that doesn't stop us from having trouble selecting which one to use! Here are some mental tricks to help you remember in a crunch:

If something happens *two* times, it happens *twice*. Both words talk about quantity. Both words are spelled with a *w*, but you actually hear it in the word *twice*. *Too*, which means *also*, has *too* many *o*'s to mistake it for *to*. (Silly? Yes, but that may help you remember it on your next test!)

■ **do / due**

The easiest way to remember the difference between **do** and **due** is to connect *due* with payment of some kind. Give credit where credit's *due*. When is the rent *due*? If we add an *s* to *due*, we get *dues*, the membership fees you pay when you belong to a club. When it's time to pay, your fees are *due*. What will you *do*?

■ **know / no**

Know is the action (verb) form of the word **know***ledge*:

How do we know what we *know*? We study to gain **know***ledge*.

No, of course, is what you say when you don't want to do something!

ACTIVITY 1.4: SPELLING TRICKS

Part 1. Choose the correct word or words to complete each sentence in the poem below.

> Every night, I watch the news,
>
> Hoping for a clue.
>
> I _____ about the weather.
> **wonder/wander**
>
> Just what will it _____?
> **due/do**
>
> The weather person smilingly tells
>
> _____ she *thinks* it will rain or snow.
> **Wear/Where**
>
> But after all her forecasting,
>
> It's clear she really doesn't _____.
> **know/no**

Who can I turn _____ for help?
to/too/two

How can I be absolutely sure

What I should lay out _____ _____
                      to/too/two wear/where

For my trip out the front door?

_____ often, there's _____ way
To/Too/Two   **know/no**

To know if my choice is just fine.

So I _____ outside with hope
    wonder/wander

That the weather each day is divine!

Part 2. Read the following sentences. In at least five, the sound-alike words have been switched. Rewrite the incorrect sentences so that they are correct.

1. It is too stormy to go outside today.
2. Did you know there is no school because of the storm?
3. You have to wonder if it's smart to wander out into this weather.
4. Wear can I where this fantastic raincoat, if not in this exciting storm?
5. To people trying two get out to their cars have been struck by lightning recently.
6. I'm going to do it anyway; I'm due some good luck!
7. I wander if you'll wonder very far before getting nervous enough to come back.
8. I no myself, and there's know way I'll get nervous.
9. I think you're more foolish then brave, but than, we'll see.
10. Well, I have to do it anyway, because my library books are due!

Part 3. Read the following letter out loud. It sounds just fine, doesn't it? If you look carefully, however, you'll notice that at least ten of the sound-alike words have been spelled incorrectly. Identify the misused words, then replace them with the correctly spelled homonyms.

Dear Fashions Editor,

I wander if you can help me. I have to attend my high school reunion in a few months, and I'm not sure what too where. It's been 25 years since I've been two a reunion with these people; I want to make a great impression. Due

I dress casually and pretend I'm really not worried about what everyone thinks, or should I go all out and really try to look fabulous? If I wonder in looking like I'm trying to hard, what will people think? Will they than expect me to live up to that glamorous image? I don't want to seem like I think I'm better then everyone else, but I really want to look great. Can you help me?

Sincerely, Kim N.

Part 4. Teamwork. In your group, discuss the letter you just read in Part 3. Should Kim N. be worried about his or her looks, or something else? Complete this sentence: **No matter how Kim is dressed, what people will notice is . . .**

Part 5. Writing prompt. Now, imagine that you are the advice columnist that has received Kim N's letter. Write the response that you will publish in your column tomorrow.

1.5   Words in space

When we talk to each other, we have clues like body language, pauses for breath, and the amount of stress a speaker puts on a word to help us understand what's being said. In writing, we use grammar, spelling, and punctuation to do the same things. Sometimes, even the spaces we put between words make a big difference in the way we interpret the meaning of a sentence.

- **a lot / alot / allot**

  Most of us say **a lot** in everyday conversation to mean an assortment, batch, crowd, cluster or large quantity. Strictly speaking, *a lot* is a parcel of land! To be more specific (and less conversational), use words and phrases like *a large number*, *a great deal*, *many*, or *several* to get across the same meaning. If you feel you must use *a lot* to indicate a conversational tone in dialogue, be sure to put a space between the two words **a** (one) **lot** (in slang, a quantity).

  Allot means to measure out, or distribute something:

  We should *allot* funds for computer upgrades this year.

- **every day / everyday**

  every day specifies how often something happens:

How often do you work out? I lift weights **every** *day*.

When the two words are separate, *every* gives you information about what *kind* of day it is: **every** day.

Now let's look at what happens when you leave out the space between these two words:

everyday describes things that are ordinary, familiar, or commonplace

His Armani suit seemed too formal for the office, so he wore his *everyday* jeans to the meeting.

I didn't do anything special that morning. I just followed my *everyday* routine.

When you put **every** and **day** together without a space in between, you're not talking about what kind of day it is anymore. You're describing what happens when you do something day after day: It becomes routine, or **everyday**.

- **each and every one / everyone**

    each and every one is a very strong way of saying *everyone*.

    everyone means the whole group, all the people involved, or humankind in general. It focuses more on the group as a unit, acting together, than on the individual members of the group.

    each and every one is used to emphasize the separate individuals in a larger group. *Each* and *every* both focus your attention on *one*:

    I expect **each** and **every** *one* of the sales staff to contribute to the blood drive.

    Although the entire sales staff--a group of people--is being urged to contribute to the blood drive, the speaker here is emphasizing the individual salespeople. He expects *each* and *every* salesperson to contribute.

    Like most common phrases, *each and every one* has been used so much that most of its power to signal emotion or enthusiasm has been lost. It's best to avoid tired phrases like this altogether. Here's another way our assertive speaker could have sent the same message:

    I expect *each of you in sales* to contribute to the blood drive.

- **all of a sudden**

    Using slang like *all of a sudden* is like wearing a swimsuit to your sister's wedding. It's fine for a casual occasion, like spending time with friends, but seems too informal for a special occasion. In a college essay or on-the-job writing, use **suddenly** to get your point across.

ACTIVITY 1.5: WORDS IN SPACE

Part 1. Read each set of sentences. Place an **X** next to the one sentence in each set which expresses its thought most clearly and correctly.

1. I told each and every one of my coworkers the story of my car trouble.

   I asked everyone of my relatives to come to the family reunion.

   Each of the paintings was hung in the new house.

2. The truck driver stopped all of a sudden when he saw the child.

   My realization that I had been completely wrong came suddenly.

   All of a sudden, everything made sense to me.

3. A lot of my time is spent cleaning up other peoples' messes.

   I really don't have alot of time to think about my decision.

   Is she ready to put in allot of effort on this project?

4. I guess my every day jacket won't be dressy enough for this occasion.

   After looking everyday for a week, James finally found the right kind of paper.

   It's not every day you get to talk to a famous author, is it?

5. Is everyone coming to Bobby's going away party?

   Each and every one in the office received an invitation.

   Every one I've asked has promised to bring an hors d'oeuvre.

Part 2. Teamwork. With your group or a partner, go back and rewrite the unclear sentences in Part I. What do you have to change? Why?

Part 3. For each blank, choose the word that will communicate most effectively with the reader.

_____, I try to spend some time learning about something that is
   Every day/Everyday

new to me. Yesterday my new topic was cloning. _____ of people
                                          Allot/Alot/A lot

are against cloning, for many reasons. The article I was reading talked about one of the reasons cloning is such a controversial practice. Scientists have found that almost _____ of the cloned creatures has some-
      each and every one/everyone/every one

thing terribly wrong with it. In one cloning experiment, young mice who had seemed normal _____ became obese. The subject of

suddenly/all of a sudden

cloning is not an _____ one; it's not something you would bring

every day/everyday

up for discussion with a fellow patient waiting for the dentist, for example. You can't deny, however, that it's one of the most interesting recent developments in science.

Part 4. Read the following selection. Pay close attention to how the underlined phrases are used. Circle those that are used correctly. Draw a line through any underlined words that are used incorrectly. Replace the incorrect words and phrases to make the letter writer's meaning clearer.

Dear Sir or Madam,

I noticed you have an ad listing an open position in your art department. I would like to express my interest in that position. I have <u>alot</u> of natural talent when it comes to art; <u>each and every one</u> of my friends tells me what an amazing artist I am. Besides being so good at art, I'm a reliable worker. I'll be at work on time <u>everyday</u>, without fail. <u>Each</u> person I've listed as a reference will tell you what a hard worker I am, so you don't need to worry about that. Give me <u>a lot</u> of work to do, and I'll have it done in no time! You'll hand me my assignment and turn around to get back to work, <u>and all of a sudden</u>, I'll be finished.

You'll see on my resume that I lost my last job. Let me explain that situation. Everything was going well when, <u>suddenly</u>, my boss decided he didn't like the way I dressed. I don't really understand why; I was just wearing my <u>every day</u> work clothes. I think I dress professionally; in fact, <u>a lot</u> of people would say that I even dress professionally during my off hours. You'll have to be the judge of that, I guess.

I get along with <u>everyone</u>; I'm sure if you take the time to interview me, you'll want to hire me. I can't wait to meet you in person!

Sincerely, A.G. Knott

Part 5. Writing practice. Do you think A.G. Knott will get the job (s)he applied for in Part 4? Why or why not? Imagine that you're writing an application letter for the same job. Rewrite A.G. Knott's letter, but this time avoid the mistakes (s)he made! Hint: The mistakes *aren't* simply in word choices!

Part 6. Working around slang.

Step 1: Use each word or phrase listed below to make sentences about one of the other subjects you're studying.

suddenly	every day	everyone	a lot
allot	all of a sudden	everyday	each and every one

Step 2: Now, read the eight sentences you've just written. In the sentences you wrote using **a lot, all of a sudden,** and **each and every one,** replace those particular words and phrases with less slangy, more professional words and phrases. Keep in mind that your replacement must carry the same emphasis and meaning as the slang it replaces. Good luck!

1.6 Writers Write: A WORD ABOUT SPELLING

John Smithnosky

When writing papers one of my worst problems is spelling. Even with spell checkers it takes a long time if every word over six letters long is spelled wrong. My methods are a lot less embarrassing than running all over the dorm asking how to spell a word.

There is no one way to learn to spell, and what works for you or me might not work for the next person. You have to find a way that works for you. Here are a few tips to help you:

■ **Keep a list of words you generally misspell.** Since this will be ready anytime you need it, you can add words at any time. This list lets you see how the words are spelled. Also, writing the list will help get the spelling in your head. After a while you will use your list less and less.

■ **Keep a dictionary on hand.** You don't have to carry a big book everywhere you go, but when you start a paper have it on your desk. Believe it or not it can save time. A dictionary has a tremendous amount of words with the correct spelling right there; it will also help you stop misusing words. Problems arise, however, when you have no clue how something should be spelled.

■ **Avoid mispronunciation.** If you don't know how to say a word correctly, chances are you are not going to spell it right. Add to the spelling word list you're already keeping. Write out the words you mispronounce in syllables. This will make it easier to spell words and it will make you sound more intelligent when you speak.

■ **Last, proofread your papers.** Even with the methods listed earlier you still might spell something wrong.

Using some or all of these methods will help you keep teacher-generated corrections down to a minimum. Remember, your papers are important and every point counts. Don't lose valuable points over something as silly as spelling.

ACTIVITY 1.6: A WORD ABOUT SPELLING . . .

Part 1. Starting your own dictionary. John Smithnosky recommended starting a card file or notebook of words you have trouble spelling. We'll give you a head start here. Each of the following ten words has a sound-alike, similar, or related word that can make it tricky for writers to use and spell correctly. Use these words to start your card file or notebook of problem words.

1. stationery–stationary
2. capitol–capital
3. principal–principle
4. who's–whose
5. alter–altar
6. accept–except
7. affect–effect
8. compliment–complement
9. farther–further
10. lay–lie

Here are some suggestions for organizing your card file or notebook:

- Find each word in the dictionary so that you'll know exactly what it means and how to pronounce it.
- Write down the meaning of each word.
- Put sound-alike words on the same card or page. When you check them later, it will be easy to see the difference between the two words.
- Use each word in a sentence to give you practice using them correctly and give you an example for your file.
- Remember that some words are variations of other words. You will probably not find them in the dictionary. Write your own definition for your notebook.

Example:

Who's = Who + is (a contraction)

Who's going on the field trip?

Part 2. Now check old papers you've written (and your memory!) for words that give you trouble. **Make a list** of at least 20 of these problem words to add to the dictionary you started in Part 1, above. As you did in Part 1, find each word in the dictionary, write down its meaning, and use it in a sentence.

Keep adding words to your file every time you come across one that gives you trouble. **You now have a valuable working resource that you put together yourself!**

Part 3. Spelling Letter

Dear Aunt Phyllis,

Next week I have a job interview, and I need you're expert advice. I would of called you, but too of my roommates are always on the phone. Anyway, your my favorite aunt, and I'd rather hear you're advice then anyone else's.

First of all, I've been wandering: should I get two the interview early or should I get they're right on time? Its important too no that! Also, what due I where? If I dress up, should I put on a blazer, to? Their are so many questions! Another question: what should I due if alot of people are their for the same interview? Is it a good idea to be friendly, or should I ignore them?

Thanks, Aunt Phyllis. I wish I had you here everyday!

Sincerely, Chris

ACTIVITIES 1.1 – 1.6: SPELL CHECKER CONFUSION

Part 1: Each of the sentences below has spelling errors. Some would be caught by your computer's spell checker software. Others wouldn't. In each set of sentences, identify the words that have been spelled or used incorrectly. Then, place an ★ beside the one sentence that would *not* be caught by your computer's spell checker.

1. a. My math test score hasn't very good.

b. I wish I'd studdied harder.

c. I honestly didn't have enogh time!

d. How does anybuddy find the time?

2. a. I thought I cooldn't go to the concert.

b. There was noway I could get off work.

c. Then this friend of mind had a great idea.

d. I offered to take Leah's Saturday shiff, and she'll take mine.

3. a. Have you ever tried to get work done on a playgrownd?

   b. Thats what it's like working at my house sometimes.

   c. It's distracting, and I'd rather play any way.

   d. Actually, I think a playground is more peaceful!

4. a. The other day, unfortunitely, I had to go car shopping.

   b. It would have been fun if I had more honey to spend!

   c. After awhile, tho, I started to have a little fun.

   d. At least now, I have a car that starts everry morning.

5. a. Let's talk about appling for a job.

   b. It's important to arrive on time for the innerview.

   c. Make sure your nails and hair are trimmed and cleen.

   d. Never tell any one in the office that this job isn't your first choice!

Part 2. Each sentence in the sets below has some strange spelling that will confuse the reader. Identify any words that are spelled or used incorrectly. Then, find and underline any sentence that would fool your computer's spell checker.

1. My hog barked loudly all way.

   The neighbors conplained to me about it.

2. That truck has a powerfull motor!

   Lily drove it right up out of hat bog.

3. Levi's computer is not cooparating today.

   Can you some over to the house and help him?

4. Which glass is taught by the toughest professor?

   I thing I'll take an easier level of astronamy.

5. After she semester ended, Tran was really ready for summer break.

   She knew that all too spoon, school woud start over again.

Part 3. Teamwork. With your group, revise each sentence in Parts 1 and 2 so it makes sense—for the spell checker *and* for the reader!

Part 4. Marcy has been experimenting with word processing software that recognizes her voice and types what she says. For several weeks, she's "trained" the software to "listen" to her voice and type what she says accurately. Now she has a cold, and the software can't seem to make sense of what she's saying. Her spell checker has located all the words that are *spelled* incorrectly, but her paragraph still doesn't make much sense. Help her fix what her spell checker missed!

Won day the wind blew my hat of. I tried to cache it, but I has too low. By favorite hat was gun must like tat! She very next bay, I went hopping for a new one. I walked though six stores in thee hours. Their cats were okay, nut not one batched by deeds. Rust when I was heady too give pup, I saw it. This mat was not blew, but I new I could live with that. It fit my heap perfectly, wish room for my biers. I've mad a bow ever to lose my hat gain!

SECTION 2: Impacting Readers with Sentence Structure

2.1   What the reader expects to see in a sentence

Readers expect to see a straight line through a sentence:

subject   →   *verb*   →   object

These elements answer the questions that a reader is most likely to be asking:

What's happening? (verb)

Who or what is making it happen? (subject)

Who or what is it happening to? (object)

The sentence may be very simple, like this:

cat   →   *ate*   →   mouse

Or, it may include an incredible amount of detail, like this:

Although we gestured wildly to shoo him away, the ginger striped **cat** that had caterwauled outside our apartment all night *ate* the small gray mouse from the research study, while lab technicians watched in horror.

The main idea is still contained in a straight path through the sentence:

subject   →   *verb*   →   object

cat   →   *ate*   →   mouse

Play with this idea the next time you're assigned a reading passage. List the subject → verb → object path through each sentence to find the main ideas. See Jessica Sullivan's notes on **Passive voice** for a special scenario in which this path runs backward (Section 4.6).

Identifying the subject of sentence

Most of the time, the subject of a sentence tells you who is doing the action of the verb. This subject → verb setup is called *active voice*, and it can help you find the subject when you need to. Most people try to find the subject of a sentence first, maybe because subjects tend to come early in the sentence. It makes more sense, however, to locate the subject *after* you've located the verb. First, find out *what's going on*; then look for who is doing it. Most likely, that's your subject!

Be sure you mentally clear away any words that distract you from the actual subject, even if they give you more information about the subject or the situation:

Although we gestured wildly to shoo him away, the ginger striped **cat** that had caterwauled outside our apartment all night *ate* the <u>mouse</u>.

Despite all the extra information, the entity that ate the mouse is still the **cat**!

When you're looking for the subject, you want the word that's *doing, being, or feeling something.* You want the person or thing that's *making things happen.* Words or phrases that describe your subject add information you may want to know, but can get you sidetracked. The subject is almost always *who or what is performing the action of the verb.*

Identifying verbs

Because *what's* happening is probably the most important element a writer is communicating, the verb is the first place to look when you're deciphering a complicated sentence. Verbs usually show some kind of action: subjects eat, run, think, write, breathe, forgive, or perform any number of other behaviors. In most sentences, subjects are *in motion*, and verbs are what moves them--even if that movement is something as serene as to think, to do, or to feel. To identify a verb, look first for the action! What's happening?

If you don't find a word that tells you what's happening, look for words like *is*, *are*, *was*, and *were*. These are special verbs (what your grammar book would call *state of being verbs*) that show who or what a subject *is* rather than the action a subject is performing:

The cat *is* black.

Smith *was* CEO of the company.

When this sort of verb is used, it usually connects the subject with words that describe (adjectives) or rename (nouns) the subject of the sentence.

(***Note:*** An object (0) is one type of a completer (C). Another type is an adjective (The people were *happy*). A third type is a word that represents the subject (Mr. Brown is the *principal*). See Chapter 4 for an explanation of SVC.)

ACTIVITY 2.1: WHAT THE READER EXPECTS TO SEE IN A SENTENCE

IDENTIFYING SUBJECTS

Part 1. In the following sentences, find the straight **subject** → **verb** path through the sentence. Draw a line through each subject. Then write your own subject in its place.

1. The rain cleaned my filthy car.

2. Several dogs got into the trash.

3. Every one of the apples had a bruise.

4. Even though the professor had asked for silence, the noisy class continued to talk.

5. With much complaining and protesting, the patient's friends and family cleared out of her room.

6. While changing a CD in her stereo, Ma'Kayla hit her head on the trunk of the car.

7. Deep in the basement of the empty house, a ticking sound reverberated through the darkness.

8. After looking through all the evidence collected that day, the detectives believed they were on to something.

9. With a shudder, the old jalopy's motor quit right in the middle of the road.

10. Too many of the people in my office like to eat the chocolate-covered donuts.

Part 2. A friend is having trouble understanding how to find the subject of a sentence. In the paragraph below, he's underlined all the words he *thinks* are subjects. You notice that some of his choices are wrong. Help him figure out the **subject → verb** path through each sentence. Put an X through underlined words that aren't subjects. Then, circle the real subject.

I had this crazy <u>dream</u> last night. In the dream, my dog was telling me all the things I do that make <u>him</u> mad. For example, we don't <u>go</u> for enough rides in the car. In the car, even on a nice day, <u>I</u> leave the windows up. For a dog, that sort of treatment is <u>torture</u>! All the dogs in the <u>neighborhood</u> have doggie doors except him. My clothes smell like other <u>dogs</u> some evenings. And that <u>crunchy</u> food is just the pits! He tells me, in this nutty dream of mine, to please buy the juicy, meaty <u>kind</u> in the can. Let's see, what else did <u>he</u> tell me? I don't rub his ears often enough or for enough time. My friend Beaux smells like a <u>cat</u>. Last but certainly not least, <u>he</u> wants me to walk him more slowly. <u>Jogging</u> keeps him from sniffing the <u>news</u> of the neighborhood. In all my <u>life</u>, I have never had such a funny dream!

Part 3. Teamwork. Now, go back to each word you put an X through in Part 2 and explain why it's *not* the subject of that sentence. Don't just give it a grammatical label! Be sure to describe <u>what the underlined word does</u>. Does it tell what happened (verb)? Does it describe something about a person, place, or thing (adjective)? Does it complete the straight **subject → verb → object** path through the sentence? If your friend can see what each word is doing in the sentence, he'll have a better chance of understanding what you're trying to tell him about subjects.

Part 4. Writing practice. Have you ever tried to see something from a totally alien perspective? Take on the persona of an animal, an inanimate object, a person from the opposite gender, or a person on the other side of a controversial issue. Write a paragraph about something you're very familiar with from that perspective.

Part 5. Below you'll find a list of words and phrases. Create sentences using 15 of the words as subjects. Don't forget: The subject of the sentence is doing the action of the verb.

lizard	quilt	notebook	ear lobe
holiday	Aunt Myrna	bay window	pillow
karaoke night	curly hair	gift wrap	dust bunnies
cubicle	globe	victim	basketball
camera	textbook	photo album	pinball machine

Example: Only one **globe** in the school is current enough to be correct.

IDENTIFYING VERBS

Part 1. Read the country song titles listed below. Underline the verb or verbs in each title.

1. I Liked You Better Before I Knew You So Well
2. I Meant Every Word That He Said
3. My Everyday Silver Is Plastic
4. Please Bypass This Heart
5. You Hurt the Love Right Out of Me
6. She Made Toothpicks Out of the Timber of My Heart
7. The Last Word in Lonesome Is Me
8. I Changed Her Oil, She Changed My Heart

Part 2. Teamwork. Have some fun! In groups, choose one or two of the song titles you saw in Activity I and come up with the "real-life" story that's behind it.

Part 3. In the following paragraph, circle each verb. Replace each circled verb with your own verb choice. Read the paragraph to be sure it still makes sense.

As we drove down the highway, we noticed a sign that said, "Snake Farm: 2 miles." Of course, my buddy Nick, the King of the Reptiles, immediately hollered, "Awesome! Turn in!" What a disappointment for me when Taylor really did slow down and roll into the dirt parking lot. "Aw, man," I protested, "I hate snakes!" The two of them just grinned at me as they slammed their car doors and strolled toward the nasty, slithering beasts.

Part 4. One of your peer reviewers is trying to help you find all the verbs in your sentences. The trouble is this: some of the words (s)he's identified as verbs aren't verbs at all! Your job is to fix her mistakes *and* then find the real verbs.

Step 1: Cross out the underlined words that are *not* really verbs.

Step 2: Underline the real verbs in these sentences, even if your helpful peer reviewer missed them! (Be sure to look for *all* the verbs in each sentence, including state of being verbs.)

The last time I <u>saw</u> Aaron, he was polishing off the <u>last</u> of the onion dip. We really need his <u>help</u> cleaning up after Mel's retirement <u>party</u>. I thought he had <u>promised</u> to stick <u>around</u>. <u>Will</u> you check <u>his</u> office? I think he might <u>be</u> downstairs in the <u>copy</u> room.

His office is <u>empty</u>, and no one <u>is</u> in the copy room. Wait, I <u>just</u> <u>heard</u> his voice.

Aaron, <u>we</u> were just looking <u>for</u> you!

Part 5. Writing practice. Write a short paragraph (at least ten sentences) describing a job you've had. Try to make it entertaining for your readers. When you're finished, circle all the verbs and underline all the subjects. Draw the path from **subject** → **verb** in each sentence.

Part 6. Teamwork. Now, show the paragraph you just wrote to your group. Together, circle all the verbs you used. How would you describe these verbs? Do they show action, description, personal qualities? Can you or your group think of any more dynamic verbs to use? Are there any ways the path from **subject** → **verb** can be made clearer? What do the changes your group suggest make happen in your paragraph?

2.2   Fragments: When a sentence isn't a sentence

Although readers look for a straight path from subject → verb → object through the sentence, a complete sentence may have only subject → verb. And, in the case of a direct command, the verb alone can signal a complete thought. *Stop!* is a sentence, because the subject *you* is assumed.

When is a sentence *not* a sentence? If it doesn't have at least the subject → verb connection, it's probably a fragment. Many fragments are thoughts that continue or lead into the sentences around them. They're not complete in themselves, and should be connected with a complete sentence so the reader doesn't get confused. Fragments also happen when writers try to give readers *so* much information at once that the subject → verb connection gets lost in a jumble of words.

Reggie Loper showed us a fragment from his writing that tries to do so much it forgets it needs a verb!

> The situation being in the conference room with all of the mayors, governors, and editors each at their boiling point, right before Jack gets thrown out of the window.

Part of this fragment does have a subject → verb pathway (Jack gets thrown out the window), but Reggie hasn't made Jack's actions stand alone as a sentence. He's just attached what happened to Jack to his description of the tension in the room. Reggie wants to keep Jack a minor player in the sentence so he can emphasize this tension. He adds a verb to keep the focus on atmosphere:

> The *mayors*, *governors*, and *editors* in the conference room *reach* the boiling point right before Jack gets thrown out the window.

2.3   Writers Write: WHY FRAGMENTS HAPPEN

Joy Collis

Fragments happen when writers don't give their readers enough information to complete a sentence. Something gets left out, so that the straightforward subject → verb → object path the reader is looking for just isn't there. Many times, the information you've promised readers is in the very next sentence, but you haven't given them enough clues to connect the ideas. Or perhaps you've signaled that more information is coming, and then stopped abruptly with a period. Joy Collis talks about her adventures with fragments.

Fragments can be thought of as math problems. Fragments are fractions of sentences; something else has to be added to make a whole! All sentences must be complete thoughts, without leaving any room for the reader to have to guess what you're trying to say.

Here's an example from one of my papers:

> **Although I enjoy the job that I am doing now. I hope to start my own advertising agency someday.**

These two statements are giving you mixed signals. The word *although* at the beginning of the first group of words signals that there's another point to be made. The period after *now* says that the first group of words has finished making its points. But, has it? Let's look at it without the second statement and see if it makes sense:

> **Although I enjoy the job that I am doing now.**

Without the second statement to give us more information, the first statement still signals that there's something it's not telling us.

If you read these two groups of words aloud, they make sense. Your mind skips over the period in the middle, and (right or wrong) fills in information gaps with the second statement. Read aloud, the two statements sound like this:

> **Although I enjoy the job that I am doing now, I hope to start my own advertising agency someday.**

You're *hearing* a comma! So, I get rid of the fragment by using a comma to *join* the two statements, instead of a period to *separate* them.

What if we just delete the word *although* and get rid of the signal that there's more to come? Here's what we'd have:

> **I enjoy the job that I am doing now. I hope to start my own advertising agency someday.**

Both of these statements are now complete sentences. There are no words that signal any information has been left out, and no words that tell us that there is any connection between them. They sound like items on a list.

Another way to get my idea across would be to delete *although* and add a different connecting word with a similar meaning:

> **I enjoy the job I have now as a clothing designer, *but* I hope to someday start my own advertising agency.**

Both *although* and *but* signal I'm going to change my mind. I *like* my job (so you'd expect me to keep it) *but* I hope to do something else in the future. Any of these revisions would clear up what I was trying to say.

> **Editor's Tip:** See Section 4 of *The Hub* for a list of common subordinating words.

ACTIVITIES 2.2–2.3: FRAGMENTS: WHEN A SENTENCE ISN'T A SENTENCE

Part 1. Even though all the items below *look* like sentences, at least 10 of them are fragments. Identify the fragments and draw a line through each one.

1. What's the deal?
2. Even though she told me it wasn't my fault.
3. How funny!
4. What a busy day.
5. After all we'd been through.
6. If she'd just send the letter changing her major.
7. Believe me.
8. Because his friends had warned him.
9. The first robin of spring.
10. Byron couldn't believe how much studying the course required.
11. Thanks to a vivid and overactive imagination, which he couldn't help.
12. It took a lot more elbow grease than expected.
13. How have you been?
14. With all the fuss over the wedding, not to mention the new job.
15. Isn't that the craziest thing?
16. I have to admit, my fears.
17. Without necessarily changing my mind.
18. What beautiful eyes you have!
19. All this is to say thank you so much.
20. Despite the butterflies in her stomach, the jelly in her arms, and the dust in her mouth.

Part 2. Teamwork. With your group, revise the fragments you found in Part 1 so that they're complete sentences. What did you have to change to make fragments into sentences?

Part 3. Each of the items below is a sentence fragment. Add your own ideas to each fragment to make it a complete thought.

Example: Even when the dog growled.

Possible answers: Even when the dog growled, Gerald continued to advance toward his goal.
Even when the dog growled, the cat held its ground.

1. Although the jokes made me laugh.
2. Without stopping for a rest.
3. After we had eaten dinner and ordered coffee.
4. We all hoped that, after much thought, her decision.
5. Deeana's high hopes, despite her previous experience.
6. Even if Kay changes her mind, all her friends.
7. Along with a healthy dose of common sense.
8. Only Matt's dogged devotion to his long-term goal of a medical degree.
9. Although the applause seemed genuine.
10. If you don't take her advice.
11. Because Javier had promised to emcee the charity fashion show.
12. After a few minutes of debate, the group's conclusion.
13. Even though I couldn't put a complete sentence together.
14. In the middle of fixing the transmission.
15. With all the excitement and drama swirling around her.

Part 4. Teamwork. Now, compare your revised sentences with those of others in your group. Did you each choose completely different ways to complete the sentences? Choose 5 fragments and use them in a paragraph. Have some fun with this!

Part 5. The following paragraph contains slogans, phrases, and sentences that might be used in an advertisement. Underline any fragments. Change the fragments into complete sentences by adding, subtracting, or changing words or punctuation.

The Sit'n'Slide is the last exercise machine you'll ever have to buy! So versatile! It slides! It jogs! And rows! Even twists! Inches slide off your waist and hips as you barely break a sweat! Cook, read, solve crossword puzzles! All while you enjoy your fabulous Sit'n'Slide! Fits anywhere! In a closet! In the bathroom! Even in the hot tub! Call now, and you'll receive a beautiful Italian leather Sit'n'Slide cover -- absolutely free! Get the Sit'n'Slide, its leather cover, AND the professionally made training videotape today! All for only $199.99! What a deal this is! Rush order only $19.99 more! Call today!

Part 6. Teamwork. Imagine that your group is a concept team at an ad agency. Read the paragraphs you each revised in Part 5 to the group. How does changing the fragments into complete sentences change the advertisement? (Hint: Think about rhythm and tone.) How will each version affect your customers (the readers)? Which version would your team decide to pay money to put on the air? Why? Which version makes your company look smart? Why? Come up with a theory about why ads tend to use fragments. Ads tend to use fragments because . . .

Part 7. As you read the paragraphs below, you'll find several fragments. Try to chart the straight **subject** → **verb** path through each statement. Underline the fragments. Then, change, add, and/or subtract words, phrases, or punctuation to turn fragments into complete sentences.

What a hike. We found out we hadn't brought enough water. After all our packing and planning! We had to ration it out carefully. Although we were very thirsty. The brambles were a problem, too. Because none of us had thought to wear protective clothing. Even though the hike leader, Bill, a longtime expert guide and ornithologist, had warned us to cover up and to bring proper supplies. Several of us had forgotten our hats, too. Along with sunscreen.

In the middle of our hike, two of the climbers, Sam and Alia, who are both beginners, are not too sure of what they're doing on the trail, and who yet wandered off. They got lost, of course! When they'd been missing about an hour, Bill and his assistant, a very capable and experienced woman and trained paramedic named Nia, who often helped on search teams for lost hikers, and who he relied on for advice about wilderness survival. When we saw them talking privately, we guessed what they were doing. Deciding whether to attempt a rescue! Finally, everyone was reunited. We were all happy to see Sam and Alia. Even though we'd been sweating in the sun while waiting for Bill and Nia to find them. We all made it back to the lodge in one piece! Thanks to Bill and Nia.

Part 8. Tiered Team Assignment: How do fragments happen? How do fragments happen? Here's your chance to find out. In the items below, we invite you *to create* ten fragments! Then we'll examine the fragments you've worked with in each activity to see if we can come up with a theory about *why* fragments sneak up on unsuspecting writers.

Step 1. Below, you'll find 10 sentences. Let's make them into fragments! You have two effective methods to make instant fragments:

■ remove the clear subject → verb path through the sentence

■ use words and phrases like *although, because, while, when, even though, if,* or *since* to signal the idea should not stand alone as a sentence.

1. That television show was supposed to be appropriate for children.
2. You can't take the job.
3. The winter solstice arrives so soon.

4. We wish we could help you with your situation.

5. Blynn was able to restore the house to its original condition.

6. All the veterinarians in the vicinity were already closed.

7. My new company's benefits package was such a good one.

8. We went to the auction looking for a desk.

9. You think I haven't figured out your trick yet.

10. His roommate was trying to study.

Step 2. Now let's look at what you just did. Look at the changes you made in each activity in this section (Parts 1–5). Which words transformed sentences into fragments, or fragments into sentences? **Make a list** of the words you *took out* or *put in* for each exercise. What kinds of connections do these words make among the ideas in each fragment? **The words I had to change....**

a. Show *who* is doing the action in the sentence.

b. Show *what* is happening in the sentence.

c. Show connections among ideas in this sentence and the sentences around it.

d. Specify which is the main idea, and which idea is less important.

e. Show that these ideas should be thought about together.

f. Show you're adding information to the original idea.

g. Show a big shift in focus from one idea to the next.

h. Help me see how these ideas move my thoughts along to the next idea in the paragraph.

i. Help me take a mental breath in the middle of several ideas.

j. Other? (you specify) _____

Step 3. Now that we know what's *missing* from fragments, let's think about why writers use them. **Why do fragments sound complete?** Using everything you've learned and discussed in Parts 1–5, decide with your group which of the following statements are true: **Fragments sound complete because they . . .**

a. seem to connect ideas, even though their punctuation tells you to disconnect them

b. continue the thought that came just before them

c. blend in with the idea that comes just after them

d. speed up the pace of whatever you're writing

e. avoid repeating the same subjects and verbs over and over

f. emphasize each item in a list—even though all the items belong together

g.   can sound like a bullet list

h.   All of these!

i.   All of these are true, but different ones are operating in different fragments.

j.   None of these are true!

Step 4. What have we left out? What did *your* investigation of fragments come up with that *we* left out? Fragments happen because _____.

2.4   Run-on sentences

Run-on sentences tend to make the reader feel rushed into finishing the sentence because there is no place to take a needed breath.

JESSICA HART

The reader is forced to read the sentence repeatedly in order to make some sense of it.

WAHKEISHA MURCHISON

With run-ons, the reader may get bored. Without an ending to each thought, the reader will feel that your piece of writing is never-ending.

JOY COLLIS

Run-ons ruin the rhythm of a paragraph.

BRIAN ROOSA

Editor's Tip: A run-on or fused sentence tries to do too much at once. Run-ons try to sandwich *two complete sentences into one*, with no punctuation or transition words to guide the reader through the mass of ideas you've accumulated. Confusion results. Readers don't know where to focus their attention, which words go with each other, and how all the piled-up ideas relate to each other.

The good news is that run-ons are easy to fix:

■ Separate your ideas into two or three shorter sentences.

■ Use transition words, commas, or semicolons to show a particular relationship between the two ideas.

2.5   How to defuse a fused (run-on) sentence

Dan Romano

Readers can get lost in a run-on. If readers don't understand the main idea of a sentence, this can cause a snowball effect: They might not understand the whole paragraph! Here's an example from one of my papers:

> The movie does just as good of a job to hide the identity of the President as the book does because in the book, you can't see the face of the person, and you have to assume that he is there.

There's too much going on here for one sentence. I decide to separate my ideas with a period. Here's my revision:

> The movie does just as good a job of hiding the identity of the President as the story does. In the book, you can't see . . .

Michael Black

If fragments can result from mixed signals, run-ons are like rush-hour traffic when none of the signals are working. They lack brakes or stopping points within the sentence. The only way to fix a run-on is to make a few alterations to it. Here are some examples of run-ons from a paper I wrote on Al Capone.

Original sentence: He ordered the murders then he should pay for them.

Possible solutions: Many people try to fix the run-on by putting a comma in between the two sentences. This would, of course, place a needed pause in the middle of the sentence, but the use of a comma would bring about the dreaded comma splice:

> He ordered the murders, then he should pay for them.
>
> comma splice

This is fixing one mistake with another. Try one of the following solutions, instead.

Solution I: *Use a semicolon.* This would fix the problem of presenting two different, complete thoughts together in a short space:

> **He ordered the murders;** *he should pay for them.*

Although this version is technically correct, it doesn't give the sentence the rhythm and flow that I want it to have in this paper.

Solution II: *Reword the sentence.* In my opinion this method is superior because it always works. Here's what I decided to do:

If he ordered the murders, **then** he should pay for them.

I like this version, because it clearly shows the relationship between the two parts of the sentence: The second part happens *because* of what the first part says. Either of these methods is technically correct. Use either one to decrease the number of run-on sentences in your works.

ACTIVITIES 2.4–2.5: RUN-INS WITH RUN-ONS

Part 1. A run-on sentence puts two complete sentences together, with no transition words or connecting punctuation to help the reader make sense of the information. At least ten of the following sentences are run-ons. Identify and draw a line through each run-on sentence.

1. Although I didn't feel nervous or scared, my heart was beating quickly.
2. We couldn't stop laughing the joke was just too funny.
3. The huge palm trees swayed in the strong winds it felt like a hurricane.
4. After Gretchen's close call, no one wanted to take a chance.
5. I watched the stone skip across the pond the ripples ran into each other.
6. According to the phone company, I'd made a shocking number of long distance phone calls.
7. Judging by his lack of tact and diplomacy, he had never been a politician.
8. Something was leaking the radiator was the obvious culprit.
9. My sister and I had already given some serious thought to the possibility that we would have to take over my aunt's bakery.
10. Samuel had to call in sick his head was aching more than ever.
11. That's crazy you can't do that!
12. All the time it took to write the book had been well worth it.
13. All things considered, I'm really glad I traded in my old car.
14. Don't miss our annual clearance everything's on sale!
15. This will take only a few minutes with two of us working on it.

16. Did he ask you for a reference are you able to do it?

17. Mary Jean wished she had said no to the job offer she was always agreeing to do things she really didn't want to.

18. I felt so sad for the lonely gorilla, living out its days in a small cement enclosure in the zoo.

19. Money was so scarce in the Keller household that each child had an after-school job starting at age 11.

20. When I was told what she had said, I was stunned my shock must have been obvious.

Part 2. Left alone, each sentence below is a run-on, confusing to the reader. In each blank, add either a transition word or a punctuation mark that will defuse the run-on sentence and clear up communication between the writer and reader.

Example: I changed the channel _____ the show I'd been watching haunted me.

Possible answers: I changed the channel, but the show I'd been watching haunted me.
I changed the channel; the show I'd been watching haunted me.
I changed the channel because the show I'd been watching haunted me.

1. The other day I decided I needed to get more exercise _____ I threw on my shorts and sneakers to go for a little jog.

2. I only made it one block _____ I started to pant.

3. I thought about calling it quits _____ it just seemed so ridiculous.

4. Instead, I gathered up all my strength _____ I stretched my muscles out one more time.

5. Taking a deep breath, I began my slow trot down the street _____ it was painful, but I knew I could do it.

6. Behind me, I heard a car coming _____ was it just me, or was it coming toward me a little too fast?

7. Just in time, I dove onto the lawn next to me _____ my knees were a little dinged up, but at least I was alive!

8. Deciding to give it another try, I limped on _____ I thought I heard laughter.

9. I turned to see some of my neighbors doubled over _____ my creative gymnastics were apparently just too much for them.

10. That was it for me _____ I turned around and headed for home.

11. I suppose that day's experiences were good for me in some way _____ next time I feel like exercising, I'm going to stay inside!

Part 3. Teamwork. Now compare the changes you made in Part 2 with the changes made by others in your group. As a group, answer these questions. Be sure you can explain why you choose the answer you come up with!

1. Which of these is more accurate:

    a. There is only one correct way to fix run-ons.

    b. There are many different ways to fix run-ons.

2. The way you fix a run-on

    a. Shows how much you know about grammar.

    b. Shows how you want the reader to group ideas.

    c. Doesn't really matter, as long as you make your ideas clear.

    d. All of these.

    e. None of these.

Part 4. Read the following selection. Underline the run-on sentences. Do they make the story confusing? Boring? Hard to follow? Write 2-3 lines describing the effect these run-ons have on you as the reader.

Just a Day at the Office

Let me tell you about my day at the office the other day it was one of the worst days of my life, although it'll probably seem funny to you. First of all, I was lucky to get to work at all that day my car was acting odd and I had to restart it about ten times on the way. By the time I got to my desk, I was pretty testy I'd already had about all the stress I could stand for the day. Apparently my boss disagreed with my feelings on that particular topic she immediately showed up to tell me that I was late and would be docked an hour's pay to make up for it. Well, I can tell you I didn't react well to that news my nostrils were flaring as I defended my tardiness in no uncertain terms. Her reaction to my frustration was to pile on the work by the time I had settled in for the day I had about ten articles that needed fact-checking. I was pretty sure she had given me everyone else's articles to work on, not just mine that suspicion was confirmed by the delighted expressions on my coworkers' faces as they received the news that they would be able to go to lunch early due to an unexpectedly light workload. Was I ever hacked off! I went ahead and did my work, but I'll admit I didn't do my usual thorough job I skipped some facts I figured were probably just fine. My boss must have suspected I would be less than careful in my unhappy state she gathered up a few of the articles I had finished and checked them after me! Uh oh. My face was red when she showed up to tell me about the misquoted "facts" I had missed luckily, she felt that I had punished myself enough. For the rest of the day, I worked hard to do my best at day's end, I was just thankful I still had a job. My car, unfortunately, wasn't quite done with me!

Part 5. Writing practice. Now, add transition words and punctuation marks to defuse the run-on sentences you just identified in Part 3. Increase the reader's enjoyment and understanding of the essay by giving a clear path through the paragraph!

Part 6. Below you'll find two short selections. As you read, choose the selection that you find to be clearer and more effective.

1. Run-ons try to force too much information into one sentence when actually two or three sentences might better serve the reader, who gets confused without solid stopping points. A writer who uses run-ons may not have readers for long, because no reader really wants to be punished with sentences that go on and on and never really seem to make a clear point they need to be broken down into shorter, more effective sentences for the reader.

2. Run-ons try to force too much information into one sentence. The reader might be better served if each run-on became two or even three sentences. Otherwise, with no solid stopping points, the reader is confused. A writer who uses run-ons may not have readers for long. What reader really wants to be punished with sentences that go on and on, never really making a clear point? Run-ons should be broken down into shorter, more effective sentences for the reader.

2.6   What's the difference between complex and compound sentences?

Complex sentences let you show sophisticated relationships among ideas.

independent clause + *dependent clause* = <u>complex sentence</u>

The main idea in a complex sentence (the straight subject → verb path the reader is looking for) is in the **independent clause**, which can stand alone as a sentence. The real fun comes when you design the *dependent clause* (which can't stand alone, even though it has a subject and verb). The *dependent clause* lets you subtly mold and reshape the main idea, adding additional information that may affect the way your readers interpret a concept.

Although he studied art, he painted houses.

(*dependent clause*)   **(independent clause)**

Compound sentences combine two complete sentences. They connect two **independent clauses** (a group of words with a subject and verb that can stand alone as a sentence) with words like *and, but, for, or, nor, so,* or *yet.* **Compound sentences** signal the reader that both sets of ideas (both independent clauses) are *equally important.*

He studied art, **but** he painted houses.

Note: **Complex** sentences and **compound** sentences will have two or more subject/verb pairs. To find the subject, first separate the sentence into its two parts. If both parts can stand alone as sentences, identify the subject in *both* parts. If only one clause can stand on its own, look for the subject in the independent clause only.

Even though Jasper had lost his confidence, he refused to give up.

Here, only the second part of the sentence, *he refused to give up,* can be a complete sentence. Since the subject of that part of the sentence is *he,* that is the subject of the entire sentence.

ACTIVITY 2.6: COMPOUND AND COMPLEX SENTENCES

Part 1. Make sentences with each of the words and phrases listed below. Which ones let you connect two complete sentences to make a compound sentence? Place an **X** beside the words that can be used to connect two equally important ideas.

because	although	according	without
if	so	and	for
but	indeed	as if	or
when	since	until	unless
to	even though	nor	yet

Part 2. Teamwork. In your group, take a look at the sentences that *don't* contain two ideas that can stand alone. What's different about these sentences? Hint: For one thing, they're complex sentences. One clause can stand alone as a sentence (independent), but the other one can't (dependent). How do we know that both ideas don't carry the same amount of importance?

Part 3. Read the following sentences. Each sentence gets its idea across, but when it is read with its companion sentence, the result is choppy. Smooth things out by making these into complex sentences. Remember, in a complex sentence, one clause can stand alone as a sentence (independent), but the other one can't (dependent). Readers will interpret the idea in the sentence that can stand alone as more important than the one that can't function as a complete sentence.

1. I had no luck that day. I was sure I would catch the biggest fish the next day.
2. She called to ask about buying my car. I told her it was sold.
3. They had been in-line skating for at least an hour. Jay and Lisette had to rest.
4. His job involved long hours. Lashawn loved it.
5. The vacation was going to be expensive. Our family had to give up some hobbies to save money.

Part 4. Read the following sentences. This time, we want to make them into compound sentences. Because you want to signal that each idea is equally important, make sure that both clauses can stand alone as complete sentences (independent clauses).

1. Kaylynn had a lot of work to do. Her friends talked her into taking a break.
2. That essay question was really tough to answer. The class only had twenty minutes!
3. Her cats had ruined the apartment's curtains. Laine had to forfeit her deposit.
4. We could swim in the pool all day. We could get dressed and see the sights.
5. Karol complained about the food. She ate every bite.

Part 4. Read the sentences below. Complete the compound sentences using the following words: *for, yet, but, and, or, so.* Complete the complex sentences using the following words or phrases: *when, if, because, even though, since.* Remember, complex sentences combine a clause that can stand alone with a clause that can't. This signals that one idea is more important than the other. A compound sentence combines two complete sentences and signals that both ideas are equally important.

_____ the parrot lunged at her, Jill shrieked loudly. The cage bars were thick and strong, _____ she was afraid of the bird anyway. The bird still looked angry, _____ Jill moved to another part of the pet store. _____ Jill was now several feet away, the parrot continued to stare at her. Jill decided she'd had enough, _____ she quickly left the store.

Part 5. Teamwork. Get together with your group to read your revisions for the previous two activities. Did you find different ways to answer Parts 2 and

3? Choose one or two sentences that different group members combined in different ways. Talk about what each version emphasized. Did different group members emphasize different parts? Was the meaning different from one group member's sentence to another's?

Part 6. Complete the compound sentences below using one of the following words: *but, so, and, or, nor, yet, for.*

1. The weather was really nasty that day, _____ Alejandra decided to postpone the picnic.
2. We'd love to help with the painting party, _____ we have to run a marathon all that day.
3. You know, you can go out house hunting with us today, _____ you can stay home and wash the car.
4. I didn't have to clean the food off the floor, _____ the dog had already done it!
5. Bailey had a lot of studying to do, _____ she had to get it done by 5:00 p.m.

Part 7. Complete the complex sentences below using one of the following words or phrases: *although, if, unless, when, after, since.*

1. _____ Kirsten had eaten the last piece of cake, she pretended she hadn't.
2. _____ he got ready without showering, Chris would be late for work.
3. _____ the wind was blowing so hard, we had to cancel the yard sale.
4. _____ all goes well at tomorrow's interview, I'll have a new job!
5. _____ changing costumes so quickly, the actor had no idea he was wearing two different shoe styles.

Part 8. Editing. Now, read the following memo. Use compound and complex sentence structures to make the paragraph less choppy, adding words like *although, but, since, yet, so, before,* and *as.* Remember, both clauses in a compound sentence can stand alone as complete sentences (independent). Both ideas are equally emphasized. In a complex sentence, one idea depends on the other, is less important, and can't stand alone as a sentence.

Memo to My Cat

Dear Fluffy,

Thank you for your recent communication. I wish you had come to me directly. Shredding my couch was very unprofessional. I understand you don't like your name. We can change it. I'm open to suggestions. "Annihilator" is what comes to mind at present.

I have issues, too. My skin is pliable. My clothes are soft. I am not a scratching post. I know it's hard to understand this. I'm bigger than you are. I'm not as tough as you are!

Here's another surprise. I don't enjoy cleaning your litter box. I promise I will keep it fresh. Keep the kitty litter in your box. I won't have more work than is necessary.

You sleep all day. You want to play at night. Your friends visit at strange hours. I work all day. I want to sleep at night. Please let me sleep. I will be cranky. You won't like that.

I hope we can work things out. Thanks for your cooperation.

Sincerely, Your roommate

Part 9. Teamwork. Compare the roommate's memo in Part 8 to your revision. How have your revisions changed the tone? Which one will Fluffy (or Annihilator) be more likely to accept?

2.7   Parallel construction in complex and compound sentences

Writers help readers follow complex ideas by balancing their sentence structures. When two or more ideas in a sentence or paragraph are very closely related, use similar words, phrases, or clauses to emphasize and clarify what you're writing. Use nouns with nouns, adjectives with adjectives, adverbs with adverbs, infinitives with infinitives, and gerunds with gerunds to make your sentence structure **parallel**. Here are a few examples.

DAVID WILLIAMS

Not parallel:
Because shyness and demureness are smiled upon in females and *less acceptable* in males, more men turn to professional therapists for help with social anxiety.

Parallel:
Because shyness and demureness are smiled upon in females and frowned upon in males, more men turn to professional therapists for help with social anxiety. This sentence uses parallel *verbs*.

JOSETTE EDWARDS

Not parallel:
What I would like to do is *creating* software.

Parallel:

What I would like to do is to create software.
This sentence uses parallel *infinitives*.

KEN SCHIRLING

Not parallel:

Show them as much love and *caring* as possible.

Parallel:

Show them as much love and care as possible.
This sentence uses parallel *nouns*.

MICHELLE FEDOR

Not parallel:

Frankenstein tells the story of a creature on a journey to find love and friendship, but instead gets tragically lost.

Parallel:

Frankenstein tells the story of a creature who goes on a journey to find love and friendship, but who gets tragically lost instead.
This sentence uses parallel *clauses* that function as adjectives.

MARTHA GOLDEN

Although **risk** of seroconversion after injury with HIV needles *is* quite low, the **likelihood** of insensitivity, pain, and resentment from an injured nurse's coworkers *is* relatively high.

This sentence uses parallel **subject** → *verb* paths in each clause:

risk → *is*	**likelihood** → *is*
(**noun** → *verb*)	(**noun** → *verb*)

It also uses parallel *adjectives*: low/high.

Editor's Tip: Using parallel structures is especially important when writing **compound** or **complex** sentences. Structure both clauses in similar ways to give your readers a sense of balance:

In a compound sentence: He studied art, but he painted houses.

In a complex sentence: Although *he studied* art, he painted houses.

ACTIVITY 2.7: PARALLEL CONSTRUCTION

Part 1. Below, you'll find ten platitudes. At least five contain parallel construction errors (one part of the sentence doesn't balance with the other). First, identify the sentences that need to be repaired. Second, underline the words or phrases that should be parallel but are not. Finally, rewrite each sentence so that it is parallel.

Example: <u>Knowing him</u> is <u>to love him</u>.
             To know him is to love him.

1. Seeing is to believe.
2. Two's company; three's too crowded.
3. Out of the frying pan, into the fire.
4. Early to bed and getting up early make you healthy, wealthy, and wise.
5. You can lead a horse to water, but you can't make him drink.
6. People who live in glass houses shouldn't throw stones.
7. The bigger they come, they fall a lot harder.
8. If at first you don't succeed, try, try again.
9. Beggars can't be choosers.
10. You'll catch more flies with honey than if you use vinegar.

Part 2. Read the parallel sentences below. In each sentence, you'll find parallel structures. Some will be nouns; others will be adjectives, verbs, infinitives, or gerunds. For each sentence, identify and underline the parallel structures. Then replace them with parallel structures of your own creation. Feel free to be silly. Be sure to replace nouns with nouns, verbs with verbs, and so on.

Example: If you choose to <u>jog</u> and not <u>walk</u>, you'll burn more calories.
             fly   **eat**

1. Add yogurt and blend for one minute.
2. Tell her to be considerate of others and to keep her cat inside.
3. Most of the staff and students were out of the building at the time.
4. Bill is the kind of professor who listens to all your worries and who gives each concern serious consideration.
5. The scout was impressed by the shortstop's hitting and fielding.

Part 3. Teamwork. Get together with your group and compare your results. Choose one sentence and write a story that goes with it. Be inventive!

Part 4. Use parallel structures to fill in the blanks below. (Don't limit yourself to one-word answers.)

Example: It is better to be _____ than _____.

Possible answers:
  A) It is better to be loved than hated.
  B) It is better to be a doer than a sitter.
  C) It is better to be progressing slowly toward a goal than running in place.

   1. Too many people are _____ instead of _____.
   2. If you aren't _____, then you must be _____.
   3. Always change your _____; never change your _____.
   4. When you truly _____, you can _____.
   5. All my friends _____, but I _____.
   6. How can you be _____ and still be _____?
   7. The wise student will remember _____ and _____.
   8. I wish I could _____ and yet _____.
   9. What good is _____ without _____?
  10. When you _____, please _____!

Part 5. In the poem that follows are five lines in which you can find parallel construction errors. Please find all five lines, then rewrite them so that they are parallel. Which way does the poem work better?

The leaves and the grass were waving goodbye
They seemed to be sighing, and they cried
Each green thing we drove past beseeching the sky
As though our loss might mean their dying.

Still, we drove on, we were trying hard not to think
Of the days passed in stillness and taking leisure
All this we would mourn, we would yet wishing to drink
From those streams which had given us pleasure.

Part 6. Use the word pairs below to form sentences containing parallel structures. Be creative.

Example: **sprinting, jumping**

Possible sentence: As we watched the athletes, we felt we were **sprinting** the
                        track and **jumping** the hurdles with them.

1. to watch, to play
2. enormous, destructive
3. enjoyed, spent
4. who ran, who ended up
5. looked up to, asked questions of
6. wickedly, nervously
7. friendship, love
8. shortest, most entertaining
9. dancing, music
10. eager tourists, entrepreneurial locals

Part 7. Teamwork. Join up with your fellow group members to compare results. Are your sentences similar or completely different? How was your use of parallel structures different from the other group members? Was one pair harder than the others? Why or why not?

2.8 Writers Write: WRITING SOPHISTICATED SENTENCES

Thad Skinner and Tarez Graban

Thad Skinner, a freshman at Marietta College, did the smart thing: When faced with a demanding writing assignment, he asked for help. Here, writing tutor Tarez Graban, whom we met in Sections 4.2 and 11.16, talks about how she helped Thad use sentence structure to mirror the complex issues he wanted to discuss.

Thad's assignment was to read an excerpt from *Achievement of Desire* by Richard Rodriguez and to write a short response. His response was to answer this question: What was the most important thing about the author's life that changed as a result of his education? Thad chose the author's attitude toward his parents. He set out to argue that the author recognized the pride his parents had in him, and finally replaced his embarrassment with respect.

Since Thad knew he had trouble writing complex sentences, he tended to stick to a very simple structure consisting of a subject, action, and an outcome. Let's see what he did.

Thad's original sentences

"He quit showing off in front of his parents and he became comfortable with
    his life."
"Rodriguez was angry."
"Rodriguez realized his parents gave him the chance they never had."
"He respected them."

We realized that these sentences contained five simpler statements or pieces of information Thad wanted to talk about.

Five simpler statements

He quit showing off in front of his parents.
He became comfortable with his life.
He was angry.
He realized his parents gave him the chance they never had.
He respected his parents.

Now we had a clear picture of just what Thad wanted to say. He began experimenting with ways to rewrite all five statements into one complex sentence. After some experimenting, Thad found two ways to combine the information in one sentence. Each version utilized a different combination of the five bits of information he wanted to convey, and each emphasized a different point:

Version one: He was *angry*, but *realized* his parents gave him the chance they never had, and *respected* them.

What this sentence does: "In this version," Thad says, "I used the last three statements. I couldn't find a way to make all five fit. The sentence structure makes "He was angry" the main emphasis. It jumps out at me because it is a definite statement. It draws the reader's attention to the anger. Also, two things happen in the sentence instead of one--he *realizes* and he *respects*."

Version two: Being *angry* at first, he *realized* his parents gave him the chance they never had, so he *respected* them and became very *comfortable* with his life.

What this sentence does: "The second version tells right in the beginning that he is going to get over his anger," Thad says. "Three things happen: he *realizes*, he *respects* and he *becomes*. The emphasis of the sentence is changed from being angry in the beginning to what happens at the end."

In both versions, Thad chose to omit the first statement--that Rodriguez quit showing off--at least as far as these sentences were concerned. Thad used it elsewhere in the paragraph, because he still thought it was important. If he had decided the idea was not important enough to keep, he could have simply left it out of his revisions.

2.9   Sentence coherence

WAHKEISHA MURCHISON

What's going on in this sentence?

Gambling opponents insist that the negative aspects of gaming; the deceptive promise of instant wealth and the personal suffering around addicted gamblers.

I know what it's trying to say, because I wrote it! My readers, however, don't understand the point the sentence is trying to make because something's missing. Here's what I meant to say:

People who oppose gaming insist that there are negative aspects of gambling. The negative aspects are the deceptive promise of instant wealth and the personal suffering around addicted gamblers.

Now the reader understands what the sentence is about, but I have two separate sentences. Could all my information fit into one sentence? Yes! I almost had it together the first time:

Gambling opponents insist *that* the negative aspects of gaming . . . (do what? I need a verb to connect this to the rest of my ideas)

The word *that* tells readers they're about to hear what gambling opponents insist. The semicolon cuts off this part of the sentence from the information in the rest. Here's what my readers need to know (what gambling opponents insist):

The negative aspects are the deceptive promise of instant wealth and the personal suffering around addicted gamblers.

That idea is already there, in my original sentence! My first version tried to hook these two thoughts together with a semicolon, but that didn't work. A semicolon has to hook together *two complete thoughts.* What I need to do is to complete that first thought with a verb:

However, gambling opponents insist *that* the negative aspects of gaming *include* the deceptive promise of instant wealth and personal suffering around addicted gamblers.

The ideas were all there in my original version. I just had to figure out how to connect them.

ACTIVITIES 2.8–2.9: SENTENCE COHERENCE

Part 1. Sometimes a writer starts off with perfectly good ideas but ends up with sentences that make no sense to the reader. When sentences are not coherent, the reader has difficulty understanding the point the author is trying to make. A reader who has to struggle to make sense of writing is likely to become disinterested or frustrated before the end of the paragraph. Coherence can mean the difference between effective communication between writer and reader and absolutely no communication at all!

At least ten sentences below demonstrate how confusing an incoherent sentence can be. Place an ⋆ beside each **coherent** sentence.

1. When the professor began to assign projects and to groups who had already begun: I felt nervous.

2. In order to change her mind about when the projects would be due, a group of students came forward to argue that an extra week would enable us to put that final polish on our projects.

3. The professor thought about our request as she taught the rest of the class period; when it was time to leave, she offered a compromise.

4. If we would and make the projects into some sort of CD-ROM compilation, of all the class projects.

5. Despite some reservations, most of us agreed it was a good compromise; although we really wanted.

6. The few extra days we'd been granted seemed to fly by, especially given the amount of work putting together that electronic compilation turned out to be!

7. On the day of our presentations, we were really proud of our results: we had formed a group identity, worked as a close-knit team, and created a product we could truly brag about.

8. A hush fell over the room the first project; on the computer screen projected up onto the wall was a work of art.

9. As soon as the professor began her critique, and as a group, we felt we were being attacked.

10. I don't think she had expected her class to react in this way; clearly, we had become united in our hard work.

11. After giving the matter some thought our confused professor although she was glad to see us working together, she felt she had a job to do.

12. She let us know first of all that if she didn't give us her critique, including both negative and positive comments, she would be letting us down.

13. After all, how could learning from hearing only the good things?

14. Secondly, she pointed out that we were a good team and she was so pleased about: but now we needed to think as individuals.

15. Her comments made sense to all of us, even though we were still hesitant to hear any criticism regarding this project that we had so lovingly put together.

16. Feeling a bit shameful as we nodded in response to her sensible suggestions, the members of the class got ready to take notes.

17. Once again, the screen magnified on the wall, we tried not to think of it as a child in need of protection.

18. Slowly but surely, as we listened carefully to our professor's constructive criticism, we found ourselves learning a little more than we had thought possible.

19. Of course, no one could deny that the positive comments were much more enjoyable than the negative ones!

20. Still, of classes I have taken; that class is the one in which I learned, through hard work, and I'm still learning today.

Part 2. Now that you've identified the sentences that are coherent, go back and reread the other sentences, the ones that made you say, "Huh?" Using the coherent sentences as a guide, rewrite those confusing sentences so that they are coherent as well. Since most of these confusing sentences leave out important information, you'll probably have to add your own ideas, drawn from your interpretation of what the sentence *should* say. Feel free to rearrange, change, add, and subtract any words and punctuation that seem to be getting in the way of clear communication.

Part 3. After all that practice, you should be ready for a real challenge. The following paragraph is a mess. Again, you may rearrange, change, add, and subtract words and punctuation in order to be sure that this author's message is not lost. When you're finished, compare your results with those of others in your group. Given the state of the paragraph you started with, you ought to have some startling differences.

The absolute last thing think about on a Sunday afternoon going back to work Monday. That's why, when my boss called me recently Sunday, my Caller ID box and let the phone ring for awhile but then I answered it. What a grim reminder his voice! He was just to remind me to set forward Daylight Saving Time the next morning. He didn't want anyone to be late; the next day's work. After I hung up the phone, I was really. Not only did I have to think: work in just a few short, but I also faced the sad, losing an hour of sleep to Daylight Saving Time. I flung down onto, groaning. I needed to think and pull myself out; it was ruining what was left! As I tried to something fun and creative with my time, and changed the clocks in my apartment. Better safe than sorry!

2.10 Writers Write: ADDING DESCRIPTIVE DETAIL

Cary Stewart

Cary Stewart is the author of "How to Make a Local Convenience Store Employee Mad," a humorous process paper featured in Section 7.2. With tongue in cheek, Cary takes readers step by step through the process of tormenting, irritating, and frustrating a hapless fast-food counter worker. Here, he talks about how he added visual imagery to his sentences to help his readers feel these emotions right along with the tormented employee.

A story, no matter what it's about, will lose the interest of the reader if there isn't any description, especially at key times. Descriptive sentences help a reader to *feel* emotions or ideas from the writer. This will help the reader form superb mental images while reading, and will inevitably make the story more enjoyable.

Here are a few sentences from a very descriptive part of a story I wrote called, "How to Make a Local Convenience Store Employee Mad." This will help you get a feel of how to use descriptive words to get across emotions and actions.

> Once you get out of your car, look inside the store and stare at the worker seated behind the deli counter. Once you have entered the store, continue on your walk to the counter.

Isn't that sentence *dull*? How can a person form images about how this scenario might develop?

These vague sentences give no indication as to how you (the customer) can start to torment the deli worker. *Vague* sentences give *vague* ideas about how to form mental images to make the story more enjoyable. A reader may lose interest in this story very quickly. What saves this story and makes it humorous are the many descriptive sentences that are placed throughout.

Compare the original sentences in the following columns to the changed versions. Adding a word or two helps with the overall design and can "back up" previous sentences.

Original sentences

Once you get out of your car, *look inside* the store and stare *at the worker* seated behind the deli counter.

Next, once you have entered the store, continue on your *walk to the counter.*

Revised sentences

Once you get out of your car, *look very intently inside* the store and stare *straight into the eyes of the prey* seated behind the deli counter.

Next, one you have entered the store, continue on your *walk to the counter. Glare and rub your hands together in a very swift motion. A good little strut may even be helpful.*

Notice the difference? The *full sentence* added at the end provides a *richer* texture.

This paragraph will help give readers images in their heads of a *scared, uneasy,* and *upset* deli worker. At the same time it gives readers clues about how the customer will continue to torment the worker, not only in this the paragraph, but throughout the overall story.

It is obvious that not everyone will form the same conclusions, actions, ideas, and emotions. But, *without the key use of descriptive words, it is guaranteed that a story will not get across to the reader that way the author intended it to be.*

ACTIVITY 2.10: ADDING DESCRIPTIVE DETAIL

Part 1. For each dull, vague, word or phrase below, offer a more interesting, more descriptive replacement.

Example: walks slowly
Possible answers: *pokes, meanders, creeps*

1. nice
2. happily
3. went
4. eating quickly
5. bad person

Part 2. Read each pair of sentences. Circle the more effective sentence from each pair. Underline the descriptive words that help the sentence communicate with its readers.

1. The dogs barked and ran toward the frightened child.

   The Rottweilers, fur bristling, barked viciously as they charged the terrified toddler.

2. The lurid news stories, full of violence and mayhem, caused my sister to have nightmares.

   The news stories upset my sister.

3. It knocked our socks off when Nick strode into the party, looking healthy and fit after six weeks in a body cast.

   We were surprised to see Nick at the party right after he'd been in a body cast.

4. Going in for jury duty made for a long, boring day.

   Jury duty, which meant sitting on a hard wooden bench listening to other potential jurors conjure up ridiculous excuses for their supposed inability to serve, was worse than a day spent counting the hairs on a poodle.

5. Sam was completely entranced by the action, noise, and sheer physicality of a live professional basketball game.

Sam really enjoyed the excitement of the basketball game.

Part 3. For each basic scenario given below, compose a detailed sentence that will give your reader a vivid mental picture of what is happening. Use descriptive words carefully, so that the meaning of the sentence is clear.

1. a race car driver winning his first race
2. a reunion between friends who haven't seen each other in ten years
3. a fire starting, then beginning to spread
4. a child eating cake at his first birthday party
5. riding a train for the first time
6. the post office on a busy day
7. driving home in a thunderstorm
8. jumping into a cold river from a tree
9. eating your favorite food
10. walking into your classroom on the first day of the semester

Part 4. Teamwork. Compare your sentences with the sentences composed by the other people in your group. How are they different? What do they have in common?

Part 5. Writing. Choose one of the scenarios in Part 3, above, and write about it. Try to get your reader to see, hear, smell, feel, and taste the scene along with you. Trade descriptions with your group. Can you experience each other's scenes? Be sure to give each other suggestions for adding specific detail to help your paragraph come alive in readers' minds.

Part 6. The lack of descriptive language in the sentences below makes it difficult for a reader to form a clear image of what is happening in each sentence. Rewrite the sentences, using descriptive words to grab the reader's interest.

1. Our baseball broke the window.
2. The washing machine made some odd noises, then stopped.
3. The eclipse was interesting to watch.
4. She gave him a dirty look.
5. Gwen thought she saw a ghost.
6. Tony told Adrian about his experience with the elephant.
7. The movie's special effects were good.

8. Les hurried to the buffet table.

9. As we drove down the road, one of our tires went flat.

10. At the zoo, the tigers were lying in the shade.

Part 7. Teamwork. Now, compare the sentences you revised for Part 4 with those of others in your group. Did you use different descriptive words? Did your sentences end up with a different meaning than their sentences?

Part 8. Writing. Choose one of the sentences you revised for Part 4. Write a paragraph about what happened next.

2.11 Writers Write: WORDINESS, VAGUENESS, AND TONE

Joy Osorio

Joy Osorio, a student at Savannah State University when she wrote this, thought she had a problem with wordiness because teachers seemed to ask her to revise her papers by editing out excess words. While developing a paper on childcare costs, however, she realized that those extra words were meant to accomplish special effects that were important to her as a writer. How could she avoid wordiness and still achieve the effects she wanted in her papers? Let's see what she came up with.

Wordiness is a problem I have when developing my papers. I have a tendency of writing words that don't need to be in a particular phrase. Sometimes, adding extra words causes me to write comma splices. [See Section 3.14 for Cary Stewart's note on comma splices.] My professor would scratch his notes on the side margin, telling me to shorten the sentences. I worried that taking these words out would lessen the quality of the paper.

What I found was that taking words out changed the *sound* of a sentence. Part of the reason I was using those extra words was to get a certain tone across. At the same time, I saw that adding descriptive words to the bare bones of my arguments helped me get my ideas across more powerfully.

This is the story of how I revised a paper on the costs of raising children to express a certain tone, while avoiding wordiness and vagueness:

1st Draft

The cost of having kids today has changed from inexpensive to extremely expensive.

In this draft, I sound very vague and lack the essential details to capture my audience. What, for example, does *inexpensive* mean? What is *today*?

2nd Draft

When I revised my paper, I decided to add details that would help the reader *see* what the cost of raising children was like. Here's my revision of the sentence I wrote in draft 1.

Draft 1:

The cost of having kids today is increasing steadily. It starts off with purchasing baby diapers and clothes, then grows to include piano lessons and Little League.

In this draft I have added quite a bit of information with just one added sentence. My first sentence still makes the same argument as it did in the first draft:

Raising kids is getting expensive!

The second sentence, however, now gives the reader specific mental images to picture. I use words that give clear mental pictures of things parents have to pay for, like diapers and piano lessons. It's much easier to imagine the cost of a stack of diapers, a piano, or a Little League uniform than it is to think about vague concepts like *expensive* and *inexpensive*.

More than that, however, the details I chose to add named concrete things that **cost more and more.** The diapers I mention in the first part of the sentence cost a few dollars, but the piano lessons I list later cost several hundred. So, my second sentence not only adds specific details, it also shows the movement from less expensive items to more expensive items.

Draft 2 is a good draft, but I worry that I'm starting to sound like a textbook. If I want real people to read my paper, I'll have to change my tone.

3rd Draft

Here's my next attempt to talk about the cost of raising children:

Babies are expensive! Today the price of Pampers alone can really hurt a person's budget.

This one presents a more friendly approach, but it is very short and loses some of the details I liked in **Draft 2**.

4th Draft

I decided to add details and return to the more formal opening sentence I'd used in my first two drafts:

In the world today, babies are expensive. The price of Pampers alone can cause a person's budget to be at risk.

I don't like this draft, either. *In the world today* and *expensive* were a little vague and *at risk* sounded like a textbook phrase.

Final Draft

Here's how I finally decided to open my paper.

Babies are expensive! After the cost of car seats, baby clothes, bottles, baby food, and hospital bills, some people may end up in debt.

This opener incorporates the friendly tone I want, as well as the concrete details I think will help a reader *see* the cost of raising a child.

What about my worries that taking words out would lessen the quality of my paper? I found out that the trick is not length, but communication: *Use the specific words you need to get your point across, and use only those words.*

ACTIVITY 2.11: WORDINESS

Part 1. For each item, a set of selections is given. One selection is wordy and does not give the reader a clear picture. The other selection uses descriptive words and specific details to communicate its ideas clearly. Circle the selection that accomplishes the more effective communication with the reader.

1.
   a. When you encounter a snake, you must always stop and think about whether or not it is poisonous or aggressive. You don't want to be near a poisonous snake, and an aggressive one might attack, so it is best to avoid either of those. If the snake begins to change its position, beware. If it coils or raises its head up, it might be thinking about striking at you. Watch its position carefully.

   b. Have you ever seen a snake ready to strike? Its body is coiled like a spring, its head raised ever so slightly. These are some warning signs to keep in mind when you find yourself looking at the business end of a snake. Is it poisonous? That's a good question, but ask yourself this: Do you really want to be bitten by any snake?

2.
   a. Rhonda sat by the window and wiped away tears. *What are my choices, anyway?* she thought miserably. Changing locks would be a temporary solution. *I always regret temporary solutions. They're no better than temporary friends or temporary housing.* She supposed she could start a new life in another town, with a new name and a new hair color. Another tear fell at the thought of leaving her cozy little cottage. *Running away.* She sighed. Such a hassle, only to be tracked and chased like a criminal!

   b. Rhonda sat and thought about her choices. If she changed the lock, she felt sure she would regret that decision for one reason or another. Changing locks was a pain in the neck, and it never really worked. That was a bad idea. Should she just move? She thought about all the trouble that moving would be, all the hauling, the packing and unpacking, the address changes, the mess. Another bad idea. She didn't like that idea at all. And anyway, by the time she got settled in, everyone would know right where to find her, whether she wanted them to or not.

3.

   a. Need a job? Tired of the same old jobs that are always listed in the newspaper's classified section? Here's an idea: Turn on your computer, access the Internet, and with a quick visit to one of the many search engines available to the World Wide Web surfer, you'll find jobs aplenty! Get your resume ready. Shine your interviewing shoes. You're in business!

   b. Anyone who is looking for a job has probably tried the newspaper classifieds. Job seekers should also consider using the Internet to search for a position. Without leaving the comfort of home, a person who needs a job can easily find opportunities in all kinds of fields. The Internet is a great job resource. If you need a job, try asking your computer first!

4.

   a. Nothing you can do is as fun as reading a good book. It can take up many hours and even days. When it's an extra good book, you'll even be sad to finish it. You'll wish you could have a few more chapters to enjoy. You'll even miss the characters you were enjoying reading about. You'll miss the book so much! Reading is a joy.

   b. Picture yourself curled up on your couch with a good book. The hours melt away as you lose yourself in the characters' lives. You can hardly stand to close the book to eat or sleep! As you close the book at the end of the final chapter, you feel an empty place inside you that only another well-crafted story can fill.

5.

   a. Every once in awhile, you'll get an e-mail warning you of a virus that may damage your computer's hard drive and erase all your files. In the e-mail, the warning will say something like "WARNING! If you receive an e-mail with an attachment labelled XXXXXXX, do NOT open it! It could erase your hard drive and all your files!" The warning goes on to tell you that if you open the e-mail, it will not only erase your hard drive and all your files, but it will also send the virus-carrying attachment to all the addresses in your e-mail address book. Be careful, though. These warnings can be hoaxes. Read them and be aware of them, but don't take them <u>too</u> seriously. A hoax can cause trouble, too, even if it can't erase your hard drive and dump your files.

   b. "WARNING! If you receive an e-mail that contains an attachment labelled XXXXXXX, do NOT open it. It contains a virus that will erase your hard drive, clear out your files, and mail itself to all the addresses in your e-mail address book!" Have you ever received an e-mail like that one? Beware! It could be a hoax. Yes, a virus could wreak havoc with your computer, but virus hoaxes, which are a form of electronic harassment, are more common than maliciously perpetrated e-mail viruses. The moral of the story? Pay attention, but don't panic.

Part 2. Read the story below. As you read, think about how you can use details and descriptive words to give the reader a clear mental picture of what the writer thinks is going on. Then rewrite the story, adding specific words and reducing the number of unnecessary, nonspecific words. Pay special attention to the viewpoint this writer is expressing. The story should be amusing; see if you can help it live up to its potential!

A Trip to the Dentist: A Cautionary Tale

Let me tell you about when I went to the dentist. After you read my story, you may want to stay away from the dentist for awhile; it's kind of a scary story! Okay, here it is. I went to the dentist one day, just to get my teeth cleaned. That's really all I wanted, but I got a lot more than I bargained for. I sat in the chair, innocently expecting some X rays, a little brushing and flossing, and maybe a lecture on dental hygiene.

Instead, Trisha the Torturer spent an hour and a half making me miserable. It was awful! Wait till you hear this! First, she made me stick the X ray plates deep into my gums. Ouch! It really hurt. She didn't listen to my complaints, though. She just kept on going. Then, after she brushed and brushed and brushed my teeth, she started poking and scraping and hurting me so badly I kept wincing and jumping and yelping.

She used a pointy metal thing to poke and scrape at my gums and teeth. I was bleeding! The Torturer didn't seem to care, no matter how much I complained, and I still had to pay $110 as I left. Let that be a warning to you!

Part 3. Teamwork. Compare the paragraph you revised for Part 2 with those of your fellow group members. You may want to come back and do a little more revising after you've seen what others have done.

Part 4. Writing. The paragraph above is a personal narrative. It's one person's perspective of events. However, there are other views of the same events. Imagine that you're Trisha the dental assistant (not torturer). You're amazed that anyone would think of teeth cleaning and x-rays as torture. You are very proud of your job and you see your job as helping people to keep their teeth healthy. Use the details listed in "A Cautionary Tale" to write Trisha's description of what *really* happened during that trip to the dentist.

Part 5. Teamwork. With your group, compare both versions of the trip to the dentist described in Part 2. What were the differences between the two versions? Think about how the different viewpoints affected your word choices, your use of specific words and detail, and (especially) your interpretation of what happened.

2.12   Special effects with transitions

Some of the same words that turn whole sentences into fragments can also make you a wizard at special writing effects. Use **subordinating conjunctions** to create all sorts of subtle shifts in meaning. Raise your readers' expectations with words like *although, even if, unless,* or *while.* Signal you're about to spring a surprise with *however* or *while.* Heighten suspense with *if only* or *as if.* Tantalize your readers with hints that a mystery is about to be revealed with *because, now that,* or *since.* Promise more detail with **relative pronouns** like *that, which,* or *who.* You can create any sort of special effect you want and guide your readers to plot twists, stunning revelations, and brilliant solutions with a deft flick of a word that shows **relationship!**

Words that show relationship also make clauses **dependent**. If you use them, be sure to do some matchmaking. Get your dependent clauses attached to an independent clause so you don't end up with the dreaded fragment. Words that show connection--like the **coordinating conjunctions** *and, or, nor, for, but, yet,* and *so*--have more stable relationships. They usually connect complete ideas. You can use them to show similarity, mild contrast, and cause and effect. They usually do not make fragments, but *so* has been known to be a troublemaker when it gets in the wrong crowd.

Here are a few special effects words to get you started. (Words that can make fragments out of sentences are bolded in blue.)

- **To add ideas, use:**

  also, another, for example, for instance, further, in addition, in fact, moreover, or **such as.**

- **To add description or more information, use:**

  that, what, whatever, which, who, whom, whomever, or **whose.**

- **To compare ideas, use:**

  another, **as if, as though,** *at the same time, equally important, in the same way, likewise, similarly,* or **than.**

- **To contrast ideas, use:**

  although, *at the same time,* **even if, even though,** *however,* **if only,** *in contrast, in spite of, instead, nevertheless, not only, on the contrary, on the other hand, otherwise,* **though, unless, whether,** or **while.**

- **To show cause and effect, use:**

  accordingly, as a result, **because,** *consequently, hence,* **if,** *if this be true, then, in fact,* **in order that,** *in short,* **provided, rather than, since, so, so that,** *therefore, thus,* or **whereas.**

- **To indicate location or order, use:**

  above, across from, adjacent to, atop, before me, below me, behind, beside me, beyond, in front of, inside, in the distance, nearby, next to, on my left, on my right, opposite to, to the left, to the right, to one side, to the front, to the rear, where, or *wherever.*

- **To indicate time order or chronological sequence, use:**

  after, again, as a result, at last, at the same time, before, during, finally, first, last, next, now that, once, second, subsequently, then, till, until, when, whenever, or *while.*

- **To summarize, use:**

  again, finally, therefore, thus, to sum up.

ACTIVITY 2.12: SPECIAL EFFECTS WITH TRANSITIONS

Part 1. Using transition words to create special effects in your writing makes your writing interesting for the reader. For this activity, you'll be using words to compare and contrast. Here are some words and phrases you may want to use: *similarly, than, even though, another, not only, in the same way, while, unless, whether, equally important, however, if only, at the same time, nevertheless, on the contrary.* By no means is that an exhaustive list of words that can be used; many more can be found in your book. Just to keep things exciting, we've mixed words used to compare with words used to contrast. Have fun!

Example: Caroline's essay was written about the perils of hitchhiking; *similarly,* John's paper explained to its readers how to avoid dangerous travel mistakes.

1. I had to admit Rebecca's drawing was better than mine; _____, I was proud of myself.

2. _____ most of the projects were turned in late, they looked so good that Professor St. Clair decided to overlook their tardiness.

3. That tent had better be waterproof; _____, we're in for a soaking!

4. Rachel was sure the doctor would say she could resume swimming; _____ , he told her to wait three more weeks.

5. The other team's hitting was much better _____ ours.

6. _____ did Robinson tell the newspaper editor of our difficulties, he enlisted the editor's help on our next edition!

7. The river rock was smooth and polished, _____ some giant hand had been rubbing it over hundreds of years.

8. The class had thought the final exam would be in short-answer format; Dr. Clooney, _____, had other ideas.

9. We found it was crucial to measure out the chemicals carefully; it was _____ to wear safety goggles while handling them.

10. _____ Deborah's thoughtful insights into Cuba's relationship with the United States, she received an average grade due to her poor writing skills.

Part 2. For the next activity, you'll be writing your own sentences. Using words that indicate time order and location, such as *atop, nearby, next to, to the rear, beyond, in front of, at last, once, subsequently, until, when, at the same time,* and *now that,* write five sentences. In each sentence, you'll need to include a word or phrase that shows location *as well as* a word or phrase that indicates time order. Again, the list of words above gives only a small number of the words that you can actually use to write your sentences.

Example: At last I found my wallet next to a pile of books in the hallway.

Part 3. Now think about cause and effect. In the next five sentences, use words such as *as a result, because, provided, consequently, if, in fact, therefore,* and *so that* (along with others) to show cause and effect.

Example: *Rather than buy two presents, one for the engagement party and one for the wedding, Mario just got one expensive gift for the couple.*

Part 4. In the following activity, you'll find five sentence stems. Each one could use a little more information. We'll build these stems into more detailed sentences using different types of transition words.

Step 1. First, we'll add more information or description. Here are some words you may want to use: *that, what, whatever, which, who, whom, whomever, whose.*

Example stem: My arm aches constantly,
Example answer: My arm aches constantly, *which makes my writing look like a monkey's!*

1. I met a man named Mr. Bateman

2. Selma, Sara, and Stan found a stray cat

3. The loudest complainer of all was the hostess

4. Alfred ate the last of the brownies

5. It was the ugliest day of the season

Step 2. Now, let's add information to the same stems with words such as *also, another, for example, for instance, further, in addition, in fact, moreover,* and *such as.* Entertain your reader with your creativity as you enliven these rather short, dull sentence stems.

Example stem: My arm aches constantly.
Example answer: My arm aches constantly; *in fact, I have to have help throwing the discus!*

1. I met a man named Mr. Bateman

2. Selma, Sara, and Stan found a stray cat

3. The loudest complainer of all was the hostess

4. Alfred ate the last of the brownies

5. It was the ugliest day of the season

Part 5. Teamwork. For the adventurous only! In your group, look over the sentences you built from the sentence stems in Part 4. Try to combine your ideas into a paragraph.

Part 6. Below you'll find ten short paragraphs. Each paragraph needs a sentence to summarize its ideas. Here are some words you may want to use: *again, finally, therefore, thus, to sum up.*

Example: My cousins run a summer camp. The kids who come there are all cancer patients. They need a place to relax and forget about all their treatments and worries. Thus, the camp counselors provide them with activities to keep them busy and happy.

1. Rattlesnakes respond to heat and movement. A rattlesnake would rather not have any sort of contact with a creature as large as a human, but it may feel it needs to strike in order to defend itself. If you come upon a rattlesnake, stop moving immediately. Be still and quiet for long enough, and this fearsome predator may slither away to safety.

2. The symptoms of meningitis tend to develop quickly and are often confused with flu symptoms. Almost all meningitis patients experience

vomiting, high fever, and a stiff neck. Other symptoms may include muscle aches, a headache, back pain, drowsiness, light sensitivity, and confusion. Patients may even experience a loss of consciousness.

3. Parrots don't make the best pets. Often, they are quite destructive. They require more attention than most working owners can provide, since many kinds of parrots are only comfortable if they feel they are part of a flock. Parrots have complicated dietary needs; seeds are not adequate food for this type of bird. They can be extremely noisy, from primitive-sounding screeches at dawn and dusk to screams for attention or freedom. The mess a parrot makes is another factor to consider when deciding whether or not to purchase one.

4. Gene therapy is now being used to treat hereditary blindness in dogs. Dogs missing a certain gene that makes an important pigment necessary to perceive light received a dose of the gene during eye surgery. Results of the surgery have been quite promising. This new therapy holds out hope for humans who suffer from retinitis pigmentosa. Human experimentation should begin within about two years.

5. When you're getting ready for a yard sale, you need to remember a few key points. First of all, have signs and newspaper notices out a week ahead of time. Second, organize your sale items by price. Third, be ready to open the doors an hour early for those eager shoppers. Next, have some change ready for the first couple of buyers.

6. There is a problem developing in e-business these days: companies are finding themselves with more and more complex technology to manage and fewer and fewer skilled workers who can manage it capably. At least two leading technology companies are working hard to create a solution to this growing problem. Soon e-businesses will be able to set up autonomous computing. These self-managing computers and computer systems will even be able to recognize and fix errors in handling data, without human intervention, before they become large problems in the system.

7. Here are some facts about venomous spiders in the United States. In general, spiders do not bite unless aggravated; in fact, black widows are nearly blind! Garages and sheds, boxes, stored clothing and linens, and dark, quiet corners are favorite spider spots. You should be aware of the different types of poisonous spiders we have in the United States: widows (not just black widows, but red and brown also), recluse spiders (eleven different types), hobo spiders, and yellow sac spiders. Although most spider bites are not dangerous, an unsure bite victim should see a doctor. It's a good idea to bring the biting spider along, just in case.

Section 2

8. When you are administering adult CPR (cardiopulmonary resuscitation), a good way to keep the steps straight is to remember A-B-C. "A" stands for "Airway." After laying the victim on a flat surface, ask "Are you okay?" If there is no response, dial 911, then tilt the head back and lift the chin to open up the victim's airway. Next comes "B" for "Breathing." Look, listen, and feel (by putting your face up next to the victim's mouth and nose) for breathing. If the victim isn't breathing, pinch the nose and breathe two full breaths into the mouth; if you need to, reposition the victim or administer the Heimlich maneuver in order to get the air into the victim. "C" stands for "Circulation," which should remind you to check for a pulse. If the victim has a pulse, continue rescue breathing (one breath every 5 seconds). If not, begin chest compressions (80 to 100 per minute, pressing the chest down about 1–1½ inches).

9. A car wash is a great place to meet people. After dropping your car off with the attendant, you wander inside and have a seat. Most of the people waiting for their cars are bored; many have already read the newspaper. So start up a conversation! If commenting on the weather seems like a run-of-the-mill way to begin, think of something unusual. Notice one particular car and ask about its owner, then offer a compliment. Ask advice about preparing your taxes. Find someone who's reading a book and ask about it.

10. Remember when you could get free stuff on the Internet? Unfortunately, that little perk may be a thing of the past. Advertisers who used to pay anywhere from $50 to $75 for every thousand users are now dropping their rates to $3 to $5, causing Web site administrators to charge customers for services previously given freely. Sites that hoped customers would try a basic service for free and then upgrade for a small fee have found this "piggyback" method to be a flop. Competition for customers continues to be fierce, and running a Web site isn't cheap.

SECTION 3: Special Effects with Punctuation

In the hands of a savvy writer, commas can sculpt rhythm, meaning, and connection. Commas guide your reader through starts and stops in your writing, show the reader whether or not words can be taken out or rearranged, and help the reader see how ideas fit together. Commas are a signal that the reader can pause briefly for a mental breath. Look at the difference, for instance, between the following sentences:

- My boss asked me to buy milk, chocolate, sugar, cookies, and chips.
- My boss asked me to buy milk chocolate, sugar cookies, and chips.

Or, which of these would you rather see on an e-mail from your department head:

- I don't want to leave you clueless, staff.
- I don't want to leave you, clueless staff.

Read on for some *writerly* suggestions about when and where to use commas.

3.1   Commas and names

When you want to make sure your reader knows you're talking *to* someone, not *about* him or her, use a comma to set the person's name apart. Here's the best example of the difference that we've every found:

> You have to eat, **Bob**.

The comma here tells the reader that we're *talking to* Bob. We're trying to persuade him to eat. If we left that comma out, Bob would be in trouble. We'd get this:

> You have to eat Bob.

Now Bob's on the menu! We're not talking *to* him; we're talking *about* him. (Now would be a good time to leave, Bob.)

ACTIVITY 3.1: COMMAS AND NAMES

Read each of the following sentences out loud just as it's written. Unless you actually see a comma, resist the impulse to pause! Did any of the sentences bring a smile to your face? Without proper punctuation, the meaning of the sentence changes completely. Add commas where needed to clear up the meaning in these sentences.

1. How are you playing Benjie?
2. That's odd-smelling Mary Lou.
3. Go ahead and taste Gil!
4. Be careful not to spill Silvio.
5. Are you crazy Karen?
6. Come meet my friend Phil!
7. Why are you sniffing Lacey?
8. What do you think of my new cat Fido?
9. Don't you ever call Jennifer?
10. He's the funniest Rafael!
11. That one's hairy Jim.
12. Go ahead and throw Melanie.
13. Put your hat on Madeleine.
14. Is it scary Martin?
15. Please don't rush Cass!
16. Is this the boat Annie?
17. Will you please drive Charles?
18. Look up John James.
19. You missed Lucille!
20. I hope we don't lose Marco.

3.2   Commas in a series

Commas make sense of lists. Any time you list three or more items in a sentence, you have a **series** of items that needs commas to make sense. The grocery list we just looked at is a series of food items; commas tell readers where to pause and which words to group together. The last word in a series is connected by what grammar books call a coordinating conjunction--words like *and, but, for, or, nor, so,* or *yet.*

You can have some fun with commas to create a particular rhythm in a series of several items. Science fiction writer Gregory Benford used commas, but **no** coordinating conjunctions, in this series to create a feeling of confusion or exhilaration, as if many things were happening at once:

Wood fragments shower up around him, tumbling, orbiting, carving the cold.

What would happen if we added conjunctions instead of commas? This writerly maneuver gives the sentence a sing-song rhythm Benford probably wouldn't like:

Wood fragments shower up around him, tumbling and orbiting and carving the cold.

The second version sounds more like the rhythm of a romance novel or children's book! Experiment with commas and conjunctions to get the tone that's right for your writing.

ACTIVITY 3.2: COMMAS IN A SERIES

The following selection lists items you might want to have on hand in the event of an earthquake. You'll notice that each list needs commas to separate the items in the series. Add commas as needed.

Earthquake Preparedness

Certain parts of the United States tend to experience earthquakes more frequently than others do. Those who live near fault lines need to have a few items on hand in order to be prepared for what might be a rather large and damaging natural disaster. What follows is a partial listing of items needed for your Earthquake Emergency Kit.

Let's start with food and water. You'll need a three-day supply (about 5–10 gallons per family member) of water stored in strong plastic containers. Some non-perishable food items to have around are juice canned foods snacks and baby formula if needed. You should keep at least a three-day supply of food items, as well. You may also want to have on hand several packets of drink mix instant coffee and tea bags sugar cubes salt and pepper and a water filtering device.

Believe it or not, hygiene is also a matter to take into consideration when you are preparing for an earthquake. You may find yourself without access to your own bathroom for several days. You will need to have ready some toilet paper soap packaged wipes toothpaste and toothbrushes a brush or comb and a towel and washcloth. Remember to have enough of each of these items to last each person in your family at least three days.

In addition to the items you may need for hygiene, a few other personal supplies should be set aside. An extra pair of glasses or contact lenses any prescription medications and any other personal items you might need should be stored with hygiene-related items in a plastic container.

A few medical supplies must be kept on hand: a splint several elastic bandages of varying widths several pairs of surgical gloves several trauma dressings plenty of gauze and a first aid manual. You may choose to keep your extra prescription medications in with the first aid supplies.

Some of the emergency equipment and protection gear you may want to consider having on hand include flashlights for each family member extra batteries spare flashlight bulbs a dozen chemical light sticks a good set of work tools and a pair of leather work gloves for each person in your family.

The last list is a grab bag of helpful items to have on hand. You should be prepared with a whistle thermal space blankets and sleeping bags a tent and a couple of tarps at least one change of clothing and shoes for each family member copies of important papers spare keys to the house and cars at least $100 cash a credit card a cooler dishwashing soap and a sponge a cell phone and some large garbage bags.

Does this seem like a lot of preparation? Many experts recommend an even larger store of items! Keep in mind that in the event of a major earthquake, these supplies might be all you have.

3.3   Commas and adjectives

Commas let you experiment with word order. If two adjectives (words that describe nouns) can change places with each other, or if you can connect them using **and** without changing the meaning of the sentence, signal this with a comma. Here's another example from Benford's science fiction:

Earth holds him in its fierce, ageless grip.

Benford uses a comma to show that these two words are both giving information about the word *grip*. Let's test this hypothesis by changing the way we connect them:

Test 1. Change the order of the adjectives:

Earth holds him in its ageless, fierce grip.

Test 2. Use *and* to connect the two adjectives:

Earth holds him in its fierce and ageless grip.

No matter how we rearrange the sentence, it makes sense. Both adjectives describe *grip*. The order they come in is up to the writer.

Sometimes, you can't rearrange adjectives like this because both words need to be read *together* in a certain order. When the adjectives fail Tests 1 and 2, they can't be separated, rearranged, or used interchangeably. They don't both carry equal weight. Signal this by *not* using a comma:

The **new** *computer* system blinked at him and died.

ACTIVITY 3.3: COMMAS AND ADJECTIVES

Part 1. In each of the following sentences, two adjectives (descriptive words) are used together to describe a noun. In at least three of the sentences, the adjectives are *interchangeable*. They can be separated by commas instead of *and*. Wherever possible, use a comma to replace the *and* between interchangeable adjectives.

1. Jaime and Mari went to dinner and to a lighthearted and funny movie.
2. Dogs and cats are usually tame and trainable pets, fun to own and love.
3. All of Electra's friends and family knew her as a kind and friendly sort, the kind of person who opens her home and heart to all.
4. At the farm where I grew up, Dad liked to plow and plant quickly, which made for long and exhausting days.
5. Eddie at first thought his neighbor was a strange and frightening person, but when he stopped and talked to the man, he realized he liked and respected Mr. Kane.

Part 2. Teamwork. Why do we do what we do? Now, get in groups of 3–5 people. Look back at the questions in Part 1. What other words have been connected by *and*? Explain why you *didn't* use commas to connect these pairs of words.

Example: In sentence one, *Jaime* and *Mari* are Proper Nouns, not adjectives. They are also the subject of the sentence.

Part 3. In each of the following sentences, two adjectives are placed together. In five of the sentences, the two adjectives are interchangeable, and should be separated by a comma. Read the sentences carefully, then place commas between interchangeable adjectives.

1. Even though she called several times that evening, Francoise kept getting a busy phone line.
2. The hungry bear cubs really made loud noises until they were fed.
3. The stereo shook with loud booming bass.
4. I was so relieved to get a helpful service manager at the car dealership.
5. Every single present was wrapped in shiny festive paper.
6. We stood staring into the pet store window, watching the playful awkward puppies.
7. After our house flooded, we bought ourselves brand new carpeting.
8. Kara couldn't believe how much the little squirming pig weighed!

Section 3

9. What made me decide not to buy the house was its ugly tile floor.

10. In the newspaper's classified section, Jay read of an interesting challenging career he might like.

Part 4. Each of the sentences below contains two underlined adjectives. These adjectives are *not* interchangeable. They need to appear in the order they're printed. Replace them with two adjectives that *can* be rearranged and separated by a comma.

Example: Sondra likes to buy the store brand instead of the <u>premium brand</u> detergent.

expensive, brand-name

1. Only the dog likes to sit on that <u>smelly couch cushion</u>

2. Mitchell and some friends chose to go on a <u>short day</u> cruise.

3. After the guests had all gone home, we stayed up late to take down all the <u>holiday party</u> decorations.

4. Can you believe Melinda buys that <u>expensive cat</u> food?

5. Dane had to call in an expert to fix a <u>complicated electronic</u> problem with his television.

3.4   Commas that emphasize

Commas can also be used to emphasize what comes just after them. Here are two more lines from Benford's science fiction:

Nigel sees the rifleman turn, steady and on guard.

Nikka gasps, suddenly alert.

The main information in each of these sentences comes before the comma:

Nigel → sees → rifleman

Nikka → gasps

The words *after* the commas heighten the tension.

ACTIVITY 3.4: COMMAS THAT EMPHASIZE

Part 1. Writers use commas to add emphasis. In each of the following sentences you'll find a phrase that needs to be emphasized. A comma in the right place will set that small section apart from the rest of the sentence. That emphasis gives the sentence, and the person reading it, a whole different feeling! Place a comma in each sentence to add emphasis where it is needed.

Example: The train's whistle sounded through the darkened house, a blaring alarm to all.

1. I cried out in my sleep my body thrashing.
2. The pitcher stretched for the fly ball tendons screaming with pain.
3. A night owl gave a piteous cry its voice echoing through the canyon.
4. My brother laughed uproariously tears streaming down his face.
5. We all sat around after dinner bellies bulging.
6. Dad came home early that day his eyes full of mischief.
7. Suddenly, Laine was at our door wide-eyed and breathless.
8. The moose we were watching turned and charged its head lowered.
9. Our professor stood silently at the front of the room arms across his chest.
10. The trees were at the mercy of the storm their branches whipping wildly.
11. I found myself walking slowly into the deserted house mouth dry as a bone.
12. Jesse told Mr. Jenkins about the hole in the wall as we watched shaking in our boots.
13. It was a campout we'd never forget broken tent and all.
14. The hours seemed to drag each one longer than the last.
15. The injured raccoon lashed out at us dark eyes betraying its fear.

Part 2. Your practice with using commas to emphasize a phrase at the end of a sentence is going to come in handy for this activity. Write five sentences. At the end of each sentence, add a phrase that gives emphasis to the key point. Be sure you use a comma to set that phrase apart and give it emphasis.

Example: She was scared, as scared as she'd ever felt.

3.5   Commas and non-restrictive clauses

You can use commas to indicate what's important in a description, and what's not. You can also use a comma to show which information is expendable or nonessential to understanding the meaning of your sentence. Watch how commas change the meaning in these two versions:

Version 1: Coffee dispensed at the space station *is cold and stale.*

Version 2: Coffee, dispensed at the space station, *is cold and stale.*

Version 1 makes sense. A particular type of coffee--the coffee that's dispensed at the space station--is cold and stale. What about **Version 2**? The commas around *dispensed at the space station* tell us that we can delete this whole phrase without changing the meaning of the sentence. What happens if you take this phrase out? Here's what you get:

Coffee is cold and stale.

Wait! Not *all* coffee, everywhere, is cold and stale! The commas in **Version 2** shouldn't have been there. They tell you that you don't need the extra information in between them--but you *do*. Now let's look at another example from Benford's writing:

Graves, his chest heaving, pauses and looks back toward the window.

Here, the commas signal that you can leave out *his chest heaving* without changing the basic meaning of the sentence. Is this true? Let's try it:

Graves pauses and looks back toward the window.

Leaving out the information between the commas gets rid of some interesting description, but it leaves the overall meaning of the sentence intact:

Graves → pauses and looks.

The commas in Benford's sentence guide the reader to what's most important about the sentence--his character's actions.

ACTIVITY 3.5: COMMAS/NON-RESTRICTIVE CLAUSES

Part 1. In each of the ten sentences below, commas have been used to show that a phrase is expendable. In at least five of the sentences, however, the commas shouldn't be there. The phrase that is set off by commas is necessary; without it, the meaning of the sentence changes completely. Place an X beside any sentences in which the commas should not be used to set off the phrase.

1. The floor, of my car, is filthy.
2. Nikki's spring hat, covered with daisies, was an attention-grabber at the party.
3. The gray dog, the hair on its neck standing up, stood its ground.
4. The flowers, on the bush outside my front door, are blooming now.
5. One of the men, in the photograph, looked very worried.

6. An acceptance letter, its envelope fat with information, came on Friday.

7. The computer, that Langston had just bought, was already on the blink.

8. Insurance rates, on my new car, are much higher than those on my old one.

9. Cary paused, muscles shaky and weak, before continuing the 5K run.

10. The price of the furniture, always a big issue with me, didn't seem to concern her.

Part 2. Some of the next five sentences use commas to set off information that shouldn't be omitted. Find these sentences and revise them so the meaning of the sentence is clear to the reader.

1. Scientists are looking closely, at "biotech foods," to be sure they are safe for us to eat.

2. Corn, that is genetically engineered, may pose health risks.

3. The corn, made to kill insects that try to eat it, could affect the environment as well as humans.

4. An Environmental Protection Agency panel, set up to study the issue, found that there is no conclusive proof that the corn is safe.

5. One concern, which will be studied carefully, is that this type of corn might cause allergic reactions in some people.

6. Any biotech corn, that breaks down slowly in a person's digestive system, is a potential allergen.

7. Results from research on biotech foods, still very new and limited, indicate so far that there is very little risk involved in eating them.

8. Most scientists still contend, that this is an area in which, more research is needed.

9. Chances are, when all research is complete, biotech foods will be judged to be safe enough for us to eat.

10. Growing crops, without using pesticides, sure sounds like a good idea!

Part 3. Below you'll find an opinion piece written about biotech foods, their usefulness, and their potential safety risks. Within the selection, there are several non-essential phrases that need to be set off by commas. Locate these phrases, and use commas to indicate to the reader that the information inside the commas is expendable.

I don't know about everyone else, but I'm of two minds on the issue of biotech foods. I can certainly see how given the health risks posed by the use of pesticides a food that fights off pests on its own could be helpful.

Every time I stand over my sink carefully washing an apple I can see the advantages of this amazing invention. Farmers who have to fight to save their crops from insects each year would certainly benefit. Studies conducted so far seem to indicate that these foods are not really harmful. All of those reasons which are good ones make me think genetically engineered food is a great idea.

I also have some concerns about the biotech foods being studied. It seems to me that considering the newness of the studies that have been published we ought to be very careful. Studies with results that show how safe these foods are for us can't really tell us anything about long-term risks. What if we start including genetically engineered food products in our daily meals and then find out about serious health risks ten years from now? Many insects that are important in keeping our environment healthy may suffer along with the pests.

I'm all for progress especially when an invention will save money and improve health but I say the jury's still out on this one.

3.6   Commas and appositives

Commas help you sneak in more information. When you want to **rename** a noun, not just describe it, you slip in the extra information with what your grammar book would call an **appositive:**

Graves, **the group leader,** took the first watch.

Commas around *the group leader* (the **appositive**) show that this is extra information. If you took it out, you wouldn't have a chance to rename Graves the group leader, but you'd still have a logical path through the sentence: Graves → took → watch.

Appositives are especially helpful to you when you're writing papers that use outside sources. Use appositives to *rename* an authority you're quoting and give him or her more credibility:

Hector Rodriguez, **an FBI agent,** reports that crime scenes are often contaminated by witnesses.

Jean Smith, **a leading advocate of pet therapy,** thinks dogs are more adaptable than cats.

Tonya Smith, **a medical technician,** found a good bit of inaccurate information about health-related topics on the Internet.

ACTIVITY 3.6: COMMAS AND APPOSITIVES

Part 1. In each of the sentences below, a noun has been renamed using an appositive. Add commas wherever they are needed to set off an appositive.

Example: Savannah a buff-colored cocker spaniel was the queen of our household.
Savannah, a buff-colored cocker spaniel, was the queen of our household.

1. The lights dimmed as the star attraction a magician who called himself The Fan Man took the stage.
2. How will we put on the play if Heather our main character is sick?
3. Professor Calvert the head of the math department is out on sabbatical.
4. Call Leigha Banyon director of student services if you need any more help.
5. Kay and Ashlyn my two best friends in the whole world came to save me from the flat tire fiasco.
6. Dessert last night Grayson's famous Four-Star Flan was the best part of the meal.
7. Keith and Ann hoped their neighbor a local firefighter could help them prepare a family fire plan.
8. The recruits breathed a collective sigh of relief when the obstacle course a grueling exercise had been successfully completed by all.
9. Since the movie a science fiction adventure was disappointing, I left early.
10. All our friends loved The Two Tones a local group of musicians for their humorous and clever lyrics.

Part 2. As you read the following paragraphs, you'll find at least ten nouns that have been renamed using appositives. Commas have been used, but not always correctly. Add, subtract, and move commas so that they are all placed appropriately. Remember, your goal is to communicate effectively with the reader!

Spring, the season when play gear once again comes out of storage is not just a time for the return of outdoor fun. Unfortunately, it's also a season of renewed danger, especially for kids. Statistics show that more accidental deaths occur among kids during springtime than any other season.

Why spring? It turns out that springtime is more dangerous for the same reasons it's more fun. There are more daylight hours available after the long, dark winter. Kids active creatures all the time are eager to get out and enjoy the warmer weather. Just being outside more exposes kids, to dangers they wouldn't encounter, sitting on the couch or in a classroom. Non-fatal injuries are caused by the same hazards, of course, but aren't tracked as carefully as fatalities.

What are some dangers we need to watch out for? One type of accidental death drowning causes about 4,000 deaths a year. Scooter accidents were responsible for more than 40,000 visits to the emergency room. The sun a leading cause of skin cancer, is a hazard we should take just as seriously in the spring as we do in the summer. UV rays are not the only sun-related danger; beware the sun's heat an enemy to those who don't keep hydrated, as it can bring about heat exhaustion and heat stroke. Bee stings and dog bites are the standouts among animal hazards; dog bites far outstrip bee stings, by more than 4.7 million to about 50 annually. Accidents with power equipment including lawn mowers and edgers are also a major problem. Don't forget hay fever! Though not usually fatal, allergies do account for plenty of visits to the hospital each spring.

There is good news as well. The figures for accidental deaths have dropped considerably in the past 20 years. Safety features have helped. For example, the"dead-man" bar on a lawn mower, a feature that automatically cuts the power to the mower when it is released has drastically reduced accidents involving lawn mowers. Cars that are better able to withstand crashes, carefully designed roads, and successful campaigns against drinking and driving have also played a part in the drop in fatalities. Air bags protective devices intended to cushion a car's passengers in the event of a wreck have also contributed to our safety. Don't forget bicycle helmets those highly decorated foam shells now seen everywhere, when you're handing out the credit!

This doesn't mean our work in reducing injuries and accidental deaths is done. Parents the example-setters in all situations must continue to consistently wear bicycle helmets, hook up seat belts, and demonstrate care in using power tools. Finally, take some simple precautions: read warning labels, cook meats thoroughly to avoid food poisoning, and put gas in your power equipment before you begin using it. Better safe than sorry!

3.7   Commas that connect clauses

Commas hook complete ideas together (with a little help). You can use a comma and a coordinating conjunction (*and, but, for, or, nor, so, yet*) to join complete sentences together without confusing the reader. Your grammar book calls groups of words that could stand alone as complete sentences **independent clauses**, because they don't need anything else to make them complete. The way you use independent clauses depends on the tone and rhythm you want to achieve.

Here's another line from Benford's science fiction:

He has his own gravitational field, and *thoughts flit like summer lightning through his streaming wash of feelings.*

Benford could have made this line into two separate sentences without breaking any grammar rules, but he chose to connect them. Read them again, but this time put a period after *field*. What changes? In Benford's version, the conjunction and comma alert the reader that these two ideas are complete on their own, but should be thought about together. Separating them with a period would be too abrupt for the tone Benford wants. (For another example of this trick, see Cary Stewart's entry on comma splices later in this section.)

If the complete ideas you want to connect are very brief and closely related, you can make them flow together without a comma, as Benford did here:

Graves takes a step forward and his arm comes up.

When Benford chose to leave out the comma in this line, he signaled that he wanted the reader to rush through the whole sentence without a pause for a mental breath.

ACTIVITY 3.7: COMMAS AND CLAUSES

Part 1. Read the sentences below. Each is made up of two complete ideas joined together with a connector like *and* or *but*. Some need to be separated by a comma, so that the reader can take a mental breath between ideas. Add commas to those sentences that require a pause.

1. On the drive home it began to snow and Maya thought again of the man on the bench.
2. The fireworks were finished but Max still stood transfixed.
3. Vernon had tried for years to win "Yard of the Month" and he wondered now if there wasn't a personal vendetta against him and his peonies.
4. She could hear the other students talking about her purple hair but she wasn't sure if it would help to confront them.
5. The bus driver fiddled with the dial and the newscast came through.
6. The lecture was fascinating yet its ideas disturbed the sociologist.
7. No one had ever asked Dan that question so it took him a few minutes to decide how to answer.
8. Did you want to eat inside or should we have a picnic?
9. Her legs were jelly and her arms hung useless like spaghetti.
10. One shouldn't completely ignore the televised news nor should one take it too seriously.

Part 2. Each item below consists of two clauses, each of which can stand alone (be used independently of the other). First, decide whether or not the two sentences should be joined into one. If you feel that they are related and should be connected, add a conjunction [and, but, or, for, nor, so, yet] to turn the two clauses into one sentence. You may have to make other changes to the sentence to make it work, as in the example. Finally, add a comma *only* if the newly combined sentence requires a pause.

Example: Bea shouldn't have said that to Del. She shouldn't have told him Kay's business.

Possible answer: *Bea shouldn't have said that to Del, nor should she have told him Kay's business.*

1. I wanted to be the one to tell him about his car. Janice beat me to it.
2. There were so many things we didn't understand. Dad had tried hard to explain the situation to us.
3. Amy started to trudge up the stairs. Alison assumed the conversation was finished.
4. Ruth Ann headed out to the barn. The cows could only wait so long to be milked.
5. The pack of dogs ran the other way. Their leader was mangy but tough.
6. The car's engine seemed to be idling smoothly. The car just quit for no apparent reason.
7. We can get some gas here. We can wait until the next town.
8. Aliyah liked the flowers. She knew she shouldn't pick them.
9. The birds woke me up that morning. I had to get to work in a hurry.
10. There were too many people. Isabel felt confused and anxious.

Part 3. The paragraph below is full of short sentences, many of which could be combined using conjunctions and/or commas. The result is a choppy, awkward piece of writing. Rewrite the selection, adding conjunctions and commas where needed to restore rhythm and tone.

Most of us know something about the American Civil War. Do you know about the role of Canadians in that conflict? Some estimate that between 40,000 and 60,000 Canadians were involved. Others will argue with those high numbers. Some were tricked into fighting. Others fought voluntarily. One trick was to put up notices advertising railroad work. The worker would show up. The only job available would be in the Federal Army. The poor man would join up. He might starve. Some volunteers were Canadians wanting to become U.S. citizens. Others had strong beliefs about the War. The stories of these men are interesting. It's sad to know so many were deceived into fighting.

Part 4. Teamwork. Compare your revisions of the paragraph in Part 3 with others written by your group members. Did you use different conjunctions? Did you choose to combine different clauses? Did you place commas where others decided not to? Most important, **how will a reader be affected by these differences?**

3.8   Commas that introduce ideas

When you want to introduce an idea at the beginning of a sentence, use a comma to give your reader a (mental) breath. Here are some ways Benford used this trick to set up a pleasant rhythm:

> *Lungs panting with the effort,* he pauses and looks back toward the crosshair window.

> *As though sprung from nowhere,* feelings and desires forked like summer lightning.

> *To dispel them growing like fresh corn,* he entered into mersion with them.

Notice that none of these introductory groups of words have a subject and verb, like a clause would. For this reason, your grammar book would call them **phrases**. Writers often use phrases to slip in more information about an idea without adding new, complete sentences. The main idea of the sentence is still carried by the subject and verb, like this:

(As though sprung from nowhere) **feelings and desires** → *forked*

Introductory phrases used in nonfiction (like this textbook) are often only one or two words:

> *However,* gambling opponents insist that gaming has negative effects.

> *In addition*, people around the gambler suffer.

> *Sadly*, many compulsive gamblers never get help.

ACTIVITY 3.8: COMMAS INTRODUCE IDEAS

Part 1. Writers use commas after introductory **phrases** and **clauses** to give readers a place to pause and take a mental breath before reading the rest of the sentence. In the sentences below, add commas as needed to allow readers to pause.

Section 3

Example: Instead of eating our dinner in the restaurant, we ordered it out and took it to a nearby park.

1. Hands waving in the air the crowd expressed its enjoyment of the music.
2. To change my mind about dessert the waiter brought me tempting samples.
3. In addition to our hot water bottles we took extra blankets to bed.
4. Too tired to think Emery fell into bed fully clothed.
5. Hanging clothes on the line Phoebe thought she saw the missing cat.
6. At three o'clock exactly the kids began to pour out of the building.
7. If just a few more people would sign up the class could go on.
8. Protected from the elements the cabin in the woods survived years of neglect.
9. When all the votes were in Charlotte was declared the winner.
10. With one fell swoop the hawk seized the field mouse in its giant talons.

Part 2. Read the following selection carefully. Look for sentences with introductory phrases that need to be followed by commas. Also look for commas that have been misplaced. Add, remove, or move commas as necessary to make the passage clear.

With Great Britain fighting an epidemic of foot-and-mouth disease the United States government has been working hard to figure out how our own country would need to react in order to contain such an outbreak. Astonishingly the Agriculture Department has made it clear, that nothing less than a full-scale response by all federal disaster agencies would be effective in handling the crises that would result.

In the past animal disease problems have been handled by state and local government agencies. Unfortunately a disease like foot-and-mouth has to be treated as a threat to human lives as well as those of livestock and other animals. This means, that a lower-level response like the ones used to contain past infections would be, at best, insufficient; at worst it could very well be devastating, its effects spreading across the country with frightening speed. Since the disease is often spread by the feces of birds that have fed on the carcasses of infected animals even wild animals would be at risk.

A surprising number of federal government agencies, have already come together to discuss their roles in a massive containment situation. At the meeting 26 different agencies, including the Departments of Defense, Interior, Health and Human Services, Commerce, and Energy, took part in an exercise that showed how quickly the disease could spread, as well as how many people would be needed to control it. The meeting was organized by, the Catastrophic Disaster Response Group, an agency originally put together to plan for bioterrorism and industrial disasters.

Our country has never been faced with a national risk like foot-and-mouth disease. It's comforting to know that the federal government is taking this risk seriously and planning ahead with speed and a high level of concern.

3.9   Commas that introduce contrast

Commas also set off contrast phrases, which emphasize a message the writer has already stated. Look how ominous the words after the comma make Benford's simple statement that his character thinks he's going to die:

He would not be returning home, *not this time.*

ACTIVITY 3.9: COMMAS INTRODUCE CONTRAST.

Part 1. Sometimes commas are used to set off a contrast phrase that the author is using to make a point. In each of the following sentences, a contrast phrase needs commas to set it apart from the rest of the sentence. Add commas where necessary to help the reader understand the point being made by the writer.

Example: It was bright and sunny rather than cloudy on the day in question.

Answer: It was bright and sunny, rather than cloudy, on the day in question.

1. That was my sister you met not me in the grocery store yesterday.
2. We had to write three term papers not one for our Mythology class.
3. Rod's car needed coolant rather than oil to get it back in working order.
4. I had to call Shelley not Bailey for the answer to my question.
5. After talking to Tina, I realized it had been the muscles in my back rather than those in my neck that had been causing me pain.
6. You'll have to change the title not the content.
7. When Vinnie took a closer look, he saw that it wasn't a rake he needed for the job but a hoe.
8. It's the message conveyed by the story not the story itself that bothers me.

9. Uncle Mitch rather than Uncle Barry ended up telling the story.

10. The instructor explained that she wanted us to show a high level of comprehension on the exam not a photographic memory.

Part 2. In the selection written below, you'll find at least ten phrases the author has added to emphasize contrast. Commas have been used, but not always wisely. Add, remove, or move commas as necessary to revise the selection.

Some companies are implementing an idea that is long overdue; they are using employees as consultants not just, workers. Employee meetings in these companies are tools that empower rather than frustrate the hard-working people who attend them. The people sitting around the table feel appreciated, even essential to the company's success. They offer suggestions that are discussed and often put into practice not shuffled under the rug.

A typical meeting in one of these forward-thinking companies might involve opening the employee suggestion box. Employees know that the contents of the box will be read, so they have put in ideas they believe will boost productivity and efficiency not jokes and insults. Each suggestion is read aloud and considered seriously; if the group decides to use the suggestion, it is often the suggestion writer who is assigned to get the job done. These are employees who now feel they have something important to contribute; they are in some ways managing themselves not, being managed.

When you think about it, the concept of using employees' ideas makes a lot of sense. After all, who knows more about the inner workings of the company than those who are right in the middle of it every day? Often a worker's idea is simple and inexpensive not difficult for the company to implement at all. The teamwork involved boosts morale, and as a bonus, many proposals are money-savers. Managers at these companies feel relieved not threatened by the fact that their employees help out more.

Of course, a mismanaged employee-suggestion program is worse than none at all. Employees who are asked to propose ideas for improvement need to see them used not ignored. Any system that does not actively pursue a fair number of the ideas offered by its employees will find itself dealing with resentful, mistrustful workers.

At least one company now invites its workers to put their ideas on a company Web site not just into a box. Another company actually requires two ideas per month from each employee. While this may seem like a lot of pressure to some, workers there know that they are, valued not taken for granted. Now that's a great idea!

3.10   Commas that help you add one final thought

Sometimes, writers want one entire group of words to describe another entire group of words. Your grammar book calls this a **final absolute phrase**, because it comes at the end of a sentence. Use a comma to show readers what you're doing, as Benford did, here:

> Graves follows through, *head turned to watch Ichino's fall.*

The descriptive words after the comma are meant to be read together, as a complete set. Benford wants readers to apply this set of words to the set of words before the comma:

> Graves **turns his head** *at the same time* he <u>follows through</u>.

Here's one more example from Benford's work:

> The blade bites into a rotten seam, *wood frags showering up around him.*

Current-day writers use the comma tricks and sentence structures we've just looked at so often that some scholars use them to define a distinctively *modern* way of writing. When you're setting up rhythm this way, think about where you want your reader to pause, or take a breath, or think about particular ideas together. Commas are a writer's tools for communication. They give the reader clues about when to pause, take a breath, or sort ideas out.

For more comma guidelines (including explanations of the grammatical structures they support), see *The Little, Brown Handbook* by H. Ramsey Fowler and Jane E. Aaron. For more examples of commaless paragraphs, see Gregory Benford's *In the Ocean of Night* (New York: Dial Press, 1972, 1977).

ACTIVITY 3.10: ADDING ONE FINAL THOUGHT

Part 1. Each of the sentences below contains a final absolute phrase, also called a final thought. The comma needed to set this final thought apart from the rest of the sentence is missing, however. Add a comma wherever a pause is needed to help each sentence communicate effectively with the reader.

1. Janice ran down the street arms flailing.
2. Our oak tree stood tall framed by the setting sun.
3. Only Ikeika turned to watch raindrops sliding down his face like tears.
4. Rae held her breath as she waited heart beating out the time that passed.

5. The street below was always busy miniature cars racing by as ant people conducted their tiny business.

6. The house on the corner looked a bit spooky shutters always closed and paint peeling in the salt air.

7. I wish you'd seen him that day eyes shifting nervously from one of us to the other.

8. Our little runaway came home the next morning tail tucked between her hind legs.

9. The movie was a sleeper hit its Oscar nomination catching most of us by surprise.

10. We hugged tightly arms locked in silent communication.

Part 2. The paragraph below contains at least ten errors in the way commas are used. Add, subtract, and move commas to clear up the meaning in this short essay.

Lucy lay on a lawn chair beside the pool head turned, toward the sun. Her thoughts raced through her head interrupting one another. *Think only of the sun*, she told, herself. She turned to stare at the pool pale aqua sparkling in the desert sun. It was no use. Emotions, obscured her vision. She saw Isabelle's face eyes brimming. Here was Isabelle's mouth lips forming accusatory words. *How can I make her understand?* It was a rhetorical question really. She'd tried already her words useless against a solid wall of blame. Lucy dove her arms slicing into the cool water.

3.11   Why quotes use commas

Writers also use commas to set up, or introduce, quotes. Whenever you're writing someone else's exact words, use a comma and quotation marks to separate *their* words from *your* words. Quotation marks enclose the *exact words someone else said or wrote*, so there's no mistake. The comma lets the reader take a mental breath before going on with the rest of the sentence or paragraph.

Example 1: "I won't stop until I've found the murderer," Rodrigo said.

Quotation marks surround Rodrigo's exact words. The comma after *murderer* signals that Rodrigo's words are over, but that the sentence is going to continue with words from the writer of the paper or story.

Example 2: According to Paula Wood, a researcher at East Coast Labs, "We're just beginning to decipher the genetic code."

In this example, the quotation comes at the end of the sentence. Everything between the two quotation marks is *exactly* what Paula Woods said or wrote. The comma after the word *labs* sets up (or introduces) the quote. A period after the word *code* signals that the end of the quote is also the end of the sentence. Notice that the period is *inside* the quotation marks, not outside, even though it ends both the quote and the sentence.

In setting up quotes, use a comma to separate your words from the words of the person you're quoting. The comma lets your reader pause between the two voices.

ACTIVITY 3.11: WHY QUOTES USE COMMAS

Part 1. In setting up quotes, use a comma to separate your words from the words of the person you're quoting. The comma lets your reader pause between the two voices. As you read the following selection, pay attention to the quotes. Add commas wherever they are needed to set up quotes.

My brother and I have always talked about running in a marathon together. When I heard our city would be hosting a marathon next spring, I called him to let him know. I thought we should begin training right away; a marathon is no walk in the park! Unfortunately, his reaction was a bit disappointing.

"Hello, Russell speaking" he answered.

"Russell! It's me. Hey, remember how we've been talking about running a marathon together? We're in luck" I practically yelled into the receiver.

Russell's answer was noncommittal. "Uh" he said.

I was still so excited, I decided to ignore his monosyllabic lack of enthusiasm. I went on "I figure we'd better start training right away if we want to be ready by April!"

"Training? April? I'm not sure" mumbled my once-eager marathon partner. "I've got a lot going on these days."

I decided to try a different tack. "Come on, Russell. You promised" I whined. "It won't be any fun to do this by myself!"

Russell wasn't moved by my play on his guilt feelings. Actually, there didn't seem to *be* any guilt feelings! "Look, Kate" he offered "I guess it seemed like a great idea before, but training for a marathon takes a lot of time and dedication. I just don't think I'm up for that right now."

"Not up for that right now! When are you ever going to have time? The time is NOW" I hollered. I was really getting steamed, and he could tell. Excitement hadn't worked. Guilt had been completely ineffective. Maybe anger would do the trick. I certainly wasn't faking it! I was sputtering with fury as I spat out "Well, thanks for nothing, Russ. Here you promised me you'd do this with me, and now you're backing out with some lame excuse. Okay for you! I'll do it without you. You'll see!"

Maybe it was a combination of all my emotions coming at him over the phone. Maybe he was afraid I'd really do it without him and show him up. Who knows? All I can say for sure is that after that last outburst of mine, Russell sat quietly on the other end of the line for what seemed like a very long time, then said "Okay, you win. We'll start training in one week, as soon as I meet this deadline. You have to agree to some terms, though, okay?"

"Terms? Okay" I answered, smiling to myself. The terms could be his battle won. I had won the war!

Part 2. Each of the following items names a person (or personification) who might be quoted in a text. Create a quote for each speaker, making sure to use a comma to set up the quote.

Example: your garage
Possible answer: *Just yesterday, my garage said to me, "Hey, how much junk do you think you can fit in me? I mean, come on!"*

   a. your car

   b. your pet (If you don't have one, imagine you do.)

   c. your neighbor

   d. your mechanic

   e. the driver sitting next to you in traffic

   f. someone walking into your house for the first time

   g. your best friend

   h. your stomach

   i. your favorite author

   j. any one of your family members

3.12   Why quotes use other punctuation

When information has been left out of a quotation, the author may use **ellipses** to let the reader know where the information would have been. Often the original quotation has been cut down to fit a limited amount of space in a photo caption or a short article. When a writer needs to add words to a quotation in order to make it clear to the reader, or when words that are clearer or more accurate need to be substituted for the speaker's original words, the added words are placed inside **brackets**.

Sometimes the sentence structure another writer or speaker has used makes it awkward to incorporate a direct quote into your own sentence structure. Writers often select key words or phrases from what another person has said or written in order to make them fit in with their own sentence rhythms. A partial quote looks like this:

> Isaacs notes a marked "inconsistency in study results" among researchers of this phenomena.

Quotation marks around *inconsistency in study results* separate Isaacs' words from those of the writer. Because the quote is not a full sentence, the reader doesn't need a comma to allow a mental pause before reading the quote.

What if you really do want to quote an entire sentence someone else has written or said, but the structure of the quote makes it awkward to mingle with your words? **Christina Sullivan** shows us some special punctuation you might want to use with quotations that have a different rhythm than your own sentences.

Ellipses

Writers use ellipses (three periods separated by spaces) to show that they have left out information in a quotation. In this example, information has been left out at the end of the speaker's words:

> "I stayed in the art teacher's house until it got warm and green outside. The law said I could stay . . ."

The next example shows something has been left out in the middle of the sentence (between *tool* and *a knowledge*):

> "There are two aspects to learning the use of any kind of *tool* . . . *a knowledge* of its fundamental theory, and actual practice in its manipulation."

> **Editor's Tip:** When you're investigating outside sources for your papers, pay close attention to quotations that leave something out of the middle of a speaker's words. Try to find the full quote in the original source: What got left out could change the way you interpret the sentence.

Brackets

Use a bracket in your writing if you need to add a word to a quotation so that it makes sense to the reader:

> Celia wrote, "There are too many people in this town, [*and there is*] too much gossip."

ACTIVITY 3.12: WHY QUOTES USE OTHER PUNCTUATION

Part 1. When information has been left out of a quotation, the author may use ellipses to let the reader know where the information would have been. Often the original quotation has been cut down to fit a limited amount of space in a photo caption or a short article. Let's say each of the following sentences needs to be trimmed in order to make it a usable quote. Pare each sentence down carefully, using ellipses to show where the information you removed used to be. Then read your answer to yourself to be sure that the quotation still makes sense.

Example: According to the Dean of Students, "Many of the students are taking too many classes not directly related to any field of study in their majors."

Revision: According to the Dean of Students, "Many of the students are taking too many classes not . . . in their majors."

1. One bus driver commented, "I'm really not sure why they've changed the routes. They seemed to work just fine. At the meeting tomorrow, I'm going to offer some reasons to keep the old routes."

2. Ray Flores, mayoral incumbent, offered the following observation: "Placing campaign signs in your front yard is merely a statement of your support. It does not necessarily say anything about your personal beliefs."

3. "We've had to revamp the plans for the park. We hope the new plans will make for a safer, more family-friendly atmosphere," said Jay Byrd, the city planner.

4. "Any phone calls received with regard to this issue will be passed along to our public health department," noted the spokeswoman. "A staff member in that office has been assigned to take care of this problem, and she will return the phone calls in the order they are received."

5. The head of the customer service department, Lynne Linnell, answered our question with the following statement: "We here at Jack's Jeeps are committed to selling only the finest quality vehicles. If you are dissatisfied with any part of your car-buying experience at our dealership, please call us and tell us, so that we can correct the situation properly."

6. The director, speaking at our weekly production meeting, made a point of saying, "It's a shame so many employees were abusing our generous sick day policy. The policy has had to be rewritten; its terms will no longer be so flexible."

7. "The Veteran's Day Parade this year was our best ever," crowed one local veteran. "So many wonderful people came to pay tribute to our soldiers, and we had the most beautiful, professional-looking floats. The people of this city should be proud!"

8. The owner of the amusement park was quick to point out, "We had all our rides inspected as recently as last month. Every effort was made to ensure the safety of our visitors."

9. With eyes brimming, the retiring vice-president of marketing said, "It's been a wonderful twenty-one years with this company. I hope to enjoy as many more in my retirement. Thank you all for your friendship, your professionalism, and your frequent reminders to call my wife!"

10. According to one of my favorite books, "Use lemon juice as a natural bleaching agent in your kitchen. Vinegar is also a useful kitchen cleanser."

Part 2. When a writer needs to add words to a quotation to make a speaker's original statement clearer to the reader, the additional words are placed inside brackets. That way, the reader knows which words belong to the person being quoted and which words were added later. After reading the following sentences, add your own words (in brackets, of course) to make each one clear.

Example: "It's obvious that it was out of control and needed to be leashed."

Revision: "Its obvious that [the dog] was out of control and needed to be leashed."

1. "We were hoping to close and never have to open again," commented one of the local shopkeepers.

2. After discussing it privately, the historical commission determined, "The property owner will not be allowed to build it, as it will substantially alter the value of this historical property."

3. With a view to ending the longstanding feud, Aunt Billie pointed out, "We really don't even know who built the house, so we can't be sure."

4. "Don't try tellin' me what to do!" yelled the old farmer.

5. With a quick nod, the agent confirmed, "You'll board in 22 minutes."

6. "That's a matter of opinion," growled the landlord, "and you all have different ones."

7. "Unless the bill is paid in full by the end of the month, privileges will be suspended," noted the letter.

8. In his comments to the press, the rock star included this little gem: "I'm the best there ever was, and I dare any of you to prove me wrong!"

9. "Unfortunately, we're going to have to suspend use until the chemicals have been completely cleared out," answered the beleaguered official.

10. After the interview, the aging starlet was heard to say, "Let's get on with it, shall we?"

3.13   Dashes and hyphens

Dashes and hyphens may look similar, but writers use them for completely different purposes. A hyphen connects words that should be grouped together, so that a reader will read them as one thought.

Example: double-edged sword

A dash is *two connected hyphens,* and is used to emphasize ideas and explanations or to set up lists of things.

Example 1:   In all that time--three years in all--no one in the town had ever complained.

Example 2: We took it all--books, snacks, puzzles, toys, and CD's.

Hyphens between words tell readers to think about the connected words as a group: a **run-on** sentence, a **non-smoker**, a **tofu-eating** vegan, an **up-and-coming** writer. We're so used to seeing hyphens connecting words together that most of us never consciously notice them. Look at what happens, however, when we put hyphens in the *wrong* places:

The study focused on older people, so there was a **relatively-high-back** injury rate.

Wait! Are we talking about an injury to something called the *relatively high back*? Let's try that again, without the misplaced hyphens:

The study focused on older people, so there was a *relatively high back injury* rate.

What about this example:

Sheila promised *to-get-her* a chocolate sundae.

Did your brain interpret the emphasized words as one word (*together*)? Or did you focus on Sheila's rather ominous promise *to get her*? The hyphens sent a strong message that you should interpret these groups of words as one unit, with a special meaning.

Writers use this almost unconscious response to make up new terms, grouping words together temporarily to make a point:

She gave me that *don't-even-think-about-it* look.

Hyphens can also signal that a group of words should be read as an adjective (a word that describes a noun or pronoun):

I got ready for my *wrap-up* meeting with the CEO.

Here, the hyphen shows that *wrap* and *up* form a temporary alliance to describe a kind of meeting. The hyphen helps the writer make *wrap-up* act as an adjective here. In this sentence, the same words have a different function:

I distribute my information and *wrap up* my meeting with the CEO.

Here, *wrap* acts as a verb. It doesn't describe the type of meeting; it tells you what action the subject of the sentence is *doing*.

Dashes are two hyphens typed together with no space in between. Writers often use them to emphasize ideas:

> We loved Southern California--*except for the traffic.*

> I expected sympathy--*not condemnation.*

Dashes can also act like a colon, to set up lists:

> He added three things to the brownies--*chocolate, walnuts, and a secret ingredient he wouldn't reveal.*

ACTIVITY 3.13: DASHES AND HYPHENS

Part 1. Dashes and hyphens may look similar, but writers use them for completely different purposes. A hyphen connects words that should be grouped together, so that a reader will read them as one thought.

Example: double-edged sword

A dash is two connected hyphens and is used to emphasize ideas and explanations or to set up lists of things.

Example 1: In all that time--three years in all--no one in the town had ever complained.

Example 2: We took it all--books, snacks, puzzles, toys, and CD's.

In the following sentences, the author has left out dashes needed to emphasize ideas and set up lists. Add dashes wherever they are needed.

1. Everything was ready for the party except the guest of honor herself.
2. The sisters were close only fifteen months apart but they couldn't have been more different.
3. When the bear came out of its sedation Sal ran wouldn't you?
4. Biff says and he appears to be serious this time that he will not be playing any more practical jokes on us.
5. That was the most spectacular photograph I'd ever seen the colors were vivid, the lighting was perfect, and the subjects were riveting.
6. My dad always told me the "idiot box" the television was draining the brain cells out of my head.
7. To change a tire on my car by myself this was a real achievement for me.
8. The pack of dogs a motley crew to say the least had the town's residents up in arms.

9. My aunt's carrot cake has three special ingredients anise, cinnamon, and a secret flavoring she won't reveal.

10. Dr. Adamson that nutty guy told Carol he'd been given an artificial pancreas!

Part 2. Teamwork. With your group, look over your revisions to the sentences in Part 1. You added dashes to practice using them, but were there any sentences you puzzled over? Could any sentences stand without a dash? What other types of punctuation could you use instead of dashes?

Part 3. Now let's spend some time with hyphens. The selection below contains at least ten errors involving hyphens. In some cases, the hyphen has been misplaced and should be removed. In others, a hyphen is missing and should be added. Read the passage carefully, then add or delete hyphens as necessary.

Example 1:   We'll ask Kevin to help, since he has a strong-back.
Revision: We'll ask Kevin to help, since he has a strong back.

Example 2: Those high backed chairs look like antiques.
Revision: Those high-backed chairs look like antiques.

Shopping for a new car or van can be quite an experience. Mine was! As soon as we arrived on the lot, out came a sweet talking sales-man. He was full of good-deals and low-prices. He talked so much my head began to swim! To counteract his run on at the mouth style, I began to ask questions. As soon as I got my answer out of him, I'd interrupt him to ask another one. That way, I could actually find out what I needed to know, while avoiding a lot of the sales-patter.

Finally, it was time to get-down-to-business. I knew that the pre ordained price on the car I wanted was too high, so I threw out a price that I knew would be too low. Immediately, our salesman's happy go lucky attitude disappeared. He acted shocked and dismayed at my ignorance. He pointed out the superior features on the car. He even intimated that I was a bit unAmerican to offer such a low price on such a fantastic American made automobile.

In the end, we were both happy. I got a new car for what I believed was a reasonable price, and he got his sale. Don't you just love happy endings?

3.14   The wily comma splice

A comma splice happens when you try to join two complete sentences with a comma. The comma "splices"--joins together--separate ideas like a film editor splices together strips of film: two scenes that were made to stand alone suddenly seem to connect. This makes it hard to tell which ideas the writer wants you to put together.

My speech was a complete disaster, by everyone's estimation it was much too long.

Just what did "everyone" estimate here?   **My speech was a complete disaster.**

Did everyone say the speech was too long?   **By everyone's estimation it was much too long.**

Or did the speaker decide her speech was much too long only after "everyone" agreed that it was a disaster?   **My speech was a complete disaster, by everyone's estimation. It was much too long.**

Now let's look at how Cary Stewart, the writer of "How to Make a Local Convenience Store Employee Mad," experimented with solutions to a comma splice in the rough draft of his process paper. Here's Cary's comma splice:

You have to be the hoagie magician, I need the hoagie magician.

(comma splice)

This, of course, splices two complete sentences together with just a comma. Now watch what Cary does in his revisions. Each of the solutions changes the way a reader "hears" and interprets his text.

Solution 1	Solution 2	Solution 3
You can add an *and*, *but*, or similar connector after the comma.	You can make the comma a period, dividing the sentence in two.	You can make the comma a semicolon, separating the two sentences while maintaining the flow.
You have to be the hoagie magician, and I need the hoagie magician.	**You have to be the hoagie magician. I need the hoagie magician.**	**You have to be the hoagie magician; I need the hoagie magician.**
Adding a connector like *and* causes the reader to pause only long enough to take a quick mental breath before reading the second half of the sentence. It can make you sound like you're *all in a rush*.	Using a period ends the sentence abruptly. There's a choppy feel to the two sentences when read together. This is good when you want to sound *nervous* or even *angry*.	Using a semicolon combines the special effects of Solutions 1 and 2, because it causes the reader to pause without stopping abruptly. Cary chose to use this solution to maintain the *easy, joking* tone of his process paper.

ACTIVITY 3.14: THE WILY COMMA SPLICE

Part 1. When you connect two complete sentences using only a comma, the result is a comma splice. At least ten of the following items are made up of two complete sentences "spliced" together with a comma. Identify and draw a line through each comma splice.

1. Although the sun was shining, there was a pronounced chill in the air.
2. We ran out of things to say, there was so much we still needed to talk about.
3. The fragrant blossoms made me feel like I was on vacation, they gave off such a tropical smell.
4. All things considered, my decision to take some time off was a wise one.
5. The leaf skittered across the pavement, finally it came to rest in a puddle of water.
6. The actors in the variety show were obviously having a wonderful time, judging by the giggles backstage.
7. After the television stopped working, we found ourselves coming up with great ideas to fill the time.
8. The car backfired several times, I thought someone was shooting a gun.
9. If they hadn't changed the rules so many times, then maybe I'd know what to do!
10. Graziela caught a cab back to work, she was running so late after lunch.
11. The house is painted hot pink, you can't miss it!
12. In the time it took to read the story, Addison fell asleep.
13. Despite his long illness, Jesse seemed as fit and feisty as he ever had.
14. Come join us for a night of music under the stars, you'll be glad you did!
15. In all the time they'd known each other, neither friend had ever taken the other for granted.
16. The walk in the woods was restorative for Adele, she felt ready to finish her work.
17. Are you ready, if she asks, can you help at a moment's notice?
18. The moment the shark's teeth bit into its prey, its eyes were covered by a protective lid.
19. Toys were strewn everywhere, as though a small whirlwind had blown through the living room.
20. After the lecture, we all went out for coffee, some of us had ice cream, too.

Part 2. Teamwork. With your group, go back over the comma splices you identified in Part 1. We're going to test how readers are affected by the different ways we fix comma splices!

Step 1. Fix each comma splice three different ways:

- Replace the comma with a semicolon
- Keep the comma, but add a connecting word like *and* or *but*
- Use a period instead of a comma to divide the two parts of the sentence into two separate sentences.

Step 2. Look at the three versions of each of the comma splices you revised. Read them aloud to the members of your group. Choose the version you like the best. Be ready to explain *why* you like it, and how a reader might respond to it.

Part 3. Left alone, each sentence below is a comma splice, confusing to the reader. In each item, add either a transition word or a punctuation mark to clear up communication between the writer and reader.

Example: I turned the fan on, the white noise might help me sleep.

Possible answers: I turned the fan on, thinking the white noise might help me sleep.
I turned the fan on so the white noise might help me sleep.
I turned the fan on; the white noise might help me sleep.

1. I went to the store yesterday, it was unbelievably crowded.
2. Even the parking lot was packed, too many people wanted to park close to the store.
3. It took awhile to find an empty space, finally, I parked far away from the store.
4. After my long trek to the door of the store, I was already tired, I needed a rest before I began my expedition into the wilds of the produce section.
5. Somewhere between the bananas and the onions, I ran into something of a traffic jam, I couldn't seem to get to the apples!
6. Escaping the produce section wasn't easy, I managed to get to the deli for some lunchmeat.
7. I was exhausted by the time I reached the bread aisle, then I headed for condiments.
8. The cereal aisle was so full of shoppers that I began to think I didn't really need breakfast at all, all I really needed was what I had managed to gather so far.

Section 3

9. I was pretty sure reaching the checkout stand would prove an insurmountable task, I wished once again to be almost anywhere else.

10. Although the customer in front of me tried to use her one hundred coupons to make sure I spent the night at the store, I managed to leave before dark, now where was my car?

Part 4. Teamwork. Now let's imagine you're trying to explain comma splices to a friend that missed class today. In your group, look again at the comma splices in Part 2. Which ones were hard to identify? What made them difficult? Does *every* comma in the items make a comma splice? Why or why not? Did some of the items seem clearer when you separated them into two or more sentences? Come up with a theory that will help your friend identify comma splices and turn them into clear sentences.

Part 5. Read the following selection, identifying the comma splices. Do they make the story confusing? Boring? Hard to enjoy? Add transition words and punctuation marks to repair the comma splices and increase the reader's enjoyment and understanding of the essay. Remember, there are three ways to revise comma splices. Choose the one that best fits the tone you think the selection should convey.

How to Scare a Phone Solicitor Away

We've all experienced this scenario, a solicitor calls just as dinner cools enough to enjoy. Have you ever wondered how to rid yourself of this nuisance, do you wish you could turn the tables on these professional dinner-ruiners? I have a few ideas you might use, just read on and learn.

First of all, keep in mind that any phone solicitor is going to be reading from a script, on the script are your probable responses to all of the salesperson's questions and comments, as well as how the salesperson should handle each question or answer you might have. If your responses aren't even close to any that appear on the script, you may be able to confuse the person on the other end of the phone. How should you do this?

Here are snippets of a sample phone call to help you, you can change a few words and names here and there to make it work for your new phone friend.

You: "Hello?"

Solicitor: "Is this Arthur Arthurson?" (to which you would normally agree)

You: "No, this is Bill Billson."

Solicitor: "Well, Mr. Billson, are you a person who is qualified to make decisions regarding telephone service at your address?"

You: "Who's Mr. Billson?"

Right away, you've thoroughly confused the caller, you gave a name as your own and then acted as though you'd never heard of that person. Surely that bizarre response cannot be found on the script, the salesperson now has to scramble to handle your odd question.

Solicitor: "Sir, didn't you just say your name is Bill Billson?"

You: "Who?"

Let's say the salesperson is particularly motivated and makes it past your little identity crisis, what can you do next? Foil that script, and you'll be off the phone in no time!

Solicitor: "Sir, how would you like to save up to $10 for every $50 you spend on long-distance phone calls?"

You: "Who are you, and how did you know I have a phone?"

Solicitor: "Sir, we're talking on the phone."

You: "Are you people spying on me?"

Solicitor: "No sir, we're just offering to help save you some money on your long-distance calling!"

You: "What's your name again? Can you see me? Where do you have your little camera hidden? What am I wearing?"

If the solicitor in question hasn't given up yet, it won't be long, keep acting confused and suspicious! No salesperson, no matter how pushy and determined, can withstand this type of onslaught for too long, once you make it clear that talking to you is a complete waste of time and money, you'll be free to laugh your way back to the dinner table.

Part 6. Teamwork. Below you'll find two short selections. Read these in your group and choose the selection that you find to be clearer and more effective in its communication with a reader. Be ready to describe *why* the paragraph you chose seems clearer.

I. When you tell a story to a friend, you pause at certain points, sometimes to take a breath and other times to give the story rhythm and drama, the story is more interesting to listen to if the listener has just a little time to think about what's being said. A piece of writing works the same way, with no stopping places or transition words, a reader may become lost and confused, reading a paragraph over and over again to try to make sense of it is no fun. So when you write, give your readers a break!

II. When you tell a story to a friend, you pause at certain points. Sometimes you pause to take a breath; other times your pause is meant to give the story rhythm and drama. The story is more interesting to listen to if the listener has just a little time to think about what's being said. A piece of writing works the same way; with no stopping places or transition words, a reader may become lost and confused. Reading a paragraph over and over again to try to make sense of it is no fun. So when you write, give your readers a break!

3.15   Colons

Colons are used for many purposes:

- to emphasize key points   His message was clear: stop smoking.
- to set up quotations   She said simply: "No comment."
- to connect closely-related sentences   I had one wish: I wanted to leave.
- to introduce lists, as the colon that introduced this bullet list did.

Colons signal a pause that's more abrupt than a semicolon, but not the full stop that a period signals. **Always make sure that what comes before the colon is a complete sentence.** Don't interrupt a sentence by putting a colon after a verb!

WILLIAM IOVINE

We all know that words like *however* take special punctuation in some cases, but sometimes, we use special punctuation when we don't need to. Here's an example I wrote:

James Thurber, *however*: depicts the greatest hero as nothing more than a below-average country bumpkin in his short story, "The Greatest Man in the World."

The colon after *however* makes readers expect something important, or the beginning of a list. A comma would have been enough:

James Thurber, *however*, depicts the greatest hero as nothing more than a below-average country bumpkin in his short story, "The Greatest Man in the World."

The commas let the reader take a breath before reading the main part of the sentence.

> **Editor's Tip:** When you're connecting *two complete sentences* with *however,* use a *semicolon*: City traffic was impassible during rush hour; *however,* a commuter train ran every thirty minutes.

ACTIVITY 3.15: COLONS

Part 1. Each of the following sentences contains a colon; however, at least five of the colons are used in ways they shouldn't have. Read the sentences, then place an **X** next to each sentence in which the colon is misplaced.

1. An ethnobotanist is a person who studies the healing properties of native plants such as: nopal, enizo, and mesquite.

2. Some medical students are even taking an interest in how these plants can be used: a group of students in one program recently took a guided tour of local medicinal plants.

3. Many medicinal plants that used to be eaten regularly are now considered inedible: most people no longer have that knowledge available to them.

4. Plants such as prickly pear cactus and purple sage can be used in several helpful ways: balms, teas, vegetable dishes, gargles, eyewashes, and more.

5. One medical student who went on a medicinal plant walk commented: "I think a lot of what I'm learning here will be useful in my practice."

6. The students have also studied the diseases that occur frequently in the area: not surprisingly, many of those diseases are treated using native medicinal plants.

7. The plants have a unique advantage over drugs created by pharmaceutical companies: the drugs have negative side effects due to their toxicity that the plants do not have.

8. The research into these plants, along with data regarding the side effects of such drugs as aspirin and ibuprofen, caused one researcher to express a strong opinion: everyone should know about these natural cures.

9. Even if you don't plan: on drinking purple sage tea the next time you have a fever, reading about these "new" cures is interesting.

10. It may not be long before the short list of the most commonly used forms of alternative medicine reads something like this: acupuncture, chiropractic medicine, and medicinal plants.

Section 3

Part 2. As you read the selection below, look for at least six misused colons. When you find a colon in the wrong place, rearrange the sentence, use different punctuation, or just remove the colon in order to clear up any confusion that may have been caused.

It's odd to think that going to the doctor was a completely different experience for our ancestors. For one thing, many people didn't go to the doctor: instead, the doctor came to them. Wouldn't that be wonderful?

Another major change in medical practice is the availability of so many drugs: painkillers, antibiotics, blood thinners, antidepressants, and so many more. Many of the treatments used long ago, even those that were quite effective: have been abandoned. Some old-fashioned treatments, such as the use of leeches to draw out a patient's blood, are being revived by a few unusual practitioners. To that particular practice, I would have to vehemently say: "No thanks!" Other traditional, less disturbing, cures have been all but lost, such as: swamp root for ulcer pain, catnip for colic, horehound for coughing, bayberry bark for congestion, and celery seeds for rheumatism. Native American healers continue to use: willow bark and tips for general pain and pinon pine as an antiseptic and expectorant, among others. Ephedra is used by Native American healers to treat congested sinuses, to purify the blood, and to stimulate the central nervous system: however, its use must be carefully monitored to prevent serious negative side effects. Pioneers were fond of: sage to stop hemorrhaging, alfalfa to relieve arthritic pain, and black walnut hulls to rid themselves of tapeworm. The many herbs mentioned here are really only the tip of the iceberg when it comes to medicinal plants used to heal by our ancestors here in the United States.

I've left out a very important change in the practice of medicine: insurance is often used these days. Although many Americans still don't have insurance: its use is common enough, and what a difference in payment methods from ancestors who often had nothing more to offer their doctors than produce from their fields!

The next time you find yourself sitting in the waiting room at your doctor's office, consider the kinds of treatments you might have been offered two hundred years ago. Which would you prefer?

Part 3. For the next activity, you'll need to use colons in four sentences. In each sentence, the colon should serve a different purpose. Examples of each purpose follow.

Set up a quotation: The healer handed me my tea, saying: "This will make your throat feel better."

Emphasize a key point:	The idea behind the program was straightforward: teach students about medicinal plants.
Introduce lists:	Some of my favorite healing plants are listed here: birch, bee pollen, red clover, and fennel seed.
Connect closely related sentences:	The students had a goal: they wanted to be able to use herbs medicinally.

3.16   Parentheses

CHRISTINA SULLIVAN

Parentheses are used to tuck information into a sentence so that the reader can better understand what the writer is saying:

The team lost yesterday (*those poor girls*).

Jamie (*the nasty woman*) yelled at the dog.

These two examples are very conversational, as if they insert the writer's unconscious thoughts about the topic into the main idea of the sentence. These comments are also called *asides.*

My allowance (*$20*) was taken away.

This example adds additional information, the amount of the allowance, to the main idea of the sentence.

> **Editor's Tip:** Parentheses tell readers to skip over the information enclosed to find a straight path through the sentence.

You also use parentheses to enclose numbers when you incorporate lists of things, like what you'll do today, into a paragraph:

I have too much to do today: (1) read my grammar book, (2) study for my exam, and (3) go to work.

In order to make dinner I need these ingredients: (1) enchilada sauce, (2) tortillas, (3) boneless chicken, and (4) cheese.

ACTIVITY 3.16: PARENTHESES

Part 1. When you want to include extra information in a sentence (as though you were whispering the added information into your imaginary reader's ear), one way to do that is to enclose the information in parentheses. The words inside the parentheses act like an aside from you to the reader.

Each of the sentences below contains non-essential information that should be put into parentheses. Add parentheses as necessary to help organize the information in each sentence.

Example: Anjetta loves to ride horses dressage as a hobby on the weekends.

Answer: Anjetta loves to ride horses (dressage) as a hobby on the weekends.

1. Centenarians those amazing people seem to have found the secret to longevity.
2. Each person doctors interview has a unique often offbeat theory about why he or she has managed to live so long.
3. One lady centenarian claims that she is alive even after a bout of pneumonia at age 93 because she has kept up her ballroom dancing.
4. A 101-year-old man a newsletter publisher, believe it or not credits his diet: he's avoided beef his entire life.
5. Yet another woman a retired teacher says her love of learning has kept her going.
6. These are perfectly good theories, because we still don't have any sort of real or even remotely close answer to the question: "What leads to a long life?"
7. Researchers are poring over each centenarian's history even their spouses in minute detail, hoping to uncover some tiny clue.
8. Does a person get to be 100 because of 1 excellent genes, 2 healthy habits, or 3 just plain good luck?
9. The eating and drinking habits intake of fatty foods and alcohol are of particular interest of centenarians have been studied extensively, for example.
10. The question, "How have these people handled stressors in their lives?" is considered as well probably more seriously by today's researchers than those in the past.
11. Scientists have also studied family members of these hardy often quite active people.

12. Their children, their siblings who often live long lives themselves, and their spouses are all studied.

13. Some of your ideas about how to live a healthy life your doctor's ideas too may be buried by the results obtained so far.

14. Centenarians who have smoked nearly all their lives are not unheard of or even uncommon, for that matter.

15. Some of these amazingly long-lived people are overweight watch your doctor's eyebrows go up at this one.

16. Their eating habits are all over the spectrum yes, even bacon is a food item consumed regularly by some, and plenty of those interviewed have admitted to a moderate daily dose of alcohol.

17. One thing scientists have discovered about these men and women is that they have managed to either avoid or delay getting the diseases diabetes, for example that often kill us as we age.

18. If a gene that carries with it long life is discovered and that's a big "if" will some enterprising company create a "long-life medicine" for everyone to take?

19. Researchers insist that such a discovery would be used to develop treatments for diseases such as Alzheimer's and heart disease, so that the lives we live would be healthier presumably, a healthier life would be longer.

20. Although that sounds like a wonderful possibility, it's doubtful that a gene or genes alone account for longevity; it's more likely that a number of factors are involved.

Part 2. Teamwork. With your group, read the sentences in Part 1 as a paragraph. What effect do all those parentheses have? Is it good to use so many in one paragraph? Why or why not?

Part 3. What other ways can you imagine to add asides to your sentences? Go back through the twenty sentences in Part 1. This time, **avoid** using parenthesis. What kinds of punctuation marks did you use?

Part 4. Teamwork. Writing. Now, get with the members of your group. Your job is to make a coherent news release out of the sentences you've been revising. Use parenthesis, other punctuation marks, and wholesale restructuring of sentences to make this story clear for news readers.

SECTION 4: The Little Mysteries of Grammar

4.1   Subjunctive mood

Subjunctive mood is special. We can suggest doubt or uncertainty just by spelling verbs a certain way! You usually hear the subjunctive mood used in "I wish" or "if" expressions, like these:

I wish I **were** a millionaire.

If I **were** a registered nurse, I would---

Using **were** with statements like *I wish* and *If → I would* tells the reader that these are speculations, not statements of current fact. You're *not* a millionaire, or a registered nurse. If you **were,** you wouldn't have to wish (as in the first example) or imagine (as in the second example).

What would happen if you used *was*, as many people do in casual conversation? You'd be sending mixed signals to your readers. The part of your sentence that said *I wish* or *If → I would* would signal you're speculating or imagining. In contrast, your verb would say you're talking about something that happened in the past:

I **was** a millionaire (until my stock crashed).

I **was** a registered nurse (until I decided to become an M.D.)

ACTIVITY 4.1: SUBJUNCTIVE MOOD

Part 1. Using the subjunctive form of a verb allows a writer to suggest doubt or uncertainty. The subjunctive mood projects readers into the future and imagines possibilities. It's a pretty neat trick, unless it's misused.

In at least five of the following sentences, the writer has abused verbs. Revise each abused sentence so that the subjunctive mood is used when it's needed, and avoided when it's not.

Example 1: Linda were a great teacher. (misused subjunctive form)
Revision: Linda was / is a great teacher.

Example 2: If Linda was a teacher, she would be a great one.
            (subjunctive form needed but not used)
Revision: If Linda were a teacher, she would be a great one.

1. If you be too tired to eat, go to bed!
2. The family get-together was somewhat marred by my cousin's outburst.
3. If she was a truly open-minded person, she wouldn't say such a thing.
4. Perry's doctor gave orders that he stay off his feet for five days.
5. That coach with the blue shorts need to change his attitude.
6. The tour guide suggests that we be ready to leave by 6:00 a.m.
7. My grandmother wishes she was an opera singer.
8. The experts recommend that a person wakes up every day at the same time.
9. If I were only interested in money, I would look for a more lucrative career.
10. According to Cindy's guidance counselor, she was two credits short.

Part 2. Imagining the future. Now, let's see where the subjunctive can take us. Write from one paragraph to 2 pages using one of the following prompts:

1. If I were rich, I'd. . .
2. If I were already through with school, I'd. . .
3. If I were married, I'd. . .
4. If you were elected class president, you'd. . .
5. If we were only free to choose, we'd. . .

4.2   Adjectives and Adverbs—What's the difference?

Writers use both **adjectives** and **adverbs** to add excitement, detail, and description to their writing. Each type of word has a specific job to do. *Adjectives* add details to what we know about nouns and pronouns; *adverbs* give us more information about verbs, adjectives, and other adverbs.

We use adjectives all the time: the *red* car, the *big* house, the *right* answer, a *bad* headache, a *good* day. Endings like *-able*, *-ful*, *-ish*, *-ive*, *-less*, and *-al* turn common words into adjectives such as like*able*, fear*ful*, book*ish*, creat*ive*, pain*less*, exception*al*. Even nouns can be used as adjectives: *risk* factors; a *business* proposal, *marriage* counseling. Many adjectives can be intensified (*more* creative, *most* likeable, prett*ier*) or downplayed (*less* fearful, *least* acceptable) by adding *-er* or pairing them with words like *more*, *most*, *less*, or *least*. Some adjectives (what your grammar book would call *absolute*) can't be intensified. Here's an example:

We dug up the *dead* plants. We wanted only *perfect* specimens.

States that can't change (like being dead or perfect) can't be intensified or downplayed: They just *are*.

Adverbs very often end with *-ly*: *sadly, quickly, surreptitiously, easily, readily, mysteriously*. But, don't be fooled! Adverbs like *fast, often, just, always, never, seldom, not*, and *almost* don't follow this rule. Many adverbs can be intensified or downplayed by using the same methods you would to intensify adjectives: add -er or pair adverbs with words such as *more, most, less, least, too*, or *very*: *faster, very* sadly, *most* easily, *too* readily.

ACTIVITY 4.2: ADJECTIVES AND ADVERBS

Part 1. In each of the following sentences, we've underlined an adjective or adverb. After reading the sentence, decide whether the underlined word is an adjective or an adverb. Write ADJ next to the sentences in which you found an underlined adjective and ADV next to those in which the underlined word was an adverb. (Remember, an adjective's job is to add detail to a noun or pronoun, while an adverb will tell more about a verb, an adjective, or another adverb.)

Examples: She took another look at the <u>expensive</u> sunglasses. ADJ
Alain <u>carefully</u> adjusted his rearview mirror. ADV

1. Over the past 50 years, <u>new</u> technologies have been developed to make our food safer.

2. Still, the chance of getting sick from the food we eat has increased <u>noticeably</u>.

3. According to the Centers for Disease Control and Prevention, the occurrence of <u>serious</u> gastrointestinal illness has risen 34% since 1948.

4. Although most of us can rely on our immune systems to keep us free of illnesses caused by food-borne bacteria, elderly people and <u>very</u> young children can be at risk from eating contaminated food products.

5. Food poisoning for them, and for others whose immune systems are not strong, can be <u>deadly</u>.

6. Eating <u>fresh</u> fruits and vegetables that haven't been cleaned properly is one way to increase the chance that you'll experience food poisoning yourself.

7. Precooked meals, such as <u>deli</u> meats, can also be contaminated.

8. The Food and Drug Administration has a hard time keeping up with inspections on the <u>wide</u> variety of foods we now have to choose from.

9. Contaminated foods <u>often</u> make it onto store shelves, escaping the notice of busy F.D.A. inspectors.

10. This problem must be taken seriously by those of us responsible for feeding the youngest and oldest members of our families, as well as by those whose immune systems are <u>already</u> compromised.

Part 2. Teamwork. Did you find *other* adverbs or adjectives in the sentences above—ones we *didn't* underline? Make a list of these and talk about what they do in the sentence.

Part 3. The following sentences are missing words that add description and detail (adjectives or adverbs). After reading each sentence, decide whether an adjective or an adverb is needed. Then have fun filling in the empty spots with words that will make the sentences interesting! Label the word you chose: was it an adjective (ADJ), or an adverb (ADV)?

Example: It seemed like shopping with my sister for her _____ dress took forever!

Possible answer: It seemed like shopping with my sister for her **prom** dress took forever! **ADJ**

1. In June, I drove home for a _____ visit.

2. My favorite uncle was in town, too, but for a _____ short time only.

3. We knew we needed to take advantage of our limited time together, so we thought _____ about what we wanted to do.

4. We could go berry-picking and have Mom make us a pie, but it was a _____ long drive to the forest.

5. Uncle Marc suggested going out to the Dickinson ranch to ride the horses, but could we carry on a _____ conversation while riding?

6. Then I thought up the _____ activity: a nature walk.

7. He laughed at my suggestion and pointed to his _____ belly, but he agreed that it would be fun.

8. We packed some tuna sandwiches and drinks, then _____ set out on our big adventure.

9. My mom and brother made fun of us, _____ dragging under the weight of our backpacks.

10. It didn't matter; the hike turned out to be so much fun, we didn't even mind our _____ muscles the next day.

Part 4. Teamwork.

Step 1. This time, *you'll* tell *us* which adjectives and adverbs to use. First, make a list of five adjectives and five adverbs in the spaces we've provided here.

Adjectives   **Adverbs**

_____   _____

_____   _____

_____   _____

_____   _____

_____   _____

Step 2. Exchange your lists of adjectives and adverbs with other members in your group. Check to make sure that all the words in the adverb list really are adverbs, and all the words in the adjective list really are adjectives. (Hint: if you're not sure whether a word is an adverb or adjective, try using it with a noun. Does it fit? Does it describe the noun?)

Step 3. Now, use words from your list to fill in the blank spaces in the paragraph below. They may not make sense, but they should make you laugh! Enjoy!

The other night I was watching this really _____ television show. It was one of the _____ "reality TV" shows. The whole time I was watching, I kept asking myself, "Would I want to be on this kind of show?" I felt _____ attracted to the idea, but I also felt I wouldn't make it for _____ long on a show like that. Usually, I'm _____ nice, and I would never even think of hurting anyone's feelings! I try to tell the truth, but if it's going to make someone feel _____, I'm gentle about it. Still, the show is _____ interesting. I can't help but watch it each time it comes on. Should I be embarrassed that I like to watch such a _____ show? I _____ ask myself that question. I can't answer that, but I can say that as a very _____ person, at least I wouldn't enjoy participating in it!

4.3 Writers Write: POSSESSIVE NOUNS

Baridilo Kponi

An apostrophe is a very small mark, but it can help make two words into one (as in a **contraction**) or make a noun signal that it owns something (**possessive**). **Baridilo Kponi** looks for two things when deciding whether or not a word is possessive: ownership and connection. Who or what does this belong to? Who or what is this connected to? Here's an example Baridilo showed us from his paper comparing American and Nigerian divorce customs:

Here is the *Nigerians* way of divorce.

Without an apostrophe, the word *Nigerians* is talking about more than one Nigerian. The focus of the sentence seems to be on a group of people from a particular place, not the method or way they do something. But then, the subject and verb don't agree: Here → is → Nigerians. "This sentence is not logical," Baridilo tells us. "We need an apostrophe after the *s* to show what I really mean." This is how Baridilo revised his sentence:

Here is the *Nigerians'* way of divorce.

Editor's Tip: Baridilo's revision emphasizes the *people* who developed the customs he's discussing by making this word possessive. Nigerians own or tend to follow a certain way of dissolving a marriage. He could have also simply dropped the *s* altogether to put the emphasis on the culture or the custom, itself. *Nigerian* is what your grammar book would call a **proper adjective**. It describes an entire people or way of life. Using it as an adjective makes it describe (rather than possess) *way*. Here's how that would look:

Here is the *Nigerian* way of divorce.

Another student offers this example of what happens when you leave out an apostrophe:

Jack moves to the window to get some fresh air, and one of the *Presidents* men pushes Jack out of the window.

"The missing apostrophe makes the sentence sound like there is more than one President," this student contributor wrote. "Using an apostrophe (*President's* men) shows the reader that the man who shoved Jack out of the window works for or is with the President."

ACTIVITY 4.3: POSSESSIVE NOUNS

Part 1. An apostrophe used to show ownership or connection changes the meaning of a word--and the sentence it is in--completely. It's a very powerful mark, so a writer should use it carefully!

Example: Jane emptied the dogs water dish.

This sentence says that Jane emptied the **dogs**! Jane → **emptied** → **dogs**. We're not sure what that involves—but it couldn't have been pleasant for the animals. How the water dish fits in is a mystery.

Jane emptied the dog's water dish.

The apostrophe in the second sentence tells the reader that there is only one dog, and that Jane emptied its **dish. Jane** → **emptied** → **dish.** The apostrophe makes this a much clearer (and more humane) sentence.

Each of the ten sentences below contains or should contain at least one apostrophe. In some sentences, the apostrophe is missing, and you'll have to add one in order to make the sentence say what it really means. In other sentences, an apostrophe is in the wrong place; you'll have to either move it to the correct spot or remove it entirely. All ten sentences need to be revised.

Example: Maggie took her clothe's out of Kays bag.

Revision: Maggie took her clothes out of Kay's bag.

1. For his senior project, Stefan was able to study Native Americans traditions.
2. Of all of the painting's Priscilla had sold, her favorite had been "Girl in Bluebonnets."
3. Seths decision affected all our live's.
4. The printers ink cartridge is almost empty.
5. Beryl's going to check to see if Jeb's shoe's are a business expense.
6. Since the fairs camel's were so testy, we tried to stay away from their teeth.
7. His bill's were really steep due to that summers high temperatures.
8. The best show we saw at the wild animal park was all about the big cats hunting habits.
9. After sightseeing, we went to visit our friends the Neiderbaum's.
10. That dish isn't your's, is it?

Part 2. In each of the following sentences, you'll find a blank space where a word that shows possession is needed. Fill in an appropriate possessive word, using apostrophes effectively in all ten sentences.

Example: I asked for the _____ name so I could recommend him to my friends.

Possible answer: I asked for the _mechanic's_ name so I could recommend him to my friends.

1. We went to my _____ favorite restaurant on her birthday.
2. The pig ate all the slop from _____ trough.
3. Each of _____ former students had something nice to say about her.
4. We all watched the _____ speech on television last night.
5. _____ homemade rhubarb upside-down cake is the best!

6. After the _____ mistake, my shirt was never the same again.

7. My last _____ disappearance was an occasion of great sadness.

8. The _____ idea was surprisingly good!

9. After seeing the _____ ridiculously high prices, Gayla decided to go somewhere else.

10. The librarian tried to fix the _____ spine.

Part 3. Make each word below possessive by adding an apostrophe plus –s, just an apostrophe, or just an –s. Then use each word in a sentence. Beware, though! Not all of the words given below need an apostrophe to show possession.

Example: thesaurus

Possible sentence: The thesaurus's many word choices have helped me more than once.

1. her

2. marketplace

3. professors

4. hypnotist

5. Jonston

6. it

7. circus

8. symphonies

9. fence

10. advertisements

Part 4. Teamwork. Look at the words in Part 2 that you **didn't** have to change to make them show ownership. Make a list of other words that may fall into the same category. What characteristics do they share? Come up with a theory that explains why these words are different.

4.4   Clauses and phrases—what's the difference?

Both **clauses** and **phrases** are groups of words used for various special effects, like adding detail, or directing how a reader should interpret a particular idea.

Clauses are groups of words that have a subject and a verb. They may be independent (able to stand alone as a sentence in themselves) or dependent (not able to stand alone). Dependent clauses have to be attached to an independent clause or they're fragments. Let's look at a line from one of **Blake Middleton's** papers:

That the bodies have a right to live on their own, *that they should be given their freedom and once again let nature take its course.*

Blake's statement is actually two (dependent) **clauses** put together. Each clause has a subject and a verb, but we know we can't read these as full sentences. Why? The word *that* signals you're *adding information* to the main point. Here's how Blake revised his statements to say what he intended:

The opposite view, *that the cloned bodies have a right to live on their own and should be given their freedom,* **is held by those who believe that nature should be allowed to take its own course.**

Two things happened to make Blake's revision work. First, he connected the ideas in the two dependent clauses with *and* to make a shorter statement. Next, he embedded this shortened dependent clause into a complete sentence (or, *in*dependent clause). Nice revision!

Phrases are also groups of words that bond together to add information to a sentence, but phrases *don't have* a subject and verb. You're probably most familiar with prepositional phrases, such as *with black fur* or *to the moon.* Writers use all sorts of other phrases, however. Here are a few examples:

Noun phrase:	*The author of the novel* led the seminar.
Infinitive phrase:	My job is *to create software* for medical files.
Gerund phrase:	*Swimming in the ocean* is exhilarating.
	(Here *swimming* is a gerund because it's used as a noun.)
Participial phrase:	The supervisor *interviewing job candidates* was my former boss.

Writers use phrases to create different rhythms in their writing, to vary the style of their sentences, to emphasize points, and to add information to the main idea of their sentences. The main thing to remember in using phrases is that they may put additional words in between your subject and verb, your pronouns and the words they refer to, or your nouns and the modifiers you use to describe them. At times, the extra words cause confusion:

The **additions** to the previous paragraph makes the essay more coherent.

The straight **subject** → verb path through this sentence is **additions** → makes. Whoops!

ACTIVITY 4.4: CLAUSES AND PHRASES

Part 1. Both **clauses** and **phrases** are used by authors to make their writing more interesting, but they have some key differences:

- **Clauses** contain a subject and a verb. **Phrases** don't.
- **Clauses** may be able to stand on their own as sentences (independent). **Example:** *The sun sets.*
- Even with a subject and verb, some **clauses** don't have what it takes to stand alone (dependent). **Example:** *before the sun sets*
- **Phrases** can **never** stand alone as a sentence. Here are some examples of phrases:

  at sunset (prepositional phrase)

  setting sun (participial phrase)

  riding into the sunset (gerund phrase)

  to enjoy the sunset (infinitive phrase)

  the sun setting behind the mountain (noun phrase)

Each of the following sentences is made up of clauses and phrases. Circle one clause and one phrase in each sentence. Write a **C** above each clause and a **P** above each phrase. Remember: phrases are often found inside clauses.

Example 1: After the train had derailed, the damaged cars were inspected.
Clause: After the train had derailed *or* the damaged cars were inspected
Phrase: damaged cars

Example 2: My writer's block disappeared when I saw her disgusted look.
Clause: My writer's block disappeared *or* when I saw her disgusted look.
Phrase: disgusted look

1. When the semester had ended, several of the students took the time to write a long letter to the dean of instruction.
2. Swimming in the pond was prohibited because of the high level of pollutants.
3. Grinning guiltily, James managed to mumble something about how hungry he was.
4. To learn all about that type of software, ask Casey when she's finished helping Rich.
5. Running up and down a basketball court, while several other people try to steal a ball from me, is not my idea of fun.
6. Unfortunately, the hovering fruit flies had also found our watermelon.
7. Even if you don't want to come with us, recommend the trip to a friend.
8. The little girl eating the snow cone is my next door neighbor.
9. The babysitter can use the cell phone number if the other number isn't answering.

Section 4

10. I tried really hard to change his mind.

11. Stuck between a rock and a hard place, Dillon found himself in a pickle.

12. Finishing the service orders before the close of business today is not possible.

13. Until the company changes its dress policy, we'll just have to make do.

14. The car drove down our street slowly, speakers blaring a techno beat.

15. You'll find that the original furnishings are still in the house.

16. Yolanda didn't want to eat anything that her mother hadn't made.

17. The owner of that house is an excellent gardener.

18. Once we were all convinced of our safety, the fun began.

19. The song started before the announcer was able to talk.

20. Selling her homemade cookies was a labor of love for Mrs. Trujillo.

Part 2. Teamwork. With the members of your group, go back and underline the subject and the verb in each of the **clauses** you circled in Part 1. Did you find that any groups of words that you had labeled clauses were actually **phrases**? If so, why did this happen? Let's find out.

Step 1. **Make a list** of all the **clauses** and **phrases** you found in Part 1.

Step 2. Make the **clauses** into **phrases.** Write a sentence with each one.

Step 3. Make the **phrases** you found in Part 1 into **clauses.** Write a sentence with each one.

Step 4. Now, we're ready to make a theory. Look at the revisions you made in Steps 1–3 and answer these questions:

- What did you have to take out, put in, or change to turn clauses into **phrases**?

- What did you have to take out, put in, or change to turn **phrases** into clauses?

- What did you have to do to make **sentences** with clauses? (Think about the ways you rearranged and punctuated each sentence.)

- What did you have to do to make **sentences** with phrases? (Think about the ways you rearranged and punctuated each sentence.)

- Clauses and **phrases** do similiar things in a sentence. we need to be able to tell them apart because. . . .

Part 3. For the next activity, we'll provide clauses and phrases. Label each group of words with a **C** for **clause** or a **P** for **phrase**, then use each one in a sentence.

1. to make a point
2. locked out of the house
3. so that we could change clothes
4. closing the store
5. where all the fun seemed to be
6. rather than eating three meals a day
7. covering her eyes
8. for three months and five days
9. which really made them nervous
10. as if he really cared
11. choosing an apartment
12. whoever showed up first
13. to hold out the longest
14. the slamming door
15. his eyes opened to new possibilities
16. who can't seem to stop talking
17. what the police officer had said
18. its tail wagging with anticipation
19. since we couldn't go last weekend
20. as he demanded

Part 4. Now, find five clauses and five phrases that *you* created and put into the sentences you wrote for Part 3. **Make a list** of all the **clauses**, and all the **phrases**, you wrote. List each one under the appropriate heading below.

Clauses	**Phrases**
_____	
_____	
_____	

4.5   Articles

Articles signal that a noun follows: *the* cat, *a* book, *an* apple. Usually the noun names something that can be counted, like *cats*, *books*, and *apples*. Things that can't be counted (made plural)--abstractions like *justice* or *mercy*, emotions like *fear* or *respect*, college majors, like *administration of justice*, or professions, like social workers--may or may not use an article.

The is more specific than *a* or *an*. *The* signals one item, in particular: Not just any book, but *the* book on the top shelf; not just social workers, but *the* social workers at Child Protective Services. For this reason, your grammar book will call *the* a **definite article**.

A and *an* are called **indefinite articles**. They don't specify a particular or specific item or idea. They simply mark one item among many: *a* table (any table, not a particular one) or *an* egg (one egg, from the dozen you just bought). We have two words that mean the same thing, but are used according to the way they sound! *A* sounds best with words that start with consonants: *a* house, *a* car, *a* democracy. *An* sounds best with words that begin with vowels, or sound like they do: *an* hour, *an* apple, *an* article. Why do we bother? Try to get your tongue around these word combinations: a hour, a apple, a article. It feels like riding down a bumpy country road in an old truck!

Section 4

ACTIVITY 4.5: ARTICLES

Part 1. In each sentence, an article is missing. Fill in the blanks with the appropriate articles. Remember to use the definite article **the** to signal a particular item (**the** two o'clock portrait session), but use the indefinite articles **a** and **an** before less specific nouns (**a** car, **an** eggplant).

1. For my Modern Art course, I was required to view _____ few paintings at a local museum.

2. Since my car wasn't performing too well, I took _____ taxi from my house.

3. When I climbed into the cab, I was met with _____ biggest smile I'd ever seen.

4. My cabbie, it turns out, was _____ extremely friendly man.

5. He turned on _____ cab's meter, then asked me where I would like to go.

6. When I told him about _____ art class I was taking, he became animated and began to gesture wildly as he spoke.

7. To my surprise, my driver explained to me that he had _____ degree in art!

8. We spent the rest of _____ trip talking about modern art.

9. What _____ amazing cab ride I had that day.

10. I know I'll never be able to repeat _____ experience I had that day.

Part 2. Now read the selection below. The indefinite articles **a** and **an**, along with the indefinite article **the**, have been misused throughout the paragraphs. Your mission is to locate any misused articles and replace them effectively. At least ten of the articles have been used improperly.

Here's the little bit of news on the health sciences front. An long-term study of a chicken pox vaccine has proven an vaccine to be 85% effective against the disease. Chicken pox may seem to be the mild disease, not worth worrying about, and it usually does turn out that way in children. In adults, however, a same disease can be very serious, leading to pneumonia and other infections. Believe it or not, before a chicken pox vaccine was introduced, about 100 people per year died of complications related to chicken pox.

Researchers are hoping this vaccine will eventually get rid of a chicken pox completely, but only if everyone takes advantage of the vaccine will the disease disappear. Many states require the chicken pox vaccination for an child entering school, and according to the Centers for Disease Control and Prevention, more than 60% of children are currently receiving vaccinations for chicken pox.

An final question remains: will children receiving the vaccine today need the booster shot, or will one vaccination in childhood give a person a immunity to the disease that will last the lifetime? Either way, we may just have one less childhood disease to contend with.

Part 3. Now that you've had some practice replacing the wrong article with the right one for the job, it's time for you to use a few articles yourself. Write ten sentences. In five of the sentences, use indefinite articles, **a** or **an**. In the other five sentences, use the definite article **the**. Try to link your sentences with a common theme to make them more interesting.

4.6   Passive and active voice

For some people, active and passive voice are very difficult to understand. What is a *voice?* What makes verbs speak in **active** or in **passive voice?** You'll find the answer in the *shape* of a particular sentence. That's what tells us how to think about the action a verb shows. Once you get the hang of it, it's not so hard.

First, find the **verb.** Verbs can ask questions, make statements, or give commands. Verbs describe the action that is happening in the sentence. Then ask yourself

Is the subject of the sentence *doing* this action?

If the subject is acting out what the verb says, the sentence is speaking to you in **active voice.** There's a straight line from start to finish through the sentence:

subject → *verb*

The **subject** does the action that the *verb* describes.

Here's an example from **Jessica Sullivan:**

Active voice: Jessica *baked* the cookies.

The **verb** *baked* tells what the **subject** *Jessica* did. Action moves from left (subject) to right (action) through the sentence:

Jessica → *baked* → cookies

Tip 1: In active voice, the subject does the action of the verb.

Sometimes, the shape of the sentence turns the action of the *verb* back on the **subject.** Instead of the **subject** acting out the *verb*, the *verb* is something that is happening to the **subject:**

The **cookies** *were baked* by Jessica.

The direction of action through this kind of sentence goes from right to left-- backwards! It looks like this:

cookies ← *were baked*

The subject, **cookies,** isn't doing anything. Something is happening *to* the cookies. When you have this kind of sentence structure, the sentence is in **passive voice.**

> **Tip 2: In passive voice, the action of the verb happens *to* the subject.**

You may have noticed that sentences written in the **passive voice** sound vague. We don't know just who really is acting out the verb:

Many essays were contributed to this textbook.

Who contributed the essays for the book? **Passive voice** tells us *what* is happening **(the verb)** and *who* or *what* receives this action **(the subject),** but it may not tell you who is doing the action of the verb. For this reason, **passive voice** is often used in things like lab reports, where *what* is happening is more important than *who* is doing it:

Ursodeoxycholic acid was found to prevent gallstones from forming in patients on very-low-calorie diets.

If you have trouble remembering all this, think about the word **passive.** It means unresisting, motionless, resigned, submissive. Imagine the subject of your sentence simply sitting there and letting the verb do whatever it wants to it!

If you do want to indicate who is actually acting out the verb, you'll have to add extra phrases to a sentence using **passive voice,** like this:

The essays were written <u>by</u> <u>students</u>.

Notice that the action still flows from **verb** to **subject:**

essays ← *were written*

That backward flow through the sentence is what makes this **passive voice.** Adding the phrase **by students** does, however, help us to know who did the action of the verb. We think the expanded sentence sounds awkward and unnatural. It seems to use its energy on getting all the details clear. Because **passive voice** tends to leave out or stumble over information about who's doing the action of the verb, most teachers will tell you not to use it very often.

ACTIVITY 4.6: PASSIVE AND ACTIVE VOICE

Part 1. Read the following sentences. Underline the subject in each sentence. Is the subject *doing* the action of the verb (active voice)? Place an **A** beside it. Is the subject is *receiving* the action of the verb (passive voice)? Place a **P** beside it. Look for at least five sentences written in active voice.

1. The computer wasn't working properly.
2. I took it in to get it fixed.
3. After two days, a message was left on my answering machine.
4. The caller said the computer was now in perfect condition.
5. Apparently, the hard disk was found to be faulty.
6. The problem was explained to me in great detail.
7. After the first sentence, I couldn't understand a word of her explanation.
8. The explanation was given by a trained technician.
9. She was using words I'd never even heard.
10. Still, the computer was fixed.

Part 2.

Step 1. The word pairs below show core sentences, a subject and a verb. Right now, the action moves from subject to verb (active voice). Write a full sentence in active voice with each of these pairs. Feel free to change the verb tenses if you need to, but keep the *voice* active.

Step 2. Now, let's change the direction the action moves. Write a full sentence in *passive* voice with each of these word pairs. Remember, in passive voice, the subject receives the action of the verb.

Example: basketball → bounced

The basketball → bounced across the court.
The basketball ← was bounced from one player to the other.

1. politician → helped
2. painting → displayed
3. wood → burned
4. airplane → landed
5. speakers → presented

Part 3. Teamwork. Compare your sentences with those written by the other members in your group. Were there any particular word pairs that gave you trouble? Why or why not? If you had to list the one thing that *all* the sentences in passive voice ignored, what would it be?

Part 4. For the activities below, first determine whether the subject in each sentence *acts out* the verb (active) or *receives* the action of the verb (passive). Label each sentence *active* or *passive*. Then rewrite each sentence so that its voice is changed.

Example: For $50, my hair was transformed at the salon. (passive)
        At the salon, Roel transformed my hair for $50. (active)

1. We planned a day at the beach.
2. A picnic lunch was packed.
3. Swimsuits were dug out of the bottoms of drawers.
4. When we were all ready, we loaded everything into the car.
5. Unfortunately, there was a problem with the car.
6. We popped the hood to see why it wouldn't start.
7. We checked to make sure we had enough fuel.
8. Jumper cables were borrowed.
9. None of our attempts to fix the car succeeded.
10. Our beach trip was postponed.

Part 5. Below are two short selections. One speaks in active voice, while passive voice is used by the other. After reading both selections, circle the selection you prefer. On the lines below the selection you have circled, give reasons to support your choice. What was it about your favorite selection that made you choose it over the other one? Below the other selection you did not choose, write the reasons you did not enjoy it as well as the other paragraph.

Selection I

At the beach, dogs were walked. Friends were made. Suntans were acquired. Many different activities were experienced at once. Romances were started, and then ended, at the beach. Sand castles were built and then washed away. Gritty snacks were eaten and enjoyed. Waves were chased, ridden, and otherwise braved. A whole world could be seen under the glaring eye of the summer sun.

_____
_____
_____
_____
_____
_____
_____
_____
_____

Selection II

The beach is a kinder, friendlier version of the real world. Walk your dog and make a friend. Bake in the sun and trade gossip. Watch the tourists do strange things. Teenagers start and end romances before your eyes. Little children build sand castles and the tide washes them away. Sand adds a gritty zest to your food. Surfers chase and ride the waves. You'll see the whole world in one afternoon under the glaring eye of the summer sun.

_____
_____
_____
_____
_____
_____
_____
_____
_____

Part 6. Teamwork. Look again at Selection II, above. Something interesting is going on in the first few sentences. Who is doing the action? How do you know? As a group, rewrite the first few sentences so that nouns are doing the action (subjects). How does this change the tone of the paragraph?

4.7   Contractions and tone

In addition to saving space, a contraction smoothes out the rhythm of a sentence and makes the overall tone of the sentence less formal. Using contractions sets up a conversational tone, as if the writer were telling the reader something not just everyone will hear. Contractions are used quite a bit in informal writing, like letters, everyday conversation, fiction pieces, and even newspaper columns. Writers also use them to invoke certain emotions in their readers.

Look at the difference in the rhythms of the following sentences:

It is dark. It is cold. It is terrifying. It is the place where nightmares breed.

It's dark. It's cold. It's terrifying. It's the place where nightmares breed.

The meaning of the two examples is the same (this is a place you don't want to be!), and only a little page space has been saved by using contractions in the second example. However, the tone of each sentence is subtly different. The first sentence (the one without contractions) slightly delays the time it takes to get to each adjective (*dark--cold--terrifying*). While this delay is only a fraction of a second, it tends to emphasize each adjective more strongly than the choppier rhythm of the second example. The rhythm or tone of the first sentence helps the writer build a sense of dread.

The second example (the one that uses contractions) zips directly to the adjectives. The reader's eye slides easily past the subject and verb of each sentence so the emphasis is on the adjectives (*dark!--cold!--terrifying!*). This version doesn't *build* a mood of impending doom. It *shakes* the reader with a nervous urgency that signals, "Get out now!" Which version is correct? Use the one that develops the tone *you* want to convey.

Are there other times when you *don't* want to use contractions? When would you *want* to create a choppy rhythm that emphasizes each word? Let's look at this example:

It is illegal. **It is** immoral. **It is** unjust. **It is** a desecration of all the values we hold dear.

You can almost see a politician pointing his or her finger at the audience to make each point! In choosing to make this presentation more formal, the writer deliberately separates each thought from the next. The goal here is to emphasize each adjective as a separate point in hope of overwhelming the reader with the sheer number of the politician's objections.

Using contractions in your writing gives it a conversational tone and a nice, smooth rhythm. On the other hand, *not* using contractions can be a handy writing strategy for an author who wants to call the reader's attention to each separate point being made.

ACTIVITY 4.7: CONTRACTIONS AND TONE

Part 1. Using contractions in your writing gives it a conversational tone and a nice, smooth rhythm. On the other hand, *not* using contractions can be a handy device if you want to be more formal, or to call the reader's attention to each separate point being made. Here are a few examples to help you think about the use of contractions:

Example 1: I can't think of anything that's more annoying than when you're in a hurry, and the guy in front of you won't turn right until the light turns green!

Example 2: I cannot think of anything that is more annoying than when you are in a hurry, and the guy in front of you will not turn right until the light turns green!

Which is the better way to write that sentence—with or without the contractions? It's really a conversational sort of sentence, isn't it? Example 2 seems much too formal, given the topic. How about these examples, though?

Example 3: We, as a people, can't stand aside and allow this kind of atrocity to take place. We won't be accused of apathy. The world must understand: we'll take action.

Example 4: We, as a people, *cannot* stand aside and allow this kind of atrocity to take place. We _will not_ be accused of apathy. The world must understand: *we will* take action.

What do you think? Did Example 3 have the same "punch" as Example 4? In writing, the choice you make between the conversational tone of contractions and the more formal and startling tone that you get without them is an important one.

For the five sentences below, replace the formal tone with a conversational one by forming contractions whenever possible.

1. Did you not know that you cannot eat that yet?
2. I will see if we are scheduled to start at 3 o'clock or at 4.
3. Can you not see that they are trying to work?
4. It does not seem like he is sure what you are talking about.
5. Tell her if it is not working out, and she will do what she can to help.

Part 2. The ten sentences in this next activity are all written in a conversational tone. At least five of them, however, might be more effective if they had a more formal tone. Identify these five sentences, and change their contractions into separate words.

1. If you're trying to scare me, it's working!
2. We'd really like to know if he's a good dentist.
3. We'll fight them in the courts, we'll fight them in the press, we'll fight them with picket lines and with boycotts.
4. I can't believe he'd actually have the nerve to say that!
5. I absolutely won't help you study if you don't put some effort of your own into it.
6. It's amazing to think about the discoveries being made daily in genetics.
7. What'll we do, and what'll we have to consider, if cloning becomes commonplace?
8. He's incompetent, he's immoral, and he's unscrupulous. He shouldn't be elected.
9. It's our responsibility, and we'll take care of it, no matter what has been said about us!
10. We're not ashamed of our actions; in fact, we're proud of what we've accomplished, and we'll stand by it.

Part 3. Let's have some fun with contractions and tone. Following are several situations you might face in college or on the job. Write **two responses**: one that uses contractions, and one that doesn't. Then tell which you'd use in the situation, and why. Check the examples above for suggestions about how contractions can affect the tone you take in each scenario.

1. You witnessed a traffic accident. You tell a friend what you saw.
2. You're refusing an invitation to dinner. This is the tenth time you've had this conversation.
3. Your apartment was broken into, but you saw the person who did it. You testify what happened in court.
4. You want to tell someone that a very scary-looking stranger is approaching. Let them know what direction the stranger is coming from, and what you think might be on his/her mind.
5. Your roommate has borrowed your favorite sweater again. You want to let him/her know, in uncertain terms, that this will be the last time.

SECTION 5: Agreement: Why Can't We All Just Get Along?

5.1   Subject-verb agreement

When subjects don't *agree* with the verbs in a sentence, they send mixed signals about how many people are acting out the verb:

They *skips* the first day of class to avoid talking to strangers.

The verb *skips* signals that *only one* entity is avoiding class--he, she, or it. The subject *they* signals that *more than one person* is involved. Confusion!

Disagreements like this are fairly easy to see when the subject and verb are close together, as in our example. Most of us run into trouble, however, when extra information comes between the subject and the verb. Look at this sentence from **Amy Moore's** pamphlet on work-site wellness:

The risk **factors** that have been shown to contribute to these health problems, such as excess weight, high blood pressure, high cholesterol, sedentary lifestyle, and smoking, *do respond* to lifestyle changes.

The straight **subject** → *verb* path through this sentence is **factors** → *do respond*, but 23 words come between the subject and the verb! Amy has skillfully inserted a good bit of information into a short space, without losing sight of what her subject and verb are doing. Let's look at some of the danger zones she avoided:

Danger zone 1

Which noun is the subject here? The first half of this sentence has several nouns: *factors, problems, weight, pressure, cholesterol, lifestyle,* and *smoking.* How do we know which one is the subject? First, *find the **verb**.* What is happening? Who or what is making it happen? Who or what is *responding?* This is the straight path through the sentence: **factors** → *do respond.* This is the pair of words that has to agree.

Danger zone 2

What about all those words after *that* and *such as?* Amy has added information that specifically describes *what kind* of **factors** she's talking about:

factors that have been shown to contribute to these health problems

The word *that* signals <u>more information is being added</u>. All of the words after *that* <u>describe</u> the actual subject, **factors.** These specific **factors** → *do respond.*

Amy adds even more information with *such as*:

such as excess weight, high blood pressure, high cholesterol, sedentary lifestyle, and smoking

The group of words after *such as* adds a list of specific examples of the kinds of **factors** (that) *do respond.* Although there are many nouns in the first part of the sentence, all but one is used to describe specific characteristics of the subject:

factors

that have been shown to contribute to these health problems,

such as excess weight, high blood pressure, high cholesterol, sedentary lifestyle, and smoking

do respond

Danger zone 3

Why isn't *risk* the subject? Risk *can* be used as a subject, if you set your sentence up this way: The *risk* is great. Let's put it in our subject → verb equation and see if it makes sense as the subject of Amy's sentence: **risk** → *do respond.* Is the risk what responds to lifestyle changes? No. Even though *risk* can be a noun, in Amy's sentence it's used to *describe* another word. It's an adjective!

Getting subjects and verbs to agree is easy, once you know how to sort through the distractions of extra information. Just find the straight subject → verb path through the sentence and make sure the subject and verb send the same signals.

ACTIVITY 5.1: SUBJECT-VERB AGREEMENT

Part 1. Some subjects and verbs just can't get along. The subject says one thing, but the verb says another. This can get confusing to the reader!

In the sentences below, at least fifteen **subject** → **verb** paths disagree about how many people or things are doing the action of the verb. In each sentence, circle the verb and underline the subject. If subject and verb disagree, place an X next to the sentence.

Examples: <u>Susan</u> always (runs) faster than her brother.
My <u>favorite</u> kind of animal in the world (are) the marsupials. **X**

1. The toy manufacturer, despite all its quality control measures, is going to recall all its Baby Dune Buggies.

2. Nothing we do to make him happy work.

3. Neither the cat nor the rabbit were happy with the new setup.

4. What are the group going to do about all the extra snacks?

5. There is too much to accomplish in such a short period of time!

6. Out in the distance glow an eerie light, making the campers jittery.

7. The minister of internal affairs, along with several of his cabinet members, have to make that decision as soon as possible.

8. The dictionary and thesaurus are helpful tools when used properly.

9. Are the team going to the playoffs?

10. Politics are not something I enjoy discussing, even with friends.

11. A contract, along with an instruction guide and some samples, are included in this packet.

12. *The Lord of the Rings* is still one of my all-time favorite books.

13. Either Mom or one of her cousins are right about the old farmhouse.

14. Athletics of any kind, whether individual or team-oriented, are of interest to me.

15. A few of the cars in the dealership parking lot were damaged by hail.

16. Sixteen years are too long to have to work in that dump.

17. The hard work put in by all the volunteers on this project, in addition to the donations given by several generous local businesses, have helped to ensure our success.

18. Peanut butter and jelly are still my brother's favorite sandwich.

19. Our cat or the neighbor's dog like to get into the trash whenever possible.

20. Each of the teachers are helping to get me ready for the exam.

Part 2. Now go back to those sentences in Part 1 where subjects and verbs disagreed. If the verb disagrees with the subject, change it so that the two agree.

Part 3. Go back one more time to those sentences in Part 1 where subjects and verbs disagreed. This time, change the subjects so that they agree with the verbs.

Part 4. For each of the following sentences, you'll find a blank space where the verb should be. Change the verb so that it's in present tense and it agrees with the subject of the sentence.

Example: One of my friends ___goes___ to the post office for me.
                                  to go

1. Whenever my family _____ on a movie, I disagree.
                              to decide

2. The director of the company's human relations department, along with
   all his employees, _____ promised to help clean up the city.
                              to have

3. When _____ the car or van going to be ready to pick us up?
            to be

4. The two hockey players, linked by one cause, _____ to help each other.
                                                      to agree

5. Every purse, box, bag, and suitcase _____ to be scanned before it
   can be loaded onto the plane.   to have

6. A casserole made up of several different ingredients _____ picky
   eaters nervous.   to make

7. Neither my doctor nor his nurse _____ thrilled with my daredevil
   activities.   to be

8. The team, loaded up onto three buses, _____ in style.
                                              to travel

9. The news always _____ me.
                      to worry

10. "Bends" _____ a word that is used differently by divers than by most
    people.   to be

11. My friend Fareed is the person who usually _____his work done first.
                                                    to get

12. The exam, as well as your answer booklet and directions, _____ in
    your packet.   to be

13. Each car, truck, and van _____ through a ten-point inspection before it
    is put out on the lot.   to go

14. The only one of the movies that I want to see _____ sold out.
                                                      to be

15. I checked to see if the number of pieces _____ to be written on the
    outside of the box.   to need

Bonus: Look again at the **prompts** that tell you what verbs to put into each blank.
What is this form of the verb called? Hint: people often split it!

Part 5. As you read the selection below, you'll find at least ten subject-verb paths disrupted by disagreements. Locate the subject and verb for each sentence. Fix any disagreements you find. In some cases, you may need to change the subject rather than the verb in order to make the meaning of the sentence clear.

If you are planning on becoming an entrepreneur, you'll need to do some planning ahead. In today's world, a good idea and a person ready and willing to put it into action is no longer enough.

First of all, every business owner and potential entrepreneur need a business plan. If you're not sure what that is or how to write one, a number of sources are available to help you. Your local library undoubtedly has at least one book that will start you in the right direction. The Internet, along with business magazines, offer plenty of sources as well. You may even want to try a business course at your local community college.

Another important area for entrepreneurs to understand before starting their businesses are the market their businesses will be targeting. Also consider these questions: who are my competition and where does my business fit in?

If neither you nor your business partners know what a balance sheet is, that's another lesson you'll need to absorb. What do a balance sheet, as well as the numbers you'll be entering into it, mean to your company?

There are a great deal more for you to learn and understand if you plan on starting and running a successful company on your own. A person who is a savvy and ambitious entrepreneur take the time to research and plan thoroughly before climbing out into the rough and tough world of business ownership!

5.2 Writers Write: THERE IS/THERE ARE

Anna Marie Mobley

Section 5

Putting the verb before the subject can upset the reader, because it disturbs the flow of the sentence. But this is what happens when you introduce ideas with *there is* or *there are*. Look at this sentence from a paper I wrote describing how gallstones develop:

There is a drug called the ursodeoxycholic acid that prevented gallstones from forming in one clinical trial of patients on very-low-calorie diets.

Although *there* comes just before the verb, it is not the subject of this sentence. It is a signal that the subject will *follow* the verb. In this sentence, **drug**, which comes *after* the verb, is the subject, so *is* is the right form of the verb to use with it.

To determine subject-verb agreement when using *there is/there are*, rearrange the word order so that the subject comes first:

The **drug** → *is* ursodeoxycholic acid.

An even better way to present my information would be to delete *there is* altogether:

Ursodeoxycholic acid was tested in a clinical trial of patients on very-low-calorie diets. The drug was found to prevent gallstones from forming in these patients.

ACTIVITY 5.2: THERE IS/THERE ARE

Part 1. Beginning a sentence with "There is" or "There are" misses out on an opportunity to make a forceful statement or give the reader key details. Try starting a sentence with its subject! Below, you'll find ten sentences that begin with "There is" and "There are." After each sentence is the revised version, but it's missing something. Add an effective subject to each revised sentence.

Example: There is a great deal of disagreement about the way children should be disciplined.

Revision 1: <u>A great deal of disagreement</u> exists about the way children should be disciplined.

Revision 2: <u>Even the experts disagree</u> about how children should be disciplined.

1. There are too many stray cats running around our neighborhood.

   _____ are running around our neighborhood.

2. There are ten kids in that family!

   _____ has ten kids!

3. There is a street named Elson Ave. in my community.

   _____ is a street in my community.

4. There are prizes for each category.

   _____ has a prize.

5. There is endless traffic on that stretch of highway.

   _____ suffers from endless traffic.

6. There is a wild tortoise living in my backyard.

   _____ lives in my backyard.

7. There are pizza coupons on the refrigerator door.

   _____ are on the refrigerator door.

8. There are three well-known authors scheduled to speak at the conference.

    _____ are scheduled to speak at the conference.

9. There is a strange car parked in our driveway.

    _____ is parked in our driveway.

10. There is a new building going up downtown.

    _____ is going up downtown.

Part 2. For this activity, you'll have to do all the work. Rewrite each "There is" and "There are" sentence so that it begins with an effective subject.

1. There are three clients waiting for you in the lobby.
2. There is an experimental treatment that you may want to try.
3. There is a meeting going on in the conference room.
4. There are two computers waiting to be fixed.
5. There is a petition that addresses the wastewater problem in our community.
6. There are donuts for everyone on the front table.
7. There are aspiring actors and actresses who never break into the business.
8. There is an online course for students interested in this topic.
9. There is an easier way to keep track of invoices.
10. There are plenty of internships available this summer.

5.3   Writers Write: WHEN VERBS GET TENSE

Jessica Hart

It is very important to keep verb tenses stable in writing. Doing this helps the reader not to get confused about when a particular action is taking place. Conflicting verb tenses don't let the reader know which tense to choose:

> My two friends and I *were* on our way to another friend's party when something happened that *changes* all of our lives.

The first verb, *were*, is in the past: an event was in motion at a particular time, but now it's over. The second verb, *changes*, is in the present, and gives the reader the feeling that events are happening now, and likely to keep happening. Putting both verbs in the same tense will help the reader to stay focused:

My two friends and I *were* on our way to another friend's party when something happened that *changed* all of our lives.

ACTIVITY 5.3: WHEN VERBS GET TENSE

Part 1. Changing verb tenses is necessary when you want to show a shift in time. However, tense shifts for no apparent reason can really confuse your readers. A reader shouldn't have to decipher what tense to use; you (the writer) are in charge of that decision!

In the sentences below, at least ten sentences have confusing changes in verb tense. Place a U (for "Unstable") beside each sentence you find that shifts tenses for no apparent reason. Then, rewrite the sentence two different ways to make all the tenses agree. Be careful, though! We've thrown in a few sentences that contain **necessary** tense changes.

Example: All the way to work, Jermaine thought about his new apartment and whether he likes the location.

Revision 1: All the way to work, Jermaine thought about his new apartment and whether he liked the location.

Revision 2: All the way to work, Jermaine thinks about his new apartment and whether he likes the location.

1. When someone asks her to try it, she turned the offer down without hesitation.
2. Belinda thinks about the long car trip to the cabin, during which she slept in the back seat of the car.
3. After you lie on the couch for awhile, it almost seemed to become a part of you!
4. Whatever I catch, I eat.
5. Seline bit down tentatively, hoping the food was cool enough.
6. Don't go so quickly that you missed the best part of the show!
7. They did all the work they could before they head for home.
8. You'll have to prove that you paid.
9. When I have dreams, I always dreamed in bright colors.
10. The whole group swam in the deep part of the river, while the camp counselor watches for any signs of trouble.
11. Please forget that I ever mentioned it!
12. The road wound around the mountainside, and we travel on it every day.

13. So many of the butterflies come through our town each spring, we have a festival to celebrate their arrival.

14. In my letter to her, I'll write about what I wore that night.

15. Even though we want him to fix the problem, we didn't mean to hurt his feelings.

16. The pitcher was mad when the opposing team's player stole home base.

17. The shirt wasn't dry yet, even though we hang it out really early this morning.

18. I can't wait to find out if she chooses to stay or to go!

19. Be careful not to fall into the hole the backhoe left.

20. Unfortunately, Kellen draws the short straw and had to clean the bathroom.

Part 2. Below, you'll find five sentences that are waiting for a verb. Fill in the blanks with verbs that continue the time line started in the first part of each sentence. Keep the verb tenses stable within each sentence!

Example: Where did Charles go after we ＿＿＿＿＿＿ him?

Possible answer: Where did Charles go after we ＿＿left＿＿ him?

1. The whole time we watched the movie, I ＿＿＿＿＿ about dessert.

2. When you dive into the water, be careful not to ＿＿＿＿＿.

3. The beginning of the poem made sense, but then it ＿＿＿＿＿ confusing.

4. If you can stand to go back in there, can you please ＿＿＿＿＿ the telephone?

5. Quite a few of the neighborhood cats had kittens, so we ＿＿＿＿＿ to adopt one.

Part 3. In the selection you'll read below, you'll find at least ten sentences that contain confusing, messy verb tense shifts. Find them and change them to eliminate shifts in time frame. It may help to circle the first verb in each sentence, so that you can refer back to it as you make your revision.

After spending the summer working as a counselor at a camp for children with debilitating illnesses, my sister begins to think about what she wants to do with her life. She had already thought about teaching, but she wasn't sure the pay is enough to live on. Becoming a pediatric nurse might be fun, but the hours are long and the work was supposed to be very difficult.

Her summer proved to be such a rewarding experience, she had a new idea: she wants to be a physical therapist for children. It isn't a job that will make her rich, and she knows that, but she decided the rewards far outweigh the disadvantages. The kids made her smile every day, no matter how tired she gets with the physical and emotional demands of the job.

She tells me just the other day that she met some wonderful people this summer, counselors who encouraged her to follow her new dream. They believe she is well-suited for a career working with children, and each one shares with her some good ideas for how to succeed in her chosen field.

As soon as she got back from her trip, she contacted the career counselor at her university. He gave her some ideas about which courses she'll have to take in order to head in the right direction. Now she's very excited about her future, when she used to be unsure and unmotivated.

I'm so proud of my sister, and I wished I had had such an enlightening experience at her age! Instead, I wandered through three different jobs before finding the one I want to stick with. What a difference a summer job can make!

Part 4. Teamwork. With the members of your group, reread the passage you just revised in Part 3. You might find that the problem with unstable verb tense has affected the whole piece of writing! **Make a list** of the kinds of decisions you had to make to eliminate each shift in verb tense. Then, use the specific examples on your list to answer these questions:

Did the meaning of the sentence or paragraph change depending on how you decided to deal with the shift in verb tense?

What did eliminating shifts in time order (verb tense) do to the overall feel or tone of the paragraph?

Part 5. The next five sentences are just fine the way they are, but we're going to play with them anyway. If a sentence is written in present tense, rewrite it so that all the verbs are in past tense. If a sentence is already in past tense, switch it back to present tense. Be careful not to introduce verb tense shifts when you change tenses!

Example: The weather is so nice, I think I'll take a walk.

Revision: The weather was so nice, I thought I'd take a walk.

1. While she wrote the words she had to, she thought about what she really wanted to say.
2. If you change your mind, you know where to find me!
3. What do you think you're doing?
4. Making that last phone call was the most difficult thing she'd had to do all day.
5. To have to choose one over the other is pure torture for me.

5.4 Writers Write: PRONOUNS THAT SHIFT IN THE NIGHT

Wahkeisha Murchison

Pronouns need to agree with, or send the same message as, the nouns or pronouns they replace:

> Job interviews make *people* reveal *their* character quirks.
>
> Job interviews make *you* reveal *your* character quirks.
>
> Job interviews make *an applicant* reveal *his or her* character quirks.

Mixing pronouns in strange ways is unfortunately easy to do. Most of us have particular trouble making pronouns agree with words like *everyone* and *anyone*.

Here's one example I wrote in a paper about interviewing for a job:

> Before *anyone* can make a great impression on the employer, *they* must first find someone who is willing to interview *you*.

My readers were very confused! Who wants to make an impression on the employer? Who is the mysterious *they*? Why would *they* interview *you*? I tried two revisions:

Revision 1.

> Before *a person* can make a great impression on the employer, *he or she* must first find someone who is willing to grant an interview.

This revision keeps the idea of *anyone* (any one) and eliminates the specific mention of *who* will be interviewed.

Revision 2.

> Before *you* can make a great impression on the employer, you must first find an employer who is willing to interview *you*.

This revision is more conversational. It speaks directly to my audience *(you)*, allowing me to use the same pronoun throughout the sentence.

ACTIVITY 5.4: PRONOUN SHIFTS

Part 1. Sometimes it's difficult to make a pronoun "match" the noun or pronoun it replaces. Unfortunately, if the pronouns and nouns in a sentence are mixed up, the reader is left wondering what exactly the author is trying to say!

At least 10 of the following sentences contain pronouns that do not agree with the words they are meant to replace. First, circle all the pronouns you find. Draw arrows to the words they refer back to. Underline each sentence where the pronouns don't agree.

1. Hilary decided not to go to her school's matriculation ceremony.

2. Everyone is allowed to make their own decision about whether or not to attend.

3. Students who don't want to attend will really miss out on an important part of her lives.

4. She told her English professor why you didn't feel like going.

5. Dr. Witherspoon was understanding, but she tried to offer Hilary some reasons for going to the ceremony.

6. First of all, a student might never again have the opportunity to go to their matriculation.

7. Secondly, matriculation might be a good place for Hilary to add to her group of friends.

8. Finally, one could only attend the dinner afterward if she had been at the ceremony.

9. After her discussion with Dr. Witherspoon, Hilary decided I had better give the issue some serious thought.

10. It seemed like any student who missed the ceremony might really regret his or her decision.

11. Her friend Annika helped Hilary make her decision.

12. Annika insisted that she would save Hilary a seat at the ceremony.

13. The two young women looked beautiful in their summer dresses as she walked through the commons area toward the general meeting hall.

14. Sitting down, Hilary and Annika noticed the professors, all dressed in their collegiate regalia, up on the dais.

15. There was an air of excitement all through the hall, as if the college knew their students were embarking on a thrilling adventure.

16. When the Dean of Students stood up to speak, everyone stopped talking and focused our eyes on the podium.

17. In a flash, the ceremony was finished; it had been short but meaningful.

18. The students seemed to enjoy their special matriculation dinner of steak, salad, and baked potatoes.

19. Hilary thanked Dr. Witherspoon and Annika for helping her to make the decision to attend the ceremony.

20. She now knew that any student who had not attended this once-in-a-lifetime event should regret their decision.

Part 2. Teamwork. With the members of your group, go back through sentences 1–20. Rewrite the sentences you underlined in Part 1 so that there's no confusion between pronouns and the words they're supposed to match.

Part 3. Here's a selection that is missing some pronouns. In order to decide which pronoun is needed to fill in each blank, you'll have to first look at the noun or pronoun it's replacing. Then fill in the appropriate pronoun. After you've finished, read the passage to yourself to be sure you've matched nouns and pronouns effectively.

Do you have a severe food allergy, or do you know someone who does? Do you have to check the labels on _____ food before you can eat? The Food and Drug Administration (FDA) recently conducted an investigation of manufacturers to find out if _____ labeled their food products properly. Certain ingredients, known to be potentially fatal allergens, were not listed on the products of approximately 25% of the manufacturers investigated.

Common allergens such as peanuts and eggs have been listed on labels less and less in recent years, even though as many as seven million Americans suffer severe allergic reactions when _____ eat products containing those ingredients. Imagine checking labels carefully to be sure that you are safe, only to find yourself in the hospital because _____ food was mislabeled! You would have to pay hospital bills and miss days of work. Depending on the severity of your allergy, you might even be lucky to be alive!

The FDA, trying to prevent this kind of carelessness in food production, studied 85 companies. The companies that were investigated used common allergens, such as nuts, as ingredients in _____ products. Even though it's a simple thing to check each product's label to be sure that all the ingredients used in _____ production are listed, only about half of the 85 companies actually did. Just checking one label from each type of product could save lives!

Part of the problem is that many people, including those in charge of manufacturing the foods we eat, are unaware that allergies can be fatal. Some people are so allergic to peanuts that _____ can't even eat food that contains peanut residue; just a tiny bit of contaminated product could cause a person's death within minutes. A company that bakes its sugar cookies on the same tray that held peanut butter cookies, for example, is putting some of _____ customers at grave risk.

Another problem is that under current FDA regulations, product labels don't have to include trace amounts of "natural" ingredients that may go into certain foods. This means cross-contamination from one type of food in a factory to another in the same factory remains hidden from consumers. Since changing regulations takes years, the FDA is working to convince manufacturers to change _____ standards voluntarily. If you're a person who must check labels in order to stay healthy, this information may be vital to _____ health.

Part 4. Sometimes pronouns in one sentence refer back to words used in a previous sentence. Readers can get lost in a paragraph of shifting pronouns! Below, you'll find ten sentences. Your job is to write *the sentence that comes next.* Your sentence should contain at least one pronoun that refers back to the information in the first sentence.

Example:

Given sentence: Elaine wasn't too thrilled when she found out about the assignment.

Your sentence: Her professor had decided each student should write a 10-page paper.

The second sentence continues the idea begun by the first sentence, and it uses a pronoun (Her) to continue talking about the original noun (Elaine).

1. Janine, Tim, Kahlil, and I went to the beach.
2. The company changed its hiring policy in May.
3. Meningitis and encephalitis often have similar symptoms.
4. Yesterday, the phone just wouldn't stop ringing!
5. The meteorologist for our local television news is predicting a cold front.
6. Yvette and Hunter met at a coffee shop to study.
7. Unfortunately, the key broke off in its lock.
8. I thought I spotted a tornado just a few miles away.
9. You'll have to ask about the newspaper.
10. Chris ran two stoplights on the way to school!

Part 5. Teamwork. Now, share the sentences you wrote in Part 4 with the members of your group. What kinds of situations did each of you write about in your follow-up sentences? Pick one situation (for example, the predicted storm, the broken key, or Chris's driving escapades) and compare your ideas about what would happen next. Write a paragraph using everyone's ideas. The bigger the differences among your ideas, the more fun you'll have making them all fit together in a believable sequence of events!

5.5   Pronoun referents

JASON LITKA

He begins to regret his decision immediately after.

Read alone, this sentence makes sense: a man begins to regret his own decision. But, what if my previous sentence mentioned *two* men, like this:

Mr. Richards and the Reverend Smithers plan to host the community outreach. He begins to regret his decision immediately after.

The reader could be confused about who *he* is referring to in the second sentence. Does Reverend Smithers regret *Mr. Richards's* decision? Does either of the men regret his own decision?

To leave no doubt about who exactly is regretting whose decision, I revised the second sentence:

Mr. Richards begins to regret *his* own decision immediately after.

ACTIVITY 5.5: PRONOUN REFERENTS

Part 1. Writers have to be careful when using pronouns such as *he, she, him, her, it, you, they,* and *them.* Each pronoun replaces its **referent**--a word that has appeared previously in the passage. If the reader isn't sure which word the pronoun refers back to, communication between writer and reader breaks down.

Example. Pat told Mick he wanted to order flowers for their mother, but he wasn't sure whether to order roses or lilies.

Who wasn't sure, Pat or Mick? Only the writer knows!

Revision: Pat and Mick wanted to order flowers for their mother. Pat wasn't sure whether to order roses or lilies, so he asked Mick.

Now it's clear to both the writer <u>and</u> the reader who he is.

Activity. Let's look at some pronouns and their referents in action.

Step 1. Underline the pronouns in each sentence. Circle the noun or pronoun that it is supposed to be replacing (its **referent**.)

Step 2. If it's not clear which word a pronoun refers to, write a question that asks for the information you need.

Step 3. Place an X beside each sentence in which the pronoun referent isn't clear to the reader.

Example: Susie and Minna had just gotten back from their walk when <u>she</u> got a phone call. X (Who got the phone call?)

1. Paolina told Lisa that she was too smart to make such a mistake.
2. Only Jacqueline said she had the information.
3. Why would the boys change their minds so quickly?
4. We saw a brochure of that new HIV study; it's very thorough.
5. I hurried to change the station on my radio.
6. We got the hinge replaced and installed a doggie door, but it came loose almost immediately.
7. In the play we saw last night, they make it seem like all people are callous and self-serving.
8. Alec and Roger both knew he would go ahead and try the jump.
9. Jamie ate every bite of the awful stuff; he even came back for more!
10. Even though the storm had scared the kids, it hadn't done any real damage.
11. We ate chicken parmesan and drank some kind of Italian lemon drink, which was really good.
12. Henry and Jack ate all his candy in one afternoon.
13. Watching the kittens fall over their littermates at the pet store was hilarious.
14. At the neighborhood pool, they try to have at least three lifeguards on duty at all times.
15. Despite the size of the box, it wasn't really heavy.
16. After the guest lecturer had finished speaking, she answered several questions from the audience.
17. After spending the entire dinner party talking to Sam and Alfie about the stock market, Sarah decided not to take his advice.

18. Talullah was obviously not willing to help either Marie or Jill; instead, she offered the two women the phone number of a physics tutor.

19. After cleaning the pine needles out of the house's gutters, Teresa and Clem complained that they never wanted to see another pine tree.

20. Jordan won't admit to any mistakes, even though it's true.

Part 2. Now, revise the ten faulty sentences you've just identified. When you're finished, each pronoun should clearly refer back to one particular noun or pronoun in the sentence.

Part 3. Let's put it all together. In this activity, you'll need to find the word that each pronoun refers back to in the sentence. If you find it, underline it. If you can't find that word (or if it really doesn't match), revise the sentence so that the reader can easily make the connection between the two words.

Once a person develops osteoporosis, they really can't do anything to stop the bones from degenerating, right? That used to be true, but at least one new drug has been developed to fight osteoporosis, and doctors are talking about it.

About 10 million Americans suffer from the effects of osteoporosis, and they need to be treated. Of course, people who include a healthy amount of calcium in the foods they eat are doing their best to prevent osteoporosis. What happens, though, when calcium is not enough? Eating more spinach and drinking more milk won't help the patients who have already begun to experience bone deterioration; they aren't able to stop the damage. Something more is needed.

The first drugs developed were aimed at reducing the fracture rate among osteoporosis patients. The success of these drugs meant that many patients who might have been wheelchair-bound for the rest of their lives were able to walk again; they were surprisingly successful. Still, no one had quite figured out how to do more than preserve the existing bone. With treatments, they could stop the degeneration, but improving bone density was still out of reach.

Now, bone regeneration is a possibility. Scientists have known for a long time about a hormone produced naturally by the human body; it regulates the balance of calcium. After many years of trying, they've finally figured out how to produce this hormone synthetically. Patients who receive this synthetic hormone can now look forward to stronger bones; they will be able to handle normal daily activities without risking dangerous fractures.

Try to imagine yourself an elderly woman with osteoporosis, living a life of constant fear. Each time you bump against a piece of furniture and each time you trip over an object or a step, you endanger your bones; it might mean a trip to the hospital with another broken hip or collarbone. You could even find yourself fighting for your life, due to complications from surgery. Now imagine that you can take a pill that will allow you to live a normal, active life. Thanks to years of research, millions of osteoporosis patients will soon be able to live this dream.

Part 4. Teamwork: Writing an explanation. Grammar books say that pronouns have to agree in **case**, **number**, and **gender**. Look up these grammatical terms and discuss them with your team members until you understand why grammar books point out these differences. Then talk about how you might explain them to a friend who just doesn't "get" grammatical terms. Together, write a script in which you 1) explain each term and 2) give examples *without using any grammatical terms*. Good luck!

5.6   Misplaced and dangling modifiers

A **modifier** is a word, phrase, or clause that modifies (changes, alters, or mutates) another word, phrase, or clause. When modifiers don't connect clearly to the words they describe, they're called **dangling** or **misplaced modifiers**. They can conjure up interesting mental images, like this one:

Example: Bill touched the strange substance to his tongue, which was dry and crumbled easily. Poor Bill!

Modifiers should stick close to the words they want to change, transform, add information to, or describe. Modifiers in awkward places can brighten your day with their unintentional humor. Watch for them as wrong answers on standardized tests for a good laugh in a tense situation!

Here are three ways to fix a sentence that contains a dangling modifier:

1. Move the modifier closer to the word or phrase that it's supposed to be modifying.

Example: Ellie wore her pajamas all day Saturday around the house.

Ellie wore her pajamas around the house all day Saturday.

2. Change the subject of the main clause so that it matches its modifier.

Example: Not wanting to offend his new friend, the topic of religion was avoided.

Not wanting to offend his new friend, Brent avoided the topic of religion.

3. Turn a dangling modifier into a complete clause.

Example: While waiting for the bus, a stray cat caught Alathea's eye.

While Alathea was waiting for the bus, a stray cat caught her eye.

Now let's look at some examples contributed by students.

JOE CRISAFULLI

When I wrote my movie review, I explained the plot in the introduction, which was frightening.

The question here, of course, is what, exactly, was frightening: the plot or Joe's introduction? To clarify things, Joe put his modifier closer to the word he wanted to describe:

When I wrote my movie review, I explained the plot (*which was frightening*) in the introduction.

JESSICA SULLIVAN

The dog was adopted by a small child *with black fur.*

Does this sound strange? It should! It paints the picture of a tiny, furry child! The modifier *with black fur* is too far away from *dog*, the word it's meant to change or give information about. Let's try that again:

The *dog with black fur* was adopted by a small child.

The second example isn't nearly as strange, but it's more accurate, we hope.

ACTIVITY 5.6: UN-DANGLING YOUR MODIFIERS

Part 1. When modifiers don't connect clearly to the words they describe, they're called **dangling** or **misplaced modifiers.** They can conjure up interesting mental images, like this one:

Example: Joan grasped the fence rail with her right leg, which was old and starting to sag.

Poor Joan!

In the folllowing sentences, look for modifiers in odd places. Underline each of these modifiers, and draw an arrow to the word the writer was *trying* to describe.

1. Never having owned a pet, the dog was the perfect gift for my friend Mike.
2. Every student has to write this paper with a major in political science.
3. The lady was looking for her car in the black suit.
4. Very loud birds, our building swarmed with grackles.
5. To change the tire, the car had to be jacked up.
6. After eating a heart-clogging, fat-rich meal, coconut pie was served for dessert.
7. Marcie had to fill out a questionnaire that took her 25 minutes about her eating habits.
8. Afraid to miss our own awards ceremony, the car seemed the only place to change our clothes on the way downtown.
9. Holding his nose, the odor became bearable for Harold.
10. Ricky's car alarm went off while eating dinner.
11. Sitting in the movie theater, Carol's cell phone rang.
12. By running a little faster, the ice cream truck came into Silvio's view.
13. Did you see a big dog running by here with floppy ears?
14. Slowly blinking out, Josie watched the library lights room by room.
15. As he broke into a gallop, Jared praised the horse.
16. After popping strangely, we watched the dishwasher silently overflow.
17. Heaving and belching sulphur, the researchers rushed to escape the erupting volcano.
18. Huge and empty, the cat ran through the open door into the lot next door.
19. To train the puppies, the floor needed to be protected.
20. Having gone to bed early, the alarm clock didn't really bother us.
21. By eating dinner early, the game wasn't missed.
22. Short on time, the museum trip had to be cancelled.
23. Before moving into our new dorm room, cleaning supplies had to be purchased.
24. On returning to the dig site, ceremonial pots were discovered in some of the grids.
25. Racing against the clock, lunch was abandoned so we could finish the presentation before the clients arrived.
26. Upon viewing the art exhibit, Martin's paintings were praised by an illustrator from D.C. comics.

27. Never imagining the earth could buckle and shift so terribly, the earthquake caught us totally unprepared.

28. We stopped at the petting zoo before we went home, which was the most popular attraction at the carnival.

29. Boring, pointless, and irritating, the task force voted to boycott the new training sessions.

30. Having already read the manual twice, the lieutenant's exam wouldn't be a problem for Jase.

31. As a paramedic, dozens of cases had been handled by Abe.

32. Running late for Grand Rounds, the shortcut through the morgue looked like the best choice to George.

33. After closing up the store, the money went to the bank for the nightly deposit.

34. On the hood of his new car, Jim examined a long, torturous scratch.

35. At age four, my favorite aunt taught me to read.

36. With drooping eyes and a pen that had run out of ink, the meeting seemed interminable.

37. Leaving the clinic after dark, the late meeting posed a safety problem for the on-call psychologists.

38. Although bruised and bleeding, the fall from the cliff only strengthened Shawn's determination to make it to the top.

39. While considering her options, a bowl of ice cream mysteriously disappeared into Leti's interior.

40. Dark and damp, Steve crept further into the cave.

Part 2. Teamwork. What's Wrong with this Picture? Look back at the dangling or misplaced modifiers you identified in Part 1. For each item, write what the next sentence would be. Then tell *why* you think that's what the next sentence should be.

Example: The shielding was designed to protect the crew and their faithful robot, which disintegrated upon reentry.

Next sentence: An official investigation was launched into the robot's sudden disappearance. (The modifier says that the *robot* disintegrated!)

Part 3. Revising. Now that you've seen the havoc that dangling and misplaced modifiers can cause, let's go back and revise those struggling sentences you've been working with. Using the methods described below, rewrite the problem sentences you identified in Part 1. Here are three ways to fix a sentence that contains a dangling or misplaced modifier. Try all three with each sentence you revise.

1. **Move the modifier closer to the word or phrase that it's supposed to be modifying.**

Example: Ellie wore her pajamas all day Saturday around the house.

> *Ellie wore her pajamas around the house all day Saturday.*

2. **Change the subject of the main clause so that it "matches" its modifier.**

Example: Not wanting to offend his new friend, the topic of religion was avoided.

> *Not wanting to offend his new friend, Brent avoided the topic of religion.*

3. **Specify a speaker or actor within the phrase.**

Example: While waiting for the bus, a stray cat caught Alathea's eye.

> *While Alathea was waiting for the bus, a stray cat caught her eye.*

Part 4. Teamwork. With your group, compare the sentences you wrote for Parts 2 and 3. Has the meaning changed? Now, write the sentence that would probably come next for the sentences you *revised* for Part 3. Tell how the meaning has changed.

Example:

Problem sentence: Joan grasped the fence rail with her right leg, which was old and starting to sag.

Revision: With her right leg, Joan grasped the fence rail, which was old and starting to sag.

Next sentence: She grabbed a branch overhead just as the rotten wood gave way beneath her. (The fence, not her leg, was starting to sag.)

Part 5. Within the passage written below, you'll find 15 dangling or misplaced modifiers. Underline each one you find, then rewrite the selection. When you're finished, all modifiers should be placed clearly next to the words they describe.

Do you consider chocolate a main course? Are you the kind of person who eats dessert foods for breakfast? If these descriptions apply to you, read on to learn the possible root of your sweet tooth.

Scientists have identified a gene found in both mice and people that may be responsible for sweetness detection. To be sure that the identified gene and the sweetness receptor really are connected, more research is needed. Still, the evidence is hard to dispute. More than one group of researchers has made the connection studying the same gene. The results of these studies this spring will be published in at least two different research journals.

Having made this initial discovery, the "sweetness gene" in the studies isn't believed to be the only one. To detect sweetness in our food, scientists believe we have more than one gene. Different "sweetness genes" might be geared toward different types of sweet foods. It's also possible that having different versions of a gene could mean that one person is more sensitive to sweetness than another. By following through with studies on these genes, there may be a link between how sweetness receptors vary and how weight gain differs among people.

While continuing their research on how we detect sweetness, studies are also being conducted with regard to salty and sour tastes. In researching our taste buds, genes for bitter taste receptors have been located; receptors for a taste called umami have probably been located which taste foods rich in protein or monosodium glutamate.

By keeping up with this kind of research, the inner workings of our bodies can be revealed to us. You don't even have to read all those challenging research journals; to find out all the newest discoveries, your daily newspaper is an excellent resource.

Now that you know it's possible to trace your sweet tooth back to genetics, who will you blame for your inability to pass up a slice of cheesecake? Is it Mom, Dad, or Uncle Jed who gave you the gene that's ruined every diet you've ever tried? After giving it some thought, the idea of being able to pass off your sugar habit on an unsuspecting relative might not seem fair. Still, it's almost as tempting as that last piece of cake, isn't it?

5.7 Writers Write: CONJUNCTIONS

Baridilo Kponi

Subordinating conjunctions show relationships between related ideas. **Coordinating conjunctions** connect words, phrases, and clauses. I used both in the same sentence in my paper on American marriage customs:

> *Although* American divorces vary from state to state, *but* there are common rules in each of the states.

Since the two words are alike in meaning, I should have used only one of them. Here are some possible revisions that would keep the flow of my writing:

Revision 1. *Although* American divorces vary from state to state, there are common rules in each of the states.

Here, the reader would like to read the remaining sentence because the use of *although* shows the sentence is not yet completed.

Revision 2. American divorces vary from state to state, *but* there are common rules in each of the states.

This version connects two complete sentences (independent clauses). I used *but* to show contrast between the two equal segments.

Revision 3. American divorces vary from state to state; there are common rules in each one.

The last version uses a semicolon to connect two complete sentences (independent clauses) without causing a comma splice or a run-on.

Editor's note: You can use conjunctions to create special effects for your readers:

Raise your readers' expectations: *although, if, unless, while, if only, as if*

Signal a change: *however, at the same time, even if, in contrast, in spite of, instead, nevertheless, on the other hand, otherwise, though, whether*

Reveal a mystery: *because, now that, since, as a result, consequently, if this is true*

Promise detail or add information: *that, which, who, such as, whose, in order that, as though, so that, also, another, for example, for instance, further, in addition, in fact, moreover, finally, to sum up*

Indicate location or sequence: *above, across from, adjacent to, before, below, behind, beside, beyond, in front of, inside, in the distance, nearby, next to, on the left, on the right, opposite to, to one side, to the front, to the rear, after, again, as a result, at last, at the same time, before, during, finally, first, last, next, now that, once, second, then, until*

ACTIVITY 5.7: CONJUNCTIONS

Part 1. Read the following sentences. In each sentence, underline the conjunctions. Then, for each sentence that contains a dependent (subordinate) clause, write an **S** above the subordinating conjunction. For each sentence that contains an independent clause, write a **C** above the coordinating conjunction. Remember, the subordinating conjunction may be a phrase, such as *by the time*.

S

Example: <u>Unless</u> my paycheck gets a lot bigger, I'm not going to be able to afford a new car.

1. When the sun sets, take a look at the mountains.
2. We'll get an invitation, provided she doesn't forget.
3. I wanted to ask about his parents, but I didn't want to make him sad.
4. Since everyone left early, cleanup was easy.
5. Jay said he had the flu, yet he played touch football.
6. I don't have any enemies, nor do I intend to make any.
7. Before I ran in the five-kilometer race, I intended to try a marathon.
8. They'll have to ask permission, and there's a good chance they won't get it.
9. While everyone else ate lunch, the hostess prepared dessert.
10. The nearest grocery store was ten miles away, so Blaine decided he really didn't need the strawberries.

Part 2. In the paragraphs below, you'll read sentences containing either coordinating or subordinating conjunctions. After **identifying** the type of conjunction in each sentence, **change** the sentences with coordinating conjunctions so that they contain subordinating conjunctions. Sentences that contain subordinating conjunctions must be changed so that they use coordinating conjunctions. You'll have to do some rearranging; it won't be enough, for example, to simply change *or* into *although*. Note: There are at least ten sentences for you to revise.

Example: Despite my resistance to the idea of taking the class, it turned out to be enjoyable.

Revision: I was resistant to the idea of taking the class, but it turned out to be enjoyable.

We all know that kids are spending more time inside these days, but do we really understand all the negative side effects of this behavior? Since video games and television shows became more of a magnet for children, parents have found it easier to keep them inside, safe from busy streets and bad guys. Many children are in daycare situations until late evening, and they may have little or no time outside during the week.

Researchers have warned parents about the potential for seriously over-weight children, yet children continue to experience most of their waking hours inside one building or another. Obesity, however, is not the only health problem that can result from decreased outdoor play. Before simply enrolling their children in gymnastics to help them stay in shape, parents should be aware that more and more children are suffering from rickets. Most readers, I'm sure, are now asking themselves, "Isn't rickets a disease that's disappeared?" We don't remember reading or hearing about rickets occurring in our era, nor do we understand how it could possibly be a problem. After all, ours is a society that has all but eliminated smallpox and tuberculosis; even measles and chicken pox are rare these days.

Because rickets is caused by a deficiency of vitamin D, we need to look at how a body gets its fair share of that vitamin. One source of vitamin D is milk, but many children are now drinking substitutes made from soy and other products. As sunlight stimulates our bodies to produce vitamin D, spending time outside is another way to avoid rickets. Exposure to sunlight, however, increases a person's risk for skin cancer, so doctors are inclined to recommend that the need for vitamin D be met nutritionally.

If your child is indoors for most of each week, consider your family's eating habits. Should more vitamin D be on your table?

Part 3. For this next activity, you'll need to revisit the first two activities in this section.

Step 1. Make two lists, one consisting of the coordinating conjunctions found in the previous sentences, the other made up of the subordinating conjunctions used. You should find at least fifteen conjunctions in all.

Coordinating	Subordinating
but	unless

Step 2. Choose three subordinating conjunctions and two coordinating conjunctions from the lists you've just compiled. Write a sentence for each conjunction. Your sentences should be about what you ate today.

5.8   What are gerunds and infinitives?

Some forms of verbs can be used as nouns! **Infinitives** combine the simple form of a verb with *to*: *to walk, to eat, to spend*. **Gerunds** use the *-ing* form of verbs: *swimming, stretching, living*. Both gerunds and infinitives can be used in the same ways nouns can:

I need *to think*. (infinitive)

Swimming is my favorite vacation sport. (gerund)

Since *–ing* words are also used as adjectives and, of course, as verbs, you have to really look at what a word is doing in order to identify it as a gerund. Here are some examples of the different ways an *–ing* word might be used in a sentence:

Example 1: My sister is *teaching* her son to swim. VERB

Example 2: They practice at the *teaching* pool at the local YMCA. ADJECTIVE

Example 3: My sister says that *teaching* him to swim is not easy. NOUN/GERUND

ACTIVITY 5.8: WHAT ARE GERUNDS?

Part 1. Can verbs ever be nouns? Surprise! They can! When writers use the **–ing** form of a verb as a **noun**, it's called a **gerund.** Since **–ing** words are also used as adjectives and, of course, verbs, you have to do some serious thinking about what a word is doing in order to identify it.

You'll find **–ing** words in all of the sentences written for this activity, but not all of them are gerunds. First, underline each **–ing** word you find. Next, decide whether it is used as a noun, an adjective, or a verb. Last, write a **G** beside each sentence in which the **–ing** word you underlined is a gerund.

1. I shouldn't have worn my jogging shorts to the store.
2. The manager was closing the store just as we arrived.
3. Wrestling is still a very popular sport.
4. I did a double-take at the sight of the coyote streaking down my street.
5. Jared can't stand shopping, unless he's in an electronics store.
6. Maggie jumped out of her sleeping bag as though it were full of ants.
7. After all the yard work we'd done that weekend, painting didn't seem so bad.
8. Instead of the carefully crafted words I'd written, the printer was spewing out papers covered with odd symbols.
9. Grinning, the two boys confessed to their misdeeds.
10. Singing in the shower has always been one of my favorite activities of the day.

Part 2. Each of the following sentences has a blank that needs a gerund. Be creative as you come up with gerunds that will effectively, maybe even humorously, finish the sentences.

Example:

I've always loved _____.

Possible answer:

I've always loved _____eating_____.

1. Let me warn you that Russell is not fond of _____.
2. _____ under the hot summer sun is pure torture.
3. Raquelle wanted to try _____, so she took lessons.
4. After plenty of research, I decided that _____ was not for me.
5. If you don't like _____, maybe you should try swimming for exercise.
6. _____ can be extremely difficult if you're not feeling creative.
7. Of all the things on my "To Do" list, _____ has been postponed the most times.
8. After _____ on one foot for 10 minutes proved too difficult, Danae decided not to take on any more ridiculous challenges.
9. _____ is, not surprisingly, against the law.
10. Anyone who thinks _____ is easy has never tried it.

Part 3. For the next activity, you'll need to move your creativity up another notch. First, change each verb into its **–ing** form, then use it as a gerund in a sentence.

Example: cry

Possible answer: (crying) Crying makes me nervous.

1. run
2. float
3. decorate
4. play
5. wait
6. write
7. sew
8. hit
9. clean
10. dance

Section 5

5.9   Split infinitives

MATT BUTLER

When a writer places a word in between the word *to* and its verb, the result is called a **split infinitive**. Here's an example I accidentally wrote in a personal narrative:

> My job for the moment is **to** *just* **cruise** the United States in a Mustang painted chrome yellow.

The way I wrote this sentence makes the word *just* into a verb! While most of my readers would still get my meaning, splitting an infinitive like this makes the sentence sound awkward. Here's one way to rewrite the sentence:

> My job for the moment is *just* **to cruise** the United States in a Mustang painted chrome yellow.

I could actually leave the word *just* out and the sentence would sound *just* fine.

Editor's Note: As long as you keep the two parts of the infinitive together, you can place additional words *before* or *after* the infinitive:

We decided **to speak** *boldly*.

We decided *boldly* **to speak**.

Each arrangement of words makes the sentence take on a slightly different emphasis. In the first sentence, we will *speak* boldly. In the second sentence, our *decision* was bold.

Let's look at the subtle changes in meaning that you can signal as you revise split infinitives:

Revision 1. Place the descriptive word *in front of* the infinitive.

Split: to **compassionately** talk

Example: The caseworker tried compassionately to talk to the scared girl.

This placement says that the caseworker's *attempt* to talk to the girl was an act of kindness.

Revision 2. Now, put the descriptive word *after* the infinitive in your sentence.

Example: The caseworker tried to talk compassionately to the scared girl.

This placement says that the caseworker's *talk* was kind. It implies that she had some trouble doing this! She *tried* to talk compassionately, but it was an effort.

Revision 3. In this version, place the descriptive word *at the very beginning* of the sentence.

Example: Compassionately, the caseworker tried to talk to the scared girl.

This placement hints that both the *attempt* to talk to the girl, and the *way* the caseworker talked, was kind.

Revision 4. Rewrite the sentence without the descriptive word.

Example: The caseworker tried to talk to the scared girl.

This version gives basic information about *what* the caseworker did, but it doesn't add any detail about *how* she did it. Was she angry? Scared? Bored? We don't know. This sentence also implies that maybe the caseworker didn't actually talk to the girl--she only tried.

ACTIVITY 5.9: SPLIT INFINITIVES

Part 1. When a writer places a word in between the word **to** and its **verb**, the result is called a split infinitive. Although split infinitives pop up all the time in conversation and in informal writing like advertisements, they're not welcome in college or professional writing.

Of the ten sentences below, at least five contain split infinitives. After identifying a split infinitive within a sentence, underline the word that separates the two parts of the infinitive. Then read the sentence to yourself without that separating word. Was that word really necessary? Try putting the word in different places in the sentence. Where would it work best?

Split: Joyce decided to quickly run to the store.

Revisions: Joyce decided *quickly* to run to the store.

Joyce decided to run to the store.

Joyce decided to run *quickly* to the store.

Joyce *quickly* decided to run to the store.

Joyce decided to run to the store *quickly*.

In this case, the last version of the sentence is probably best, but of course, that depends on what message the author is trying to send the reader.

Now try it yourself! (Note: If you absolutely have to, you may dispense with the infinitive form of the verb altogether.)

1. After practice, the coach told us to not come to the game late.
2. It's best to quietly watch the pandas.
3. She always wanted to just eat the cookie parts.
4. Last night, I made an effort to carefully watch what I ate after six o'clock.
5. At first glance, the kids seemed to happily be playing on the swings.
6. This spring, that tree appeared to suddenly come to life.
7. What a surprise to almost eat a bug!
8. My goal is to possibly lose 25 pounds.
9. In the past few days, the car has tried to pathetically sputter to a halt twice.
10. Can you help me to safely get to my car tonight?

Part 2. In the following paragraph, at least ten infinitives have been split apart by other words. By removing or moving the other words, revise any splits you find.

Would you like to soon see fat cells help rather than frustrate people? You may be in luck. Researchers hope to strategically place fat cells in damaged areas of our bodies in order to actually repair them. In experiments conducted at three different universities, stem cells from fat have been used to surprisingly create new bone, cartilage, and muscle in laboratory animals. The fat used to carefully harvest the stem cells came from liposuctions, which means that researchers have an almost unlimited supply of fat to draw from!

Stem cells, the kind of cells taken from the fat, are amazing in that they are so primitive; thus, a stem cell has the potential to practically become any type of tissue the body might need. Stem cells are useful in so many different ways, both for researchers and for doctors, that having a plentiful source is very important. Believe it or not, the fat we want to gladly toss into the trash is worth a lot of money to scientists!

In about five years, researchers will be able to hopefully begin using humans in the first clinical trials of this new study. At that time, we'll get to finally enjoy our fat cells. Would you be willing to bravely be one of the first humans to really benefit from this groundbreaking research?

Part 3. Now that we've edited the split infinitives in someone else's work, let's work with them in our own. Each item below is an infinitive split by a descriptive word. Using the steps below, write sentences that experiment with placing the descriptor in different places. How does the **place** you put the descriptive word change the **meaning**?

1. to quietly enjoy
2. to happily offer
3. to gently convince
4. to often fool
5. to usually have
6. to sweetly tell
7. to matter-of-factly eat
8. to partly change
9. to confidently contact
10. to mostly please

Step 1. Place the descriptive word *in front of* the infinitive. What does your sentence mean?

Example: to daily open

The owner of the deli planned daily to open his restaurant at 10 a.m.

This placement makes it sound like the owner planned every day**.**

Step 2. Place the descriptive word *after* the infinitive in your sentence. Does this change the meaning?

Example: The owner of the deli planned to open his restaurant daily at 10 a.m.

This placement makes it clear that *daily* gives us more information about when the restaurant will *open*.

Step 3. Place the descriptive word *at the very beginning* of the sentence. What does this do to the meaning of the sentence?

Example: Daily, the owner of the deli planned to open his restaurant.

Like the first example, this placement makes it sound like the owner *planned* daily.

Step 4. *Remove* the descriptive word entirely. What happens then?

The owner of the deli planned to open his restaurant at 10 a.m.

Removing the descriptive word changes the meaning of the sentence. Opening at 10:00 a.m. no longer sounds like a routine. We may be talking about one particular day that's different from the rest.

Part 4. Teamwork. Now let's think a bit more about how the **place** you put the descriptive word changes the **meaning** of the sentence. Read the sentences you wrote for Part 2 to the other members of your group. Together, imagine what the next sentence would be.

Examples:

Descriptor placed before the infinitive: The owner of the deli planned daily to open his restaurant at 10 a.m. Every day, late deliveries thwarted his plan.

Descriptor placed after the infinitive: The owner of the deli planned to open his restaurant daily at 10 a.m. Opening late would miss the before-work crowd, but would be the perfect time for students on their way to classes at the university.

Descriptor placed at the beginning of the sentence: Daily, the owner of the deli planned to open his restaurant at 10:00 a.m. Red tape made him postpone his plan time after time.

Descriptor removed: The owner of the deli planned to open his restaurant at 10:00 a.m. However, the bank robbery across the street kept the deli closed until long after lunch.

Part 5. Tiered team project. Why do we split infinitives?

People split infinitives all the time in everyday conversation. Why is this? Let's find out!

Step 1. With your group, look back at the split infinitives you encountered in Parts 1, 2, 3, and 4. **Make a list** of the words that you had to remove to bring split infinitives back together. Using this list, answer these questions:

What do these words *do* in the sentence?

Does grammar have a name for these kinds of words?

Does moving these words to another position in the sentence make it easier or harder for these words to do their function?

What would happen if you left the words out (used *only* to + a verb)?

Step 2. Now that we know what kinds of words make infinitives split, let's think about why writers use them. Look at the different versions of the sentences you wrote in Parts 3 and 4. Each version asks you to put the descriptive word in a different place. How does moving the descriptive word affect the meaning of each sentence? For each sentence, complete this statement: **In this sentence, the descriptive word . . .**

      a. sounded better when it split the infinitive.

      b. drastically changes the meaning of the sentence, depending on where you put it.

      c. doesn't affect meaning at all.

      d. subtly changes the meaning of the sentence, depending on where you put it.

      e. adds detail about the action in a sentence, but could be left out.

Step 3. Why do we split infinitives? Now we're ready to think about why infinitives get split. What do we gain from inserting a descriptive word in the to + verb combination? Use the things you learned in Steps 1 and 2, and examples from any of the activities in this section, to answer these questions. **Split infinitives sound right because they . . .**

      a. preserve a smooth rhythm in a sentence

      b. allow the descriptive word to be close to the verb it describes

      c. make a sentence sound more like real-life conversation

      d. allow you to emphasize a particular quality of the action (the verb)

      e. eliminate misinterpretations or subtle differences in meaning

      f. Other? _____

Step 4. What have we left out? What did *your* investigation of split infinitives come up with that *we* left out? Split infinitives clarify/confuse meaning in a sentence because _____.

5.10   Writers Write: PARAGRAPH BREAKS

Kimberly Woodfork

A paragraph is a cluster of sentences that support a main idea. *When the main idea changes, another paragraph should be started.* In a pamphlet I wrote for new parents, I opened with a story about a clueless new father who ruined the family microwave trying to heat up the baby's formula. Once I had the readers laughing, I switched to giving advice. In my rough draft, I ended the narrative about the clueless dad like this:

> . . . and put out the fire. That's right, folks. Now they had a worthless microwave on their hands and a baby that was *still hungry!* To prevent that situation from happening to you, here are step-by-step instructions for how to fix a cereal bottle. First, . . .

You can hear the switch in tone between the two sections; I'm shifting from an anecdote to a serious discussion of how to feed babies safely. The exclamation point gives me a perfect punch line for my story. Yet, there are no spaces to give the reader room for a short chuckle.

The melding of the two paragraphs made the pamphlet seem to drag on. I didn't want my readers to become bored and lose interest before they got to the main points I wanted to make. Here's what I did for the finished pamphlet:

> . . . and put out the fire. That's right, folks. Now they had a worthless microwave on their hands and a baby that was *still hungry!*
>
> To prevent that situation from happening to you, here are step-by-step instructions for how to fix a cereal bottle. First, . . .

ACTIVITY 5.10: PARAGRAPH BREAKS

Part 1. An author starts a new paragraph to tell the reader that it's time to switch gears. A new main idea means a new paragraph. Rewrite the selection given below, inserting paragraph breaks wherever a new topic begins. Remove any unnecessary paragraph breaks by rejoining the related sentences in one paragraph.

Do you have a specialized skill within the field of information technology? Are you able to learn quickly? Do the latest trends in technology fascinate you? You may want to consider working as a contractor. Before you commit yourself to this type of career, you'll need to know what contract work is all about. As a contract worker, you'll be working for a new company every few months. You'll have to learn new skills for each company, as well. After your time at the company has ended, you'll have to leave the new friends you've just made. These are the facts of life for a contractor, and you may not have a problem with any of them. In fact, you may be the kind of person who relishes the ever-changing world of contract work. Boredom certainly isn't a problem for contractors! Contract work offers a unique advantage to all who are willing to stick with it: contractors amass a vast array of skills as they move from company to company. A contractor whose impressed employers are willing to provide excellent recommendations just might be able to pick and choose among several high-paying regular jobs, once the fun of contracting wears off. Wouldn't it be nice to have such a dazzling resume? Companies often hire contract workers for financial reasons; a contractor doesn't receive the benefits package that must be funded for a full-time worker. In addition, the contractor will come in and meet any temporary special needs the company may have, leaving as soon as the project is completed. After the job is done, the company can stop paying that employee. Meanwhile, the contractor is being paid for yet another project, so everyone benefits from the situation. Contracting can be helpful to both employer and contractor in an entirely different way. The employer who is looking to fill a full-time position may offer that job to a contractor who does particularly nice work. The employer has had a month or two to evaluate this employee; if the employee doesn't meet the company's standards, the employer is under no obligation to hire him or her. The contract worker has the advantage of being able to experience the company's atmosphere and the employer's attitude, among other things. If the job offer is made, the worker can make an informed decision to accept or reject the offer. There are plenty of contractors who have chosen to avoid full-time work for one company. Some have hobbies they wish to pursue during their off-time; others quickly become bored at one company, using only one set of skills. Quite a few are using their pay and their extra time to go back to school. Contracting work doesn't have to be a "loner" kind of career; according to contractors, it's what you make of it. Often, a contractor will return to a company over time in order to complete different projects. When this happens, friendships are renewed and the contractor finds it easy to blend in with the company's regular employees. In between jobs, contract workers may even keep in contact with friends at various companies. Are you cut out for contract work? Consider the following: your ability to be flexible, both in hours worked and in type of work completed; your need for a predictable schedule; your required income level; and your tolerance for change. It may be a real opportunity for you.

Part 2. It's time for you to make some decisions about arranging your own writing into paragraphs. Write a piece that explains why you would or would not be the kind of person who would enjoy and benefit from contract work. Group your main ideas into at least five paragraphs—and be sure to put breaks in between them!

Part 3. Teamwork: Editing. Select one of your own papers that your group members haven't seen before. It can be the first draft of a paper you're working on for this class, or any draft of any paper for another class. Make a backup copy of this paper on your computer (keep the original intact!). In the backup copy, remove all paragraph breaks, so that one sentence runs into the next. Bring this copy to your group. Ask them to tell you where paragraph breaks seem to be needed.

VISIT *NEW DIRECTIONS FOR WRITERS* ON THE WEB

Visit our Web site to see how *you* can contribute *your work* to the next edition of the Hub!

http://www.nd-connect.net

This Web site is refreshed with new material regularly, so be sure to return to it again and again.

THE READINGS

Heaven Is a Bookstore in Paris

Allison Bruner

1   I settle Indian-style onto a tattered carpet, squeezing between a bed on my left and three-foot stacks of old books serving as a table on my right. A gray-haired man in a worn-out cardigan stands in the middle of the room, reading from a script. His voice alters between a roar and a whisper, and the room, filled to capacity, is silent except for the occasional *ping, ping, clink of* spoons as a few listeners stir their tea. I can tell the man's prose is captivating, because no one flinches when tiny beads of saliva spray over those closest to him while he reads. I listen to the words, but I do not take them in—I'm more fixated on the notion that I'm in Paris, at Shakespeare and Company bookstore, where dozens of the most talented literary figures of the 20th century have visited or even spent a few nights.

2   I try to imagine a similar scene in the spring of 1937, at 12 rue de L'Odéon, in a neighborhood not far away at a bookstore by the same name. There, Ernest Hemingway read excerpts of *Winner Take Nothing* to an audience that included James Joyce, Janet Flanner and André Gide. Owned by Princeton, New Jersey, native Sylvia Beach, the original Shakespeare and Company was the most famous bookshop/lending library in the world, where Joyce's *Ulysses* was first published and books like *Lady Chatterly's Lover,* banned in England and the United States, were available. Until the Nazis forced Beach to close her shop in 1941, it was ground zero for members of the Lost Generation—Hemingway, F. Scott Fitzgerald, T.S. Eliot, Ezra Pound, Thornton Wilder, Samuel Beckett, Katherine Anne Porter and others.

3   The Shakespeare and Company now nestled in the Left Bank's Latin Quarter became a spiritual successor to Beach's store when it opened in 1951. A new generation of expatriates, who descended on Paris after World War II, gravitated to the little shop at 37 rue de la Bûcherie to hear William S. Borroughs read from his controversial and racy novel, *Naked Lunch,* and Allen Ginsberg recite *Howl.* Beat poet Lawrence Ferlinghetti took refuge in one of the guest rooms to write his doctoral thesis on T.S. Eliot's poetry, and Henry Miller, Anaïs Nin and Richard Wright visited regularly to read and discuss books. Meanwhile, students and young bohemians published literary magazines out of the store with articles by Miller, Beckett and Jean-Paul Sartre.

4   Black-and-white photographs of Miller, Ginsberg, Ferlinghetti—and of the ubiquitous Beach, Hemingway and Joyce—hang between the book-crammed shelves of the writer's room where I'm seated among other guests who've come here for inspiration, conversation, a place to dream or simply for a good book and a quiet corner. I spot a few of the rare volumes once housed at the first Shakespeare and Company, and I realize that the spirit of the Lost Generation has taken up permanent residence here—and that is why I've come: to be a part of it.

5   When George Whitman opened what he calls his "rag and bone shop of the heart," he called it The Mistral, then renamed it on the 400th anniversary of Shakespeare's christening, in memory of Beach. He also refers to it affectionately as the Tumbleweed Hotel, with a motto painted in black letters above the doorway on the second floor: "Be not inhospitable to strangers lest they be angels in disguise." He takes it seriously: Traveling writers, artists and vagabonds are sometimes permitted to stay in one of the guest rooms. In exchange, they must work at the cash register, clean up (an endless task in this dusty little place), serve tea and, most important, write a short autobiography for the store's archives and retire early at night to read a book.

6   When I arrived in Paris this morning with a few hundred francs and a backpack that held one change of clothes, a journal and my toothbrush, I was at the mercy of Whitman's generosity. Since no one at the store answers the phone—I'm not even sure if one is plugged in—I couldn't call ahead. Realizing that I'd have to sleep along the quai of the Seine if Whitman would not invite me to stay, I approached him nervously

7   "We're full!" he told me gruffly in a raised voice. I felt my entire body begin to frown. "But I like your smile. Do you write?"

8   I told him I was a writer, and he offered me a room on the third floor, where Ferlinghetti had stayed in the '50s. Then, he invited me to tea with the visitors and guests upstairs, in the writer's room where I'd be staying.

9   Getting to the stairs was navigating an obstacle course of people, old paintings, posters and portraits, a dried-up well full of pennies, and books stacked on tables, falling out of boxes, stuffed into and in front of shelves. Faded Persian carpets conceal much of the brick tile floors, and between wooden ceiling beams, the plaster is cracked and discolored. The stairway was the steepest and most narrow I had ever seen, and at the top, a black cat was snoring on a refrigerator while a gray one, lying next to it, seemed to be smiling in her sleep. In the entire building, you can hear about a dozen languages being spoken, and though the musty rooms smell vaguely of cat urine and dust, I sensed that I was in the middle of something magical.

10   In the backroom library, two women debated while shoving their backpacks next to books piled under beds. "Squeezing a tubeful of orange paint on a canvas and giving it a title doesn't make it art," said one.

11   "Apparently you know little about the Modernists," argued the other.

12   Nearby a couple sat back-to-back on the floor, reading. One was holding *Tropic of Cancer*, the other *War and Peace*.

13   Across the hall, I peeked into a room with a view of Notre Dame towering majestically over the Seine and of the green book stalls that border the Left Bank. A bed was littered with half a baguette, crumbs and an orange, and on the desk in front of the window a dirty coffee cup looked like it was glued into place. A complete set of diaries by Nin, and some of her fiction, lined the shelves above the bed. I heard clapping come from the top of the stairs nearby, where the tea party was being held.

14   *Smack!* Back on the third floor my thoughts are interrupted when a woman abruptly slaps her leg. When it occurs to me that she's sitting on the bed where I'll be sleeping, I look at her. "These bloody bed bugs are driving me bonkers!" she exclaims.

15   I thought bed bugs didn't exist, I tell her, that they're a myth.

16   "Well, Shakespeare and Company is like the stage of a fairy tale. But these are real," she insists, pointing at her ankles and calves dotted with red bumps.

17   She introduces herself as Fiona Kennedy, Irish-born but raised by her aunt in London. Her dream is to become an aromatherapist, a psychologist or an actress—or maybe she'll join the circus, she muses—but for the time, the heavily freckled woman with braided black hair spends her summers doing road construction in England then traveling Europe and Japan from fall until spring. Thus far, she's learned French, Spanish and a little bit of Swedish and Japanese.

18   She doesn't believe me at first when I tell her that I've been invited to stay in the writer's room; she says Whitman reserves it for special guests only.

19   As we talk, I hear Whitman yelling at someone downstairs.

20   Fiona explains that a guest named Jeff had been caught sneaking in past midnight last night. Whitman is fed up with him because he never helps with the chores or with running the bookstore, and four weeks after arriving he has yet to complete his autobiographical essay. Whitman is a generous man, she points out. But if you take advantage of his generosity, it infuriates him.

21   After graduating from Boston University and before studying at Harvard and the Sorbonne in Paris, Whitman journeyed penniless through North and Central America and wrote articles about his experiences. He had also been drafted by the U.S. into WWII, and later worked in a peace camp for orphans in France. Since opening what Miller called this "wonderland of books," Whitman has hosted thousands upon thousands of wayfaring writers and artists—his way, he says, "of repaying the hospitality I received in many countries when I was a vagabond."

22   Whitman, almost 90, has a big heart and an imagination to go with it. He likes to pretend he's king of the castle, where his male guests are tumbleweeds drifting across his flower garden of girl guests who are angels in disguise. As his guest, I feel like I'm part of a fairy tale full of eccentric characters, in a place where anything is possible.

23   Later in the evening, the king of the castle, with his shirt wrinkled and his hair sticking up in random places, emerges from his bedroom where he'd been reading for hours. He pulls a large metal pot off a shelf then starts chopping potatoes. I offer to help.

24   "Nah," he says. "You just read one of my books." An hour later he leaves me a bowl of potato soup and peach slices, then returns to his room.

25   As I finish my meal, I hear drum beats approaching outside. I walk over to the window and see students from the Sorbonne playing tom-toms while gathering in a circle in front of the store. They pass around a bottle of red wine, and each, in turn, takes a swig then resumes the cadence: *thump, bap-bap, thump, thump.*

26   Outside a golden-pink sunset casts long shadows over the students and the people browsing through used paperbacks in front of the store. One by one, the street lamps illuminate, and I notice a man at an easel painting pigeons bathing in the fountain on rue Bûcherie.

27   *Thump, bap-bap, thump, thump.*

28   Then a man begins reading something aloud in Portuguese, pauses and clumsily hurls a handful of roses in the window directly below mine. Seconds later the roses come flying back out and the window is slammed shut. The man lowers his head forlornly under a shower of red petals.

29   *Thump, bap-bap, thump, thump.* The cadence is hypnotic. A late-spring breeze blows gently into my room, and I breathe deeply to soak up the energy of this place. The beating of the tom-toms is like the collective pulse of the dreamers, tourists and vagabonds who come and go year after year. Here in the Fifth Arrondissement, one of the most vivacious neighborhoods in Paris, I feel like I've come home, to a place where we gather inspiration, and where one day we return to share the stories of our adventures. In Paris, where art and literature are as important as romance and red wine, the spirit of the Lost Generation lives in the hearts of a new generation of expatriates.

Allison Bruner, "Heaven Is a Bookstore in Paris," *AAA World*: July–Aug. 2001: 34–37.

Give Us Jobs, Not Admiration

Eric Bigler

1   Tuesday I have another job interview. Like most I have had so far, it will probably end with the all-too-familiar words, "We'll let you know of our decision in a few days."

2   Many college graduates searching for their first career job might simply accept that response as, "Sorry, we're not interested in you," and blame the rejection on inexperience or bad chemistry. For myself and other disabled people, however, this response often seems to indicate something more worrisome: a reluctance to hire the handicapped even when they're qualified. I have been confined to a wheelchair since 1974, when a high-school diving accident left me paralyzed from the chest down. But that didn't prevent me from earning a bachelor's in social work in 1983, and I am now finishing up a master's degree in business and industrial management, specializing in employee relations and human-resource development.

3   Our government spends a great deal of money to help the handicapped, but it does not necessarily spend it all wisely. For example, in 1985 Ohio's Bureau of Vocational Rehabilitation (BVR) spent more than $4 million in tuition and other expenses so that disabled students could obtain a college education. BVR's philosophy is that the amount of money spent educating students will be repaid in disabled employees' taxes. The agency assists graduates by offering workshops on résumé writing and interviewing techniques, skills many already learned in college. BVR also maintains files of résumés that are matched with help-wanted notices from local companies and employs placement specialists to work directly with graduates during their job search.

4   Even with all this assistance, however, graduates still have trouble getting hired. Such programs might do better if they concentrated on the perceptions of employers as well as the skills of applicants. More important, improving contacts with prospective employers might encourage them to actively recruit the disabled.

5   Often, projects that *do* show promise don't get the chance to thrive. I was both a client and an informal consultant to one program, Careers for the Disabled in Dayton, which asked local executives to make a commitment to hire disabled applicants whenever possible. I found this strategy to be on target, since support for a project is more likely when it is ordered from the top. The program also offered free training seminars to corporations on how they can work effectively with the disabled candidate. In April of 1986—less than a year after it was started and after only three disabled people were placed—the program was discontinued because, according to the director, they had "no luck at getting [enough] corporations to join the program."

6   Corporations need to take a more independent and active part in hiring qualified handicapped persons. Today's companies try to show a willingness to innovate, and hiring people like myself would enhance that image. Madison Avenue has finally recognized that the disabled are also consumers; more and more often, commercials include them. But

advertisers could break down even more stereotypes. I would like to see one of those Hewlett-Packard commercials, for instance, show an employee racing down the sidewalk in his wheelchair, pulling alongside a pay phone and calling a colleague to ask "What if . . . ?"

7   Corporate recruiters also need to be better prepared for meeting with disabled applicants. They should be ready to answer queries about any barriers that their building's design may pose, and they should be forthright about asking their own questions. It's understandable that employers are afraid to mention matters that are highly personal and may prove embarrassing—or, even worse, discriminatory. There's nothing wrong, however, with an employer reassuring him or herself about whether an applicant will be able to reach files, operate computers or even get into the bathroom. Until interviewers change their style, disabled applicants need to initiate discussion of disability-related issues.

8   **Cosmetic acts:** Government has tried to improve hiring for the disabled through Affirmative Action programs. The Rehabilitation Act of 1973 says institutions or programs receiving substantial amounts of federal money can't discriminate on the basis of handicap. Yet I was saddened and surprised to discover how many companies spend much time and money writing great affirmative-action and equal-opportunity guidelines but little time following them. Then there are the cosmetic acts, such as the annual National Employ the Handicapped Week every October. If President Reagan (or anyone else) wants to help the disabled with proclamations, more media exposure is necessary. I found out about the last occasion in 1985 from a brief article on the back of a campus newspaper—a week after it had happened.

9   As if other problems were not enough, the disabled who search unsuccessfully for employment often face a loss of self-esteem and worth. In college, many disabled people I have talked to worked hard toward a degree so they would be prepared for jobs after graduation. Now they look back on their four or more years as wasted time. For these individuals, the days of earning good grades and accomplishing tough tasks fade away, leaving only frustrating memories. Today's job market is competitive enough without prejudice adding more "handicaps."

10   About that interview . . . five minutes into it, I could feel the atmosphere chill. The interviewer gave me general information instead of trying to find out if I was right for the job. I've been there before. Then the session closed with a handshake, and those same old words: "We'll let you know." They said I should be so proud of myself for doing what I am doing. That's what they always say. I'm tired of hearing how courageous I am. So are other disabled people. We need jobs, and we want to work like anyone else.

11   But still, I remain an optimist. I know someday soon a company will be smart enough to realize how much I have to offer them in both my head and my heart.

12   Maybe then I'll hear the words so many of us really want to hear: "You're hired."

Eric Bigler, "Give Us Jobs, Not Admiration," *Newsweek* 1987.

Hold the Mayonnaise

Julia Alvarez

1   "If I die first and Papi ever gets remarried," Mami used to tease when we were kids, "don't you accept a new woman in my house. Make her life impossible, you hear?" My sisters and I nodded obediently and a filial shudder would go through us. We were Catholics, so of course, the only kind of remarriage we could imagine had to involve our mother's death.

2   We were also Dominicans, recently arrived in Jamaica, Queens, in the early 60's, before waves of other Latin Americans began arriving. So, when we imagined who exactly my father might possibly ever think of remarrying, only American women came to mind. It would be bad enough having a *madrastra,* but a "stepmother." . . .

3   All I could think of was that she would make me eat mayonnaise, a food I identified with the United States and which I detested. Mami understood, of course, that I wasn't used to that kind of food. Even a madrastra, accustomed to our rice and beans and tostones and pollo frito, would understand. But an American stepmother would think it was normal to put mayonnaise on food, and if she were at all strict and a little mean, which all stepmothers, of course, were, she would make me eat potato salad and such. I had plenty of my own reasons to make a potential stepmother's life impossible. When I nodded obediently with my sisters, I was imagining not just something foreign in our house, but in our refrigerator.

4   So it's strange now, almost 35 years later, to find myself a Latina stepmother of my husband's two tall, strapping, blond, mayonnaise-eating daughters. To be honest, neither of them is a real aficionado of the condiment, but it's a fair thing to add to a bowl of tuna fish or diced potatoes. Their American food, I think of it, and when they head to their mother's or off to school, I push the jar back in the refrigerator behind their chocolate pudding and several open cans of Diet Coke.

5   What I can't push as successfully out of sight are my own immigrant childhood fears of having a *gringa* stepmother with foreign tastes in our house. Except now, I am the foreign stepmother in a gringa household. I've wondered what my husband's two daughters think of this stranger in their family. It must be doubly strange for them that I am from another culture.

6   Of course, there are mitigating circumstances—my husband's two daughters were teen-agers when we married, older, more mature, able to understand differences. They had also traveled when they were children with their father, an eye doctor, who worked on short-term international projects with various eye foundations. But still, it's one thing to visit a foreign country, another altogether to find it brought home—a real bear plopped down in a Goldilocks house.

7   Sometimes, a whole extended family of bears. My warm, loud Latino family came up for the wedding: my *tía* from Santo Domingo; three dramatic, enthusiastic sisters and their families; my papi, with a thick accent I could tell the girls found hard to understand; and my mami, who had her eye trained on my soon-to-be stepdaughters for any sign that they were about to make my life impossible. "How are they behaving themselves?" she asked me, as if they were 7 and 3, not 19 and 16. "They're wonderful girls," I replied, already feeling protective of them.

8   I looked around for the girls in the meadow in front of the house we were building, where we were holding the outdoor wedding ceremony and party. The oldest hung out with a group of her own friends. The younger one whizzed in briefly for the ceremony, then left again before the congratulations started up. There was not much mixing with me and mine. What was there for them to celebrate on a day so full of confusion and effort?

9   On my side, being the newcomer in someone else's territory is a role I'm used to. I can tap into that struggling English speaker, that skinny, dark-haired, olive-skinned girl in a sixth grade of mostly blond and blue-eyed giants. Those tall, freckled boys would push me around in the playground. "Go back to where you came from!" *No comprendo!* I'd reply, though of course there was no misunderstanding the fierce looks on their faces.

10   Even now, my first response to a scowl is that old pulling away. (My husband calls it "checking out.") I remember times early on in the marriage when the girls would be with us, and I'd get out of school and drive around doing errands, killing time, until my husband, their father, would be leaving work. I am not proud of my fears, but I understand—as the lingo goes—where they come from.

11   And I understand, more than I'd like to sometimes, my stepdaughters' pain. But with me, they need never fear that I'll usurp a mother's place. No one has ever come up and held their faces and then addressed me, "They look just like you." If anything, strangers to the remarriage are probably playing Mr. Potato Head in their minds, trying to figure out how my foreign features and my husband's fair Nebraskan features got put together into these two tall, blond girls. "My husband's daughters," I kept introducing them.

12   Once, when one of them visited my class and I introduced her as such, two students asked me why. "I'd be so hurt if my stepmom introduced me that way," the young man said. That night I told my stepdaughter what my students had said. She scowled at me and agreed. "It's so weird how you call me Papa's daughter. Like you don't want to be related to me or something."

13   "I didn't want to presume," I explained. "So it's O.K. if I call you my stepdaughter?"

14   "That's what I am," she said. Relieved, I took it for a teensy inch of acceptance. The takings are small in this stepworld, I've discovered. Sort of like being a minority. It feels as if all the goodies have gone somewhere else.

15   Day to day, I guess I follow my papi's advice. When we first came, he would talk to his children about how to make it in our new country. "Just do your work and put in your heart, and they will accept you!" In this age of remaining true to your roots, of keeping your Spanish, of fighting from inside your culture, that assimilationist approach is highly suspect. My Latino students—who don't want to be called Hispanics anymore—would ditch me as faculty adviser if I came up with that play-nice message.

16   But in a stepfamily where everyone is starting a new life together, it isn't bad advice. Like a potluck supper, an American concept my mami never took to. ("Why invite people to your house and then ask them to bring the food?") You put what you've got together with what everyone else brought and see what comes out of the pot. The luck part is if everyone brings something you like. No potato salad, no deviled eggs, no little party sandwiches with you know what in them.

Julia Alvarez, "Hold the Mayonnaise," *The New York Times Magazine* 12 Jan. 1992.

The Kitchen

Alfred Kazin

1   In Brownsville tenements the kitchen is always the largest room and the center of the household. As a child I felt we lived in a kitchen to which four other rooms were annexed. My mother, a "home" dressmaker, had her workshop in the kitchen. She told me once that she had begun dressmaking in Poland at thirteen; as far back as I can remember, she was always making dresses for the local women. She had an innate sense of design, a quick eye for all the subtleties in the latest fashions, even when she despised them, and great boldness. For three or four dollars she would study the fashion magazines with a customer, go with the customer to the remnants store on Belmont Avenue to pick out the material, argue the owner down—all remnants stores, for some reason, were supposed to be shady, as if the owners dealt in stolen goods—and then for days would patiently fit and baste and sew and fit again. Our apartment was always full of women in their house-dresses sitting around the kitchen table waiting for a fitting. My little bedroom next to the kitchen was the fitting room. The sewing machine, an old nut-brown Singer with golden scrolls painted along the black arm and engraved along the two tiers of little drawers massed with needles and thread on each side of the treadle, stood next to the window and the great coal-black stove which up to my last year in college was our main source of heat. By December the two outer bedrooms were closed off, and used to chill bottles of milk and cream, cold borscht and jellied calves' feet.

2   The kitchen held our lives together. My mother worked in it all day long, we ate in it almost all meals except the Passover *seder,* I did my homework and first writing at the kitchen table, and in winter I often had a bed made up for me on three kitchen chairs near the stove. On the wall just over the table hung a long horizontal mirror that sloped to a ship's prow at each end and was lined in cherry wood. It took up the whole wall, and drew every object in the kitchen to itself. The walls were a fiercely stippled whitewash, so often rewhitened by my father in slack seasons that the paint looked as if it had been squeezed and cracked into the walls. A large electric bulb hung down the center of the kitchen at the end of a chain that had been hooked into the ceiling; the old gas ring and key still jutted out of the wall like antlers. In the corner next to the toilet was the sink at which we washed, and the square tub in which my mother did our clothes. Above it, tacked to the shelf on which were pleasantly ranged square, blue bordered white sugar and spice jars, hung calendars from the Public National Bank on Pitkin Avenue and the Minsker Progressive Branch of the Workman's Circle; receipts for the payment of insurance premiums, and household bills on a spindle; two little boxes engraved with Hebrew letters. One of these was for the poor, the other to buy back the Land of Israel. Each spring a bearded little man would suddenly appear in our kitchen, salute us with a hurried Hebrew blessing, empty the boxes (sometimes with a sidelong look of disdain if they were not full), hurriedly bless us again for remembering our less fortunate Jewish brothers and sisters, and so take his

departure until the next spring, after vainly trying to persuade my mother to take still another box. We did occasionally remember to drop coins in the boxes, but this was usually only on the dreaded morning of "mid-terms" and final examinations, because my mother thought it would bring me luck. She was extremely superstitious, but embarrassed about it, and always laughed at herself whenever, on the morning of an examination, she counseled me to leave the house on my right foot. "I know it's silly," her smile seemed to say, "but what harm can it do? It may calm God down."

3   The kitchen gave a special character to our l lives, my mother's character. All my memories of that kitchen are dominated by the nearness of my mother sitting all day long at her sewing machine, by the clacking of the treadle against the linoleum floor, by the patient twist of her right shoulder as she automatically pushed at the wheel with one hand or lifted the foot to free the needle where it had got stuck in a thick piece of material. The kitchen was her life. Year by year, as I began to take in her fantastic capacity for labor and her anxious zeal, I realized it was ourselves she kept stitched together. I can never remember a time when she was not working. She worked because the law of her life was work, work and anxiety; she worked because she would have found life meaningless without work. She read almost no English; she could read the Yiddish paper, but never felt she had time to. We were always talking of a time when I would teach her how to read, but somehow there was never time. When I awoke in the morning she was already at her machine, or in the great morning crowd of housewives at the grocery getting fresh rolls for breakfast. When I returned from school she was at her machine, or conferring over *McCall's* with some neighborhood woman who had come in pointing hopefully to an illustration—"Mrs. Kazin! Mrs. Kazin! Make me a dress like it shows here in the picture!" When my father came home from work she had somehow mysteriously interrupted herself to make supper for us, and the dishes cleared and washed, was back at her machine. When I went to bed at night, often she was still there, pounding away at the treadle, hunched over the wheel, her hands steering a piece of gauze under the needle with a finesse that always contrasted sharply with her swollen hands and broken nails. Her left hand had been pierced through when as a girl she had worked in the infamous Triangle Shirtwaist Factory on the East Side. A needle had gone straight through the palm, severing a large vein. They had sewn it up for her so clumsily that a tuft of flesh always lay folded over the palm.

4   The kitchen was the great machine that set our lives running; it whirred down a little only on Saturdays and holy days. From my mother's kitchen I gained my first picture of life as a white, overheated, starkly lit workshop redolent with Jewish cooking, crowded with women in housedresses, strewn with fashion magazines, patterns, dress material, spools of thread—and at whose center, so lashed to her machine that bolts of energy seemed to dance out of her hands and feet as she worked, my mother stamped the treadle hard against the floor, hard, hard, and silently, grimly at war, beat out the first rhythm of the world for me.

Alfred Kazin, Excerpt from "The Kitchen" in *A Walker in the City* (New York: Harcourt Brace & Company, 1979). (Original © 1951).

Fishy Business

Roz Batt

1   Never have I seen so much blood and guts. The concept of fish bleeding as they are prepared to become food had never occurred to me until now, as I stand and make notes—inconspicuously, I hope—to one side of the Wah Fat Fish Market in San Francisco's Chinatown. Until now, I have done all my fish buying from supermarket chains, where I have been presented with fish that have been perfectly filleted, washed clean, and sanitarily wrapped in plastic. Here at Wah Fat, however, I am forced to come face to face with the real thing.

2   Around the edge of the market are huge water tanks filled with grotesque-looking fish. I have not encountered such species before, let alone eaten them. The floor is slippery and covered with black mats. Miles of hose pipe lead from one tank to another. The walls, floor, and counter appear filthy, and the machinery is rusty. But the salty, sea smell of the market is of today's freshly caught fish, and above the humming of the tanks and refrigerators is the sound of someone's car stereo in the street, booming out the sounds of rap music, making us aware of lives being lived.

3   Although it is a sunny day outside, here in the market it is damp, cool, and rather dark. The atmosphere feels comfortable somehow; the dim ceiling lights do not offend my eyes. Standing here, I suddenly realize how much I dislike the feeling of treading on the automatic door opener of a supermarket entrance. The large, metal-framed doors heave themselves open, and as I enter the impersonal surroundings, the mass of fluorescent light fixtures make me squint. It always takes me a moment to recover and adjust to these efficient but somehow hostile places.

4   In the center of the fish market is a huge, wooden preparation table; above it hang all manner of deadly looking weapons. Standing behind the table are three men, each clothed in identical, blood-stained white overalls and black-rubber boots. One is wearing an uncharacteristic blue baseball cap—the influence of America in this bustling Asian enclave of the city. Although the men are not speaking to each other and have no expressions that I can discern on their faces, they are clearly working as a team. Each is performing his own laborious task. One slices off the fishes' fins, another scrapes off the scales, and the third slams the fish down onto the wooden board and chops off its head. They are all masters at using the cleaver, a terrifying instrument twice as long as their hands.

5   As I watch and wait for the men to speak to one another, I realize that they communicate through body language, working closely, side by side, in unison, almost as though they were in a silent, carefully choreographed dance. It feels as though these fishmongers have worked together for years, as though they are related. I wonder whether this is a family owned business.

6   Still, none of them has uttered a word. Their eyes are fixed on the job at hand. Then one looks up to scan the front of the market for possible customers. I am discovered. The

older man in the baseball cap is coming toward me. His face looks hard and tired. How many hours has he been working today? My suspicion is since very early morning.

7   "You want something?" he asks.

8   "Not right at this moment, thank you," I reply, fingering my notepad awkwardly.

9   He walks away, clearly disappointed at a "no sale."

10   The market is now alive with all manner of customers—young and old, women and men—each determined to purchase the best catch of the day. Unlike in a supermarket, there is no question of picking a numbered ticket to be served in the order of arrival. No, here in the market we face more of a challenge. If you want a particular fish, you had better elbow your way to the front and speak up, or someone else will buy it first. Survival of the fittest.

11   Something in the atmosphere of the market has changed. Perhaps my presence has made the men self-conscious. They utter a few, brief words to each other, but I cannot hear what they are saying. The two younger men's eyes flash toward me. They resume their work, but at a slower, disjointed pace. Finally, the youngest of the trio places his cleaver carefully on the work table, and the others watch him intensely as he walks in my direction.

12   "Are you from Health, IRS, or what?" he asks me. His voice is timid, hesitant, the voice of the immigrant not yet at home in America and wondering what he has done wrong this time.

13   Quickly, I slip the pen and pad into my pocket and say, trying to put him at ease, "No, no, sorry, I'm writing a college assignment and I'm truly fascinated by your work."

14   There is relief on his face as he walks away. Embarrassed by my intrusion, I feel compelled to buy some fish.

15   Next to casting a line and catching the fish myself, or waiting for the early morning fishing trawlers to come to the dock to sell their products, purchasing my dinner at the fish market and watching it being made ready seems to me the most authentic option. I choose a Rock Cod from one of the bubbling tanks. The fish is huge, with orange and brown speckles and vicious-looking fins. It is not particularly appealing to the eye, but I know from experience that it will taste delicious. Inspired by the smells wafting into the market from the numerous Chinatown restaurants close by, I begin to imagine steaming the fish with ginger, garlic, green onion, and soy sauce. Of course, it is possible to create wonderful meals from food that is bought from the supermarket, but having experienced the Wah Fat Fish Market, I feel it is not quite the same. Our supermarkets do not provide us with any connection between the food we buy and its live source. No intrigue. No uncomfortable feelings. No reality. And no sense of the hard work that has gone into its making.

16   My assignment complete, I leave the fish market with my dinner tucked under my arm, feeling pleased that my purchase has cost me only three dollars. I have mixed feelings about my visit to the fish market—as do the fishmongers, who are still keeping an eye on me. I feel badly about how hard they are working to make a living, especially as I can see that the fish trade is not making them rich. However, they do have something money cannot buy: dedication and teamwork and pride in their expertise, in their ability to work

efficiently and well with what supermarkets would regard as the most primitive of conditions and equipment.

17   In 20 years time, will we be able to find such personal service in food stores? Will markets like the Wah Fat Fish Market still exist? Or will all food stores be pristine, sterile, and lacking any kind of human character? Will we even remember the presence of the "invisible" men and women who work so hard behind the scenes to bring us the "perfect" products, totally removed from the natural world, that today's consumers seem more and more to desire?

Roz Batt, "Fishy Business," *We, Too, Sing America,* ed. Chitra B. Divakaruni (Boston: McGraw-Hill, 1998). [Student Essay] 223–225.

My Ecumenical Father

José Burciaga

1   ¡Feliz Navidad! Merry Christmas! Happy Hanukkah! As a child, my season's greetings were tricultural—Mexicano, Anglo and Jewish.

2   Our devoutly Catholic parents raised three sons and three daughters in the basement of a Jewish synagogue, Congregation B'nai Zion in El Paso, Texas. José Cruz Burciaga was the custodian and *shabbat goy*. A shabbat goy is Yiddish for a Gentile who, on the Sabbath, performs certain tasks forbidden to Jews under orthodox law.

3   Every year around Christmas time, my father would take the menorah out and polish it. The eight-branched candleholder symbolizes Hanukkah, the commemoration of the first recorded war of liberation in that part of the world.

4   In 164 B.C., the Jewish nation rebelled against Antiochus IV Epiphanes, who had attempted to introduce pagan idols into the temples. When the temple was reconquered by the Jews, there was only one day's supply of oil for the Eternal Light in the temple. By a miracle, the oil lasted eight days.

5   My father was not only in charge of the menorah but for 40 years he also made sure the Eternal Light remained lit.

6   As children we were made aware of the differences and joys of Hanukkah, Christmas and Navidad. We were taught to respect each celebration, even if they conflicted. For example, the Christmas carols taught in school. We learned the song about the twelve days of Christmas, though I never understood what the hell a partridge was doing in a pear tree in the middle of December.

7   We also learned a German song about a boy named Tom and a bomb—*O Tannenbaum*. We even learned a song in the obscure language of Latin, called "Adeste Fideles," which reminded me of, *Ahh! d'este fideo,* a Mexican pasta soup. Though 75% of our class was Mexican-American, we never sang a Christmas song *en Español*. Spanish was forbidden.

8   So, our mother—a former teacher—taught us "Silent Night" in Spanish: *Noche de paz, noche de amor.* It was so much more poetic and inspirational.

9   While the rest of El Paso celebrated Christmas, Congregation B'Nai Zion celebrated Hanukkah. We picked up Yiddish and learned a Hebrew prayer of thanksgiving. My brothers and I would help my father hang the Hanukkah decorations.

10   At night, after the services, the whole family would rush across the border to Juárez and celebrate the *posadas,* which take place for nine days before Christmas. They are a communal re-enactment of Joseph and Mary's search for shelter, just before Jesus was born.

11   To the posadas we took candles and candy left over from the Hanukkah celebrations. The next day we'd be back at St. Patrick's School singing, "I'm dreaming of a white Christmas."

12   One day I stopped dreaming of the white Christmases depicted on greeting cards. An old immigrant from Israel taught me Jesus was born in desert country just like that of the West Texas town of El Paso.

13   On Christmas Eve, my father would dress like Santa Claus and deliver gifts to his children, nephews, godchildren and the little kids in orphanages. The next day, minus his disguise, he would take us to Juárez, where we delivered gifts to the poor in the streets.

14   My father never forgot his childhood poverty and forever sought to help the less fortunate. He taught us to measure wealth not in money but in terms of love, spirit, charity and culture.

15   We were taught to respect the Jewish faith and culture. On the Day of Atonement, when the whole congregation fasted, my mother did not cook, lest the food odors distract. The respect was mutual. No one ever complained about the large picture of Jesus in our living room.

16   Through my father, leftover food from B'nai B'rith luncheons, Bar Mitzvahs and Bat Mitzvahs, found its way to Catholic or Baptist churches or orphanages. Floral arrangements in the temple that surrounded a Jewish wedding *hutpah* canopy many times found a second home at the altar of St. Patrick's Cathedral or San Juan Convent School. Surplus furniture, including old temple pews found their way to a missionary Baptist Church in *El Segundo Barrio*.

17   It was not uncommon to come home from school at lunch time and find an uncle priest, an aunt nun and a Baptist minister visiting our home at the same time that the Rabbi would knock on our door. It was just as natural to find the president of B'nai Zion eating beans and tortillas in our kitchen.

18   My father literally risked his life for the Jewish faith. Twice he was assaulted by burglars who broke in at night. Once he was stabbed in the hand. Another time he stayed up all night guarding the sacred Torahs after anti-semites threatened the congregation. He never philosophized about his ecumenism, he just lived it.

19   Cruz, as most called him, was a man of great humor, a hot temper and a passion for dance. He lived the Mexican Revolution and rode the rails during the Depression. One of his proudest moments came when he became a U.S. citizen.

20   September 23, 1985, sixteen months after my mother passed away, my father followed. Like his life, his death was also ecumenical. The funeral was held at Our Lady of Peace, where a priest said the mass in English. My cousins played mandolin and sang in Spanish. The president of B'nai Zion Congregation said a prayer in Hebrew. Members of the congregation sat with Catholics and Baptists.

21   Observing Jewish custom, the cortege passed by the synagogue one last time. Fittingly, father was laid to rest on the Sabbath. At the cemetery, in a very Mexican tradition, my brothers, sisters and I each kissed a handful of dirt and threw it on the casket.

22   I once had the opportunity to describe father's life to the late, great Jewish American writer Bernard Malamud. His only comment was, "Only in America!"

José Antonio Burciaga, "My Ecumenical Father," Reprinted from *Drink Cultura: Chicanismo* (Santa Barbara, CA: Joshua Odell Editions, 1993).

First Job: Ka-Ching!

Margaret Atwood

1   I'll pass over the mini-jobs of adolescence—the summer-camp stints that were more like getting paid for having fun. I'll pass over, too, the self-created pin-money generators—the puppet shows put on for kids at office Christmas parties, the serigraph posters turned out on the Ping-Pong table—and turn to my first real job. By "real job," I mean one that had nothing to do with friends of my parents or parents of my friends but was obtained in the adult manner, by looking through the ads in newspapers and going in to be interviewed—one for which I was entirely unsuited, and that I wouldn't have done except for the money. I was surprised when I got it, underpaid while doing it, and frustrated in the performance of it, and these qualities have remained linked, for me, to the ominous word "job."

2   The year was 1962, the place was Toronto. It was summer, and I was faced with the necessity of earning the difference between my scholarship for the next year and what it would cost me to live. The job was in the coffee shop of a small hotel on Avenue Road; it is now in the process of being torn down, but at that time it was a clean, well-lighted place, with booths along one side and a counter—possibly marble—down the other. The booths were served by a waitressing pro who lipsticked outside the lines, and who thought I was a mutant. My job would be serving things at the counter—coffee I would pour, toast I would create from bread, milkshakes I would whip up in the obstetrical stainless-steel device provided. ("Easy as pie," I was told.) I would also be running the customers' money through the cash register—an opaque machine with buttons to be pushed, little drawers that shot in and out, and a neurotic system of locks.

3   I said I had never worked a cash register before. This delighted the manager, a plump, unctuous character out of some novel I hadn't yet read. He said the cash register, too, was easy as pie, and I would catch on to it in no time, as I was a smart girl with an M.A. He said I should go and get myself a white dress.

4   I didn't know what he meant by "white dress." I bought the first thing I could find on sale, a nylon afternoon number with daisies appliquéd onto the bodice. The waitress told me this would not do: I needed a dress like hers, a *uniform*. ("How dense can you be?" I overheard her saying.) I got the uniform, but I had to go through the first day in my nylon daisies.

5   This first humiliation set the tone. The coffee was easy enough—I just had to keep the Bun filled—and the milkshakes were possible; few people wanted them anyway. The sandwiches and deep-fried shrimp were made at the back: all I had to do was order them over the intercom and bin the leftovers.

6   But the cash register was perverse. Its drawers would pop open for no reason, or it would ring eerily when I swore I was nowhere near it; or it would lock itself shut, and the

queue of customers waiting to pay would lengthen and scowl as I wrestled and sweated. I kept expecting to be fired for incompetence, but the manager chortled more than ever. Occasionally, he would bring some man in a suit to view me. "She's got an M.A.," he would say, in a proud but pitying voice, and the two of them would stare at me and shake their heads.

7   An ex-boyfriend discovered my place of employment, and would also come to stare and shake his head, ordering a single coffee, taking an hour to drink it, leaving me a sardonic nickel tip. The Greek short-order cook decided I would be the perfect up-front woman for the restaurant he wanted to open: he would marry me and do the cooking, I would speak English to the clientele and work—was he mad?—the cash register. He divulged his bank balance, and demanded to meet my father so the two of them could close the deal. When I declined, he took to phoning me over the intercom to whisper blandishments, and to plying me with deep-fried shrimp. A girl as scrawny as myself, he pointed out, was unlikely to get such a good offer again.

8   Then the Shriners hit town, took over the hotel, and began calling for buckets of ice, or for doctors because they'd had heart attacks: too much tricycle-riding in the hot sun was felling them in herds. I couldn't handle the responsibility, the cash register had betrayed me once too often, and the short-order cook was beginning to sing Frank Sinatra songs to me. I gave notice.

9   Only when I'd quit did the manager reveal his true stratagem: they'd wanted someone as inept as me because they suspected their real cashier of skimming the accounts, a procedure I was obviously too ignorant to ever figure out. "Too stunned," as the waitress put it. She was on the cashier's side, and had me fingered as a stoolie all along.

Margaret Atwood, "Ka-Ching," *The New Yorker* 23 & 30 Apr. 2001: 72.

First Job: Coins of the Realm

Nicholson Baker

1   In 1973, when I was sixteen, I got a job in building maintenance at Midtown Plaza, Rochester's then flourishing downtown shopping mall. I spent a day pulling nails from two-by-fours—loudly whistling Ravel's "Bolero" while I worked, so that the secretaries would know that I knew a few things about French music—before being apprenticed to the mall's odd job man, Bradway. Bradway taught me how to move filing cabinets (you walk with them on alternating corners, as if you were slow dancing with them), how to snap a chalk line, how to cut curves in Sheetrock, how to dig a hole for a no parking sign, and how to change the fluorescent bulbs in the ceiling of the elevator. He wore funny-looking glasses, and he sang "Paper Doll" to the secretaries, embarrassing them and me, but he was a decent person and a good teacher. For reasons I still don't understand, he was disliked by one of the carpenters in the maintenance department, who referred to him as "a proctologist's delight."

2   One day, Bradway told me he was going to teach me how to sweep up the pennies in the fountain. Midtown Plaza's fountain had a fifteen-foot-high inward-curving spray, and there were four or five low mushroom fountains to one side, lit from below; the water went around and under a set of stairs rising up to the mall's second level. People sometimes threw pennies in from the landing on the stairs and while standing at the railing on the second level, but mostly they tossed them in as they walked past. I had thrown in pennies myself. The thing to do when you wished on a penny was to memorize where it landed. It was the penny with the two very tarnished pennies just to the left of it—or no, was it one of the ones in that similar constellation a foot away. Every day, you could check on your penny, or the penny you had decided must be your penny, to see how it was doing.

3   So when Bradway said that I—a maintenance worker earning two-fifty an hour—was going to be sweeping up all the coins, I experienced a shiver of mastery. We went down to the basement, and I put on a pair of rubber fly-fishing boots. Bradway showed me the switch that turned off the pump for the fountains. I pressed it. There was a clunk.

4   Back upstairs, the water was almost still. I stepped over the marble ledge, squeegee broom in hand, and began pushing around other people's good luck. The pennies, moved along by the squeegee, formed planar sheets of copper, arranging themselves to fit into each other's adjoining curves, until finally a row would push up, make peaks, and flip back, forming a second layer, and then a third, and eventually there was a sunken reef of loose change in one corner of the pool. "That's it, just keep sweeping them toward the pile," Bradway said. He gave me a black bucket with holes in it, and, rolling up my sleeves as high as I could, I used a dustpan to scoop up the change and pour it, entirely underwater, into the bucket. The sound was of anchor chains at the bottom of the sea.

5　　Bradway went off while I swept further afield, and I looked out with a haughty but weary look at the people walking by: I was the maintenance man, standing in the water; they were just pedestrians in a mall. "Are you going to keep all that money?" a man said to me. I said no, it was going to charity. "I'm a good charity, man," he said. By the time I got the strays out into the open blue tilework and scooted them along in a cloud of pale, sluggish dust, I felt like a seasoned cowboy, bringing the herd home.

6　　Bradway came back, and together we pulled the black bucket out, letting the water pour from the holes. It was extremely heavy. We set it on a two-wheeled dolly. "Feel that slime?" said Bradway. I nodded. "The bank won't take the money this way." We went down the freight elevator to a room in the basement, where he showed me an old yellow washing machine. Together we dumped the money in, and Bradway turned the dial to regular wash; the coins went through a slushy-sounding cycle. After lunch, I scooped out the clean money and wheeled it to the bank— As I'd been told, I asked to see Diane. Diane led me to the vault, and I slid the black bucket off the dolly next to some dirty sacks of quarters.

7　　Every week that summer, I cleaned the fountain. Every week there was new money there to sweep up. I flipped more coins in myself; one nickel I deliberately left in place for a few weeks while I maneuvered away all the pennies around it, so that my wish-money would have more time to gather momentum. Eventually, I swept it along with the rest, trying, however, to follow its progress as a crowd of coins lined up like piglets on the sow of the rubber blade. There were momentary collisions and overturnings, and the wavelets of the water added confusion. My coin slid over another coin and fell to the right, and then, as I pushed them all into the corner pile, a mass of money avalanched over it, and it was lost to view.

Nicholson Baker, "Coins of the Realm," *The New Yorker* 23 & 30 Apr. 2001: 146.

First Job: Boxing Days

Jonathan Franzen

1   For three years when I was in high school, I was the packing boy for a German émigré couple, Erika and Armin Geyer, who operated a small business, Erika Imports, in the basement of their gloomy house in suburban St. Louis. Several afternoons a week, I left behind a pleasant-smelling world of liberty and sanity and climbed the stairs to the Geyers' dark front porch and peered into a living room where Erika and Armin and their overfed schnauzer were typically sprawled, snoring, on old wooden-ankled German chairs and sofas. The air inside was heavy with schnitzel grease and combusted cigarette. On the dining-room table were ruins of *Mittagessen:* plates flecked with butter and parsley, a partially trashed whipped-cream cake, an empty Moselle bottle. Erika, in a quilted housecoat that gaped to reveal an Old World bra or girdle, continued to snore while Armin roused himself and led me to my workstation in the basement.

2   Erika Imports had exclusive contracts with workshops in Communist East Germany that produced handmade giftware—enamelled Easter Bunny and Santa figurines, cunningly painted wooden eggs, deluxe carved crèche sets, hardwood tangram puzzles, candle-propelled Christmas carrousels in sizes up to three feet tall—that gift shops throughout the central tier of states were forever mad to buy. Erika could therefore be high-handed with her customers. She sent out broken merchandise or merchandise reglued, by Armin, with insulting carelessness. She wrote her invoices in a German cursive illegible to Americans. She slashed the orders of customers who'd fallen out of favor; she said, "They want twenty—ach! I send them three."

3   My job in the basement consisted of assembling cardboard cartons, filling them with smaller boxes and excelsior, checking the invoices to be sure the orders were complete, and sealing the cartons with paper tape that I wetted with a sea sponge. Since I was paid better than the minimum wage, and since I enjoyed topological packing puzzles, and since the Geyers liked me and gave me lots of cake, it was remarkable how fiercely I hated the job—how I envied even those friends of mine who manned the deep-fry station at Long John Silver's or cleaned the oil traps at Kentucky Fried Chicken.

4   I hated, in part, the arbitrary infringements of autonomy: the Saturday afternoons torpedoed by Erika's sudden barking on the telephone, "ja, komm immediately!" I hated the extravagant molds that grew on the sea sponge in its pan of scummy water. There was also the schnauzer and everything relating to the schnauzer. There was Armin's stertorous breathing while he pecked out U.P.S. slips on a manual Olivetti. There was Erika's powerful body odor and the powerful perfumes with which she failed to mask it. And there was the seasonal flood of Styrofoam bells and sentimental snowmen and plastic toys that recalled all too vividly the aesthetic wasteland of heartland hospital gift shops.

5   The main reason I envied my friends in the fast-food kitchens, though, was that their work seemed to me so wonderfully *impersonal.* They never had to see their supervisor's

blue-veined stomach falling out of her housecoat, a toppled glass of cheap champagne soaking into the rug by her feet. Hamburger fragments and parsleyed potatoes weren't decaying in a dog's bowl at their job sites. Most important, their mothers did not feel sorry for their bosses.

6   My own mother was always after me, in the years following high school, to stop in at the Geyers' and "visit" with them when I came home from college, or to greet them after a church service, or to send them postcards when I went to Europe. My mother herself, in a spirit of Christian charity and masochism, sometimes invited the Geyers to dinner and a game of bridge, during which Erika, at escalating volumes and with a diminishing ratio of English to German, abused Armin for his sins of bidding and his crimes of card-play, and Armin went crimson and began to bray in self-defense. Although my mother fervently believed in personal responsibility, she resorted to the most transparent ruses if I was in the house when Erika called. She handed me the phone ("Jonathan wants to say hello to you!") and then, when I tried to return the phone, she made me tell Erika that she would call her back "next week." Poor Erika and Armin, with their blood clots, their broken bones, their abrupt hospitalizations! Each step of their downward progress was faithfully reported by my mother in her letters to me. Now everyone is dead, and I wonder: Is there no escaping the personal? In twenty-five years, I have yet to find a work situation that isn't somehow about family, or loyalty, or sex, or guilt, or all four. I'm beginning to think I never will.

Jonathan Franzen, "Boxing Days," *The New Yorker* 23 & 30 Apr. 2001: 153.

First Job: Legal Aide

Lorrie Moore

1   In the nineteen-seventies, a new para-profession was getting a foothold in urban law firms—that of the legal assistant, or paralegal—and some college graduates, uncertain how to pay the rent or fund their art, were venturing into this day job. In New York, these jobs paid slightly better than entry-level publishing positions but involved a level of exploitation that had actually caused the paralegals at one prominent Manhattan firm to strike. Upon graduation from college, fresh from editing the school literary magazine, perplexed at the number of people I knew going in an automatic fashion to law school (when I asked them what it was a lawyer did exactly, none of them could say), I entered this strange professional racket. I would find out what a lawyer did exactly. Others I knew at the time who also embarked on this pursuit included a woman with a just completed master's thesis on Carlyle's "Sartor Resartus" (who promptly used her employer's legal services to change her last name from Schmunk) and a high-school teacher with a deep case of burnout.

2   Paralegals did not type! This was a kind of rallying cry. Nonetheless, I often coveted the jobs of the secretaries who did, for if they stayed after five they were paid overtime, and the kind of mindless typing they did looked restful to me. I, meanwhile, had to organize documents—which fell under the category of "exhibit preparation" and, murmuring into a Dictaphone, to digest depositions into a kind of telegraphic code ("W can't recall Palm Too din. w/ Stutz"), reducing the testimony of deposed witnesses to what was optimistically called its "essence." I also had to make the occasional and terrifying court appearance to get an adjournment on a motion. This is now almost always done by attorneys, but in the seventies Manhattan paralegals were a cheap substitute. "In this city you would make more money as a paraplegic than as a paralegal," I was continually told by one of the associates.

3   I was twenty-one and mute with shyness. Up until this point in my life I had lived only in tiny towns in northern New York. The midsized, midtown firm I worked for comprised a dozen lawyers, all Jewish, all men, with names like Ira and Julian, which to a provincial ear did not even properly sound like boys' names. The staff was not Jewish: the goyim served, grumblingly and winkingly; everyone smoked and drank too much coffee. My boss, the senior partner, had apparently made his name with some big case for Sears, Roebuck in the nineteen-forties, and he had coasted on this reputation for years. With his money he bought antiquarian books, boxes of which he ripped open hungrily when they arrived, as well as some Calder prints, which he displayed in the firm's lobby and which made a big impression on me. His clients still tended to be department stores, and the case he had me working on involved the firing of the chairman of Bonwit Teller, whose makeup counters I dreamily visited during lunch hours. My boss was alternately tetchy and expansive—he spoke loudly and crazily, as all bosses, in my experience from summer jobs, did. By the time I came on board, he was also a little hard of hearing. When

after two years I told him I was leaving for graduate school in writing, he thought I'd said "riding" and made a crack about horses.

4   But this is what my first real job brought me: my first gay friend, my first African-American friend, and what I thought of as my first grownup friend (a lawyer fifteen years my senior who remains my friend to this day). And though I envied the chicly dressed young women who worked in the Pace Gallery and at Cambridge University Press, housed in the same building and sharing the elevators, my own exquisitely wrong job did bring me, for a brief period, a life in Manhattan improvised, lonely, exhilarating. I lived on Eighteenth Street and First Avenue, above a restaurant, and was always broke, though it was middle-class poverty—temporary, part of youth and art, more a game to be played than a true condition. It produced in me an eccentric economy. Tired from work and fearful of the subways at night, I would get into a cab and say, "Give me a dollar-fifty's worth, please," then hop out at Murray Hill. I had one suit, which I wore all week—the jacket on Monday with slacks, the skirt on Tuesday with a blouse, the jacket and skirt together at last!—on Wednesday, and so on. I ate hamburgers but not cheeseburgers, which cost ten cents more. Still, I spent twenty-five dollars to see Bette Midler on Broadway, and another twenty-five dollars to see Liza Minnelli at Carnegie Hall. I was like a fourteen-year-old gay boy escaped to the bright, big city from the farm—which is perhaps what, in my heart, given even the slimmest of paychecks, I continue to be.

Lorrie Moore, "Legal Aide," *The New Yorker* 23 & 30 Apr. 2001: 158.

First Job: Early Inklings

John Updike

1　"You're hired": sweet words, in this life of getting and spending. I have heard them rather rarely; my last regular paycheck was issued when I was twenty-five and poised to anoint myself a self-employed writer. My first paying job that I can recall was swatting flies ten for a penny on my family's side porch. The pay rate, considering the number and sluggishness of Pennsylvania flies, seems high; perhaps I broke my employers' bank. Though I was keen and eager, at the age of six or so, the job did not open out into a career.

2　Next, at the age of twelve, I worked for a weekly pass to the local movie theatre. I and some six or eight other boys would gather at the Shillington, with its triangular marquee and slanting lobby, on Saturday mornings, and be entrusted with bundles of little tinted leaflets, folded once like a minimal book, advertising the week's coming attractions. Shows, some of them double features, changed every other day and took Sundays off—gangster films, musicals, Disney cartoons, romantic comedies, Abbott and Costello, Biblical epics, all offering a war-beset, Depression-haunted America ninety minutes of distraction from its troubles. We boys were dispatched in pairs, some of us to territories as remote as Mohnton and Sinking Spring, and scampered up and down the concrete steps of hilly Pennsylvania to leave our slithering beguilements on expectant porches where tin boxes held empty milk bottles and rubber mats said in raised letters "Welcome." When the leaflets were gone—some very bad boys, it was rumored, would dump theirs down a storm drain—we returned to the theatre for our magic pass. More than once, to save the seven cents the movie-house proprietor had given us for the trolley car, my partner and I would saunter the several miles back to Shillington, between the shining tracks.

3　Next, a dark chapter. I must have been sixteen when I was deemed eligible to work in a lens factory in the gritty city of Reading. They were sunglass lenses, at least in our end of the plant—they came mounted on hemispheres fitted, in turn, onto upright hubs that held them under rotating caps in a long trough full of a red liquid abrasive called "mud." They had to be changed every twenty minutes, as I remember; I was always falling behind, and a foreman kept coming around to chalk rejection marks—white X's—on my over-cooked hemispheres, with their blank and slippery eyes. The red sludge got all over you, inexpungeably, into hair, ears, and fingernails. A wan, Dickensian boy about my age tried to teach me the ropes, but my only prowess emerged at the brief lunch break, when a country skill at quoits enabled me to outscore my malnourished city-dwelling co-workers.

4　On the vast factory floor, various machines mercilessly thrummed around me, and my stomach churned. In my nervous moments of repose, I smoked cigarettes, flipping the butts right onto the scarred old floor. I could smoke all I wanted; the adults around me didn't care. But the consolation fell short: if this thrumming, churning misery marked the entrance to adulthood, childhood wasn't so bad. I quit after three days, promising my parents to work profitably instead at my strawberry patch on the farm to which we had moved. Agricultural labor is as mirthless as industrial, but the strawberry season lasted only three weeks of straddling the wide rows, as the sun baked your bare back and daddy longlegs waltzed up your arms. For the rest of the summer, I tried to write a mystery novel.

5   When I was eighteen, between high school and college, the editor of the Reading *Eagle* told me I was hired, as a summer copyboy. This was even better than swatting flies. It paid a bit better, too—thirty-four dollars and change in a small brown envelope every Friday. My duties were to hang around the editorial room, doing a breakfast run for the doughnut-prone, coffee-addicted staff and carrying copy into the Linotype room, where men in green eyeshades tickled the keyboards of the towering Mergenthaler Linotype machines. Their activity was noisily industrial, and smelled of hot lead and human confinement, but its product made sense to me. A copyboy's last duty of the day was to bring up a stack of fresh, warm newspapers (the *Eagle* was an afternoon paper) from the roaring pressroom and distribute them, with a touch of ceremony, to the editors, the reporters, and even the paper's owner, a local magnate who sat patiently in his grand front office. He always thanked me. I felt part of a meaningful process, a daily distillation, an installment of life's ceaseless poetry. This was my element, ink on paper.

John Updike, "Early Inklings," *The New Yorker* 23 & 30 Apr. 2001: 173.

Appendix A

Formal Outline

This formal outline is based on the revised essay "Socialization" found on pages 120–121.

Thesis: Socialization can be defined as a learned behavior acquired in childhood through formal and informal situations.

I. Two types of socialization
    A. Formal learning occurs in schools and through the media.
        1. School
            a. Teachers teach social behavior.
            b. Teachers help students solve problems.
        2. Media
            a. Assigned readings can teach social behavior.
            b. Educational television teaches values.
    B. Informal learning occurs at home, through friends, and through the media.
        1. Parents
            a. Parents teach children right from wrong.
            b. Parents instill other family values.
        2. Friends
            a. Friends teach kids what to wear.
            b. Friends teach peers how to act to be socially acceptable.
        3. Media
            a. Children learn how to socialize from watching television.
            b. Children learn from reading books and magazines.
            c. Children learn from using computers.
II. Importance of having social skills
    A. World is becoming smaller.
        1. Internet brings people together.
        2. Television brings other cultures closer.

      B. People are spending more time socializing.
         1. People use e-mail.
         2. People chat online.
      C. The more adept a person is at socializing, the more easily that person can adapt to his or her native culture and that of others.
      D. It is especially important for people who are interested in social science to understand how the process of socialization works. [Note that this is a new idea.]

When writing a formal outline, keep the following tips in mind:

- Write the thesis separately at the beginning.
- Use Roman numerals for the main categories, capital letters for the next levels and numbers and lowercase letters for subsequent levels.
- Provide at least two subdivisions for each category (A and B, or 1 and 2).
- Be consistent in using sentences or phrases except for major headings.
- Don't be a slave to your outline; change it if necessary as your ideas develop in various drafts.

Appendix B : Proofreading Symbols and Abbreviations

Proofreading Symbols

Proofreaders use the following symbols when correcting typeset material. Many instructors also use them in marking student papers.

Symbol	Meaning
¶	begin a new paragraph
No ¶	do not begin a new paragraph
⊙	add a period
⌄ ⌄	add double quotation marks
#	add space
∩	transpose elements (usually with *tr* in margin) (releive)
⌄	add an apostrophe
◯	close up
∧	add a comma
ℯ	delete
∧	insert

Correction Symbols and Abbreviations

Symbol	Meaning
‖	lack of parallelism
ab	faulty abbreviation
adj	improper use of adjective
adv	improper use of adverb
agr	faulty agreement
amb	ambiguous expression or construction
awk	awkward expression or construction
cap	faulty capitalization
cs	comma splice

dgl	dangling construction
frag	fragment
lc	use lowercase
num	error in use of numbers
p	faulty punctuation
ref	unclear pronoun reference
rep	unnecessary repetition
r-o	run-on sentence
sp	spelling error
ss	faulty sentence structure
t	wrong verb tense
tr	transpose elements
vb	wrong verb form
wdy	wordy writing

CREDITS

INDEX